Brilliant Biruni

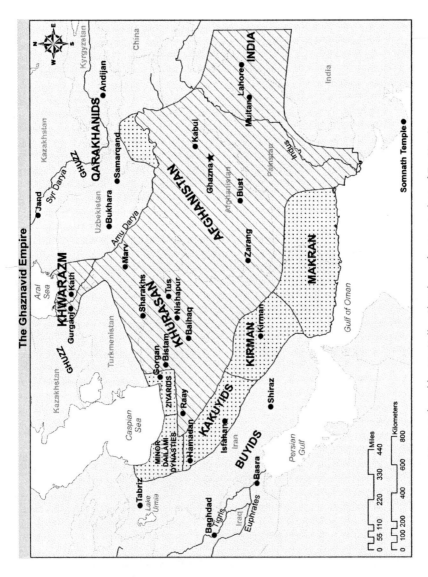

The Ghaznavid Empire

Map produced by Mr. Kelley Slettebo, a former student of Dr. Kamiar.

Brilliant Biruni

A Life Story of Abu Rayhan Mohammad Ibn Ahmad

M. Kamiar

THE SCARECROW PRESS, INC.
Lanham, Maryland • Toronto • Plymouth, UK
2009

SCARECROW PRESS, INC.

Published in the United States of America
by Scarecrow Press, Inc.
A wholly owned subsidary of
The Rowman & Littlefield Publishing Group, Inc.
4501 Forbes Boulevard, Suite 200, Lanham, Maryland 20706
www.scarecrowpress.com

Estover Road
Plymouth PL6 7PY
United Kingdom

British Library Cataloguing in Publication Information Available

Library of Congress Cataloging-in-Publication Data
Kamiar, Mohammad.
  Brilliant Biruni : A life story of Abu Rayhan Mohammad Ibn Ahmad / Mohammad S.
Kamiar.
     p. cm.
  Includes bibliographical references and index.
  ISBN-13: 978-0-8108-6243-2 (pbk. : alk. paper)
  ISBN-10: 0-8108-6243-3 (pbk. : alk. paper)
  ISBN-13: 978-0-8108-6244-9 (ebook)
  ISBN-10: 0-8108-6244-1 (ebook)
  1. Biruni, Muhammad ibn Ahmad, 973?–1048. 2. Muslim scientists–Iran–Biography.
3. Scientists–Iran–Biography. 4. Geography–History–To 1500. 5. Biruni, Muhammad
ibn Ahmad, 973?–1048–Sources. 6. Science, Medieval. 7. Science and civilization. I.
Title.
  Q143.B5K36 2009
  509.2–dc22
  [B]   2008029120

Contents

Preface

My real encounter with Biruni was little over a quarter of a century ago when I was a graduate student of geography at Michigan State University. At that time, all students were required to take a course called "GEO 852: Philosophy of Geography." I took this course with Professor Lawrence Sommers in the fall term of 1979. I selected Biruni, as a Muslim geographer, as a topic for one of my research papers.

The formal research paper had to be only five pages. It was filled with technical terms and jargon and included three pages of footnotes and references. For the first time, I learned that Biruni was able to calculate the height of a mountain by measuring its shadow. I also found out about Biruni's theory of location of landmasses opposite to Eurasia. Thus, he knew about the Americas five hundred years before the Europeans discovered the New World. Fortunately, Dr. Sommers enjoyed reading my paper. In his comment at the end of my paper, he used the word "excellent" and believed that it was a publishable paper. This encouragement and support inspired me to collect all references written about Biruni, including his own research works.

This collection was published as *A Bio-Bibliography for Biruni* by the Scarecrow Press in 2006. This book has a brief biography and geography of Biruni's birthplace, and all available references related to him were put together under a single title. For the first time, names of all of Biruni's 183 books in Arabic, Persian, Transliteration, and English, with brief annotations, were given in one place. Again, for the first time, some selected resources available on Biruni on the Internet were provided.

The aforementioned more technical book about Biruni makes research very convenient for the students and scholars in the fields of geography, classical works, medieval research, and Islamic civilization. It is, however, to be used for serious research and investigation in related fields with specific agendas. This means that *A Bio-Bibliography for Biruni* is not geared toward public consumption. Therefore, I was led to write the present book for that purpose. In the book in your hand, I have tried to give the reader a simplified version of the life of one of the greatest scholars in the history of the world. This is the life story of the boy who became Biruni, a life story of the survival of a scientist who brightened the dark skies of the Middle Ages.

It is only smart for the public to be entertained and educated about other cultures. Post–September 11 is a very critical time in our history. With knowledge alone can we fight against the misconception and resultant discrimination and prejudices so persistent all around the world. A great majority of the people in the world have not heard Biruni's name, a man who worked for the peace and prosperity of mankind.

I would like to acknowledge all the help I received from all librarians at Michigan State University, Florida Community College at Jacksonville, and the Library of Congress. Finally, I would like to thank my wife Molouk, my daughter Anahiat, and my son Arash for the time they allowed me for this public service. However, any problem in this book should be referred to me. I assume responsibility for any mistakes.

CHAPTER ONE

Village of Vasemereed, Khwarazm, South of Lake Aral, Central Asia

It was moments before daybreak and the roosters were getting ready to sing. It was a windy, squally, and very cold day. Large drops of semifrozen rain were striking the wooden door of the little house. It had been raining all night and the sky was filled with thick black clouds. One could still hear the wailing of hungry wolves and the cry of jackals from afar.

The village of Vasemereed was not very different from other such lonely places on the northern edge of this desert-like steppe, which was a grazing land for several Turkish tribes collectively known as the Ghuzz. It was small, and it was lonesome. At this hour, the village was sleeping within its own mud walls on this desert without a horizon. The endless darkness and late autumn's bitter cold would force even the more experienced peasants to stay indoors in such weather.

A little house bedaubed by mud in the northeastern corner of the village was where Professor Abu-Jafar Ahmad Ibn Ali Andijani's family lived. It was located at a considerable distance from the other houses that circled the water-mill. After his death, Professor Andijani's widow and his seven children, four sons and three daughters, were living here. The native villagers addressed them as the Birunis, or "those who came from outside" or just "outsiders." In Persian the word *Birun* means "outside." The reason they were called by this name was that they had emigrated from the city of Khwarazm. This family was still seen as strangers by the local population.

The village of Vasemereed was composed of some houses in irregular rows lacking order and planning. The facades of the houses were arranged in various directions. The village had a square shape and was surrounded by a high mud wall reaching almost eight meters in height. In each corner, there was a watchtower with holes for looking out. Behind these watchtowers, there were some platforms three meters high made of brick for defensive purposes. Whenever the village was attacked, the villagers would climb onto these platforms to repel the attackers with arrows and spears.

The houses in the village contained one or two rooms, with a porch that was usually a few steps higher than the yard. This yard was enclosed with mud walls. In one corner it had a small storage area, and in the other corner, for animals of many types, a stable was built. More often during the colder season, from late autumn through early spring, smoke coming out of little holes in the flat roofs of the houses would indicate the continuation of the struggle for life on the plateau of Persia and nearby regions. Villages, for centuries, had a few things in common: A *qanat* system, which is a man-made spring (Kamiar, 1983), a water-mill, a mosque, and a bazaar. Together, they represented life near many deserts, big and small. Life was a continuous struggle against the sun's burning rays during the day and the cold winds and darkness of the night.

Vasemereed was still in peace with itself and other places. It was the late tenth century, but the death and annihilation sweeping across the East had not visited this village yet. It took another three centuries for the eastern storm of death and destruction to throw the dust of misery over most human settlements in Persia. These storms from the Gobi Desert and Mongolia would later change the shape of these places and uproot people's happiness, hope, and prosperity.

The day was just beginning. In the large room in Professor Andijani's house six children were sleeping next to their mother, Mehrana. The eldest son was away. He was now a soldier in the army of a local khan. Mehrana was originally from the city of Nishaboor (Nishapour). She was sleeping near the *tanoor*, sometimes called *tandoor*, an oven-like hole made in the ground for baking bread and warming the room. She was sleeping over an old *geleem*, a short-napped coarse carpet, and was covered by a quilt filled with goat hair. The children were still gently snoring. The rain and wind were also at work. Mehrana was the first to wake up everyday. She was happy that her family had a roof over their heads. Mehrana, now forty-four years of age, was still a beautiful woman. She had long, dark hair; beautiful, big, black eyes; and swarthy skin. She was slim and well-built. But each morning as she woke up she was filled with worries and a sense of helplessness.

The Persian New Year celebration of Norouz was three months and ten days away, but she had been unable to pay any of her late husband's debts, buy new clothes for her children, or purchase a pair of cows to replace the pair that she had to sell. Her husband, Professor Andijani, died too soon, leaving her all alone with too many problems to solve.

Their home was the most important asset they had. They had a farm too, which was located nearly a *farsang* (or *farsahk*), about six kilometers, away from the village. They had thirty sheep, twenty-eight goats, a dozen chickens, hens, and roosters, a spindle, a few rugs, and an expensive Persian carpet. Nevertheless, they were refugees. They had been forced out of the city. By borrowing money and selling some possessions, including Mehrana's jewelry, they somehow managed to purchase a house and a farm. But life had not been good to them. In the seven years that they had lived in Vasemereed, they had seen two drought years, one flood, and a war. One year, they planted fruit trees, but unfortunately they were all frozen due to a very cold winter. One year, their farm was flooded. And one year the Ghuzz attacked the village and totally destroyed their harvest.

Professor Andijani was not a good farmer, and he was not a fortunate man. His hands were not made for farming. He was an astronomer by education. Until recently, he was working at the Gurganj Observatory. It was a wrong destiny for an astronomer to be working as a peasant farmer under the burning sun in central Asia.

The call for prayer was coming from the minaret of the only mosque in the village. Mehrana was wide awake and was staring at the ceiling with sadness. It was not too bright yet for Mehrana to see clearly the blackened ceiling covered by twelve wooden beams. She knew, however, that her fate was black as the ceiling. After the death of her husband, their life had been stripped to a bare minimum. The worst was the loans and the interest that she had to repay. Thus, their life was simply work, and work without any hope or happiness. After a deep and painful sigh, she finally stood up and looked outside from the one little window in the room, which was covered by very thin Chinese paper. The sky was still black and ominous. The flood was heading toward the desert. She walked toward her son Mohammad, who was still asleep. She touched his shoulders and said in a whisper, "Wake up, wake up dear son, it is morning." Mohammad did not respond. Morning sleep was delicious, especially after a night filled with storm and thunder. His nap was so delightful, he might not have heard his mother call him.

Mehrana called one more time. The boy of fourteen years of age was in deep sleep, covered by a heavy quilt made of goat hair. It seemed he was sleeping in the best bedroom of a palace covered by silk. With a murmurous sound, Mehrana called again, "Wake up, wake up please. Today is the time to take the livestock out for grazing."

On one side of the *tanoor*, the three daughters—Zareen-Geesoo (golden-haired), Ziba (the beautiful), and Negareen (fair-faced)—were sleeping. On the other side, her three sons—Mohammad, Mehdi, and Mohsen—were still not awake. Mehrana's oldest son, Mahmud, who was nineteen years old, was a soldier. And Mohammad, although only fourteen years of age, was the man of the household. Zareen-Geesoo was sixteen, Ziba twelve, Negareen ten, Mehdi eight, and Mohsen was six years old. Mehrana gently touched Mohammad's shoulders again. "I go to start the fire, please wake up and take the herd out as soon as possible." Then she called Zareen-Geesoo. "Please go and milk the cow, please hurry." In this little mud-walled house, life began again.

Mohammad had a hard time waking up. Mehrana touched her son's forehead. It was somewhat warmer than usual. Shaking her head, she began to get worried. Mohammad somehow opened his eyes and said, "Forget it Mother."

"Why don't you get up and take the herd out?"

"It is too early; let me go back to sleep!"

Mehrana said, with a motherly softness in her voice, "I know it is too hard. But what can I do? Especially after Mahmud's departure, most of the hard tasks have fallen on your shoulders. It has been four days since the animals have eaten anything. They might die." Complaining, the young boy said, "It is still too early!" Mehrana said, "But it is cloudy; if it was not so, you could see the Morning Star." Mohammad said, "Dear mother, then it would become a caravan killer."

Yawning, Mohammad sat in his bed. Darkness still covered everything. He could only see the few red charcoals in the fireplace. The tanoor still was somewhat warm, giving off heat to the room. Mohammad was aimlessly touching the quilt. Zareen-Geesoo too was complaining that it was too early to wake up. She said, "Mohammad, maybe you are afraid to go." Mohammad asked, "What kind of fear are you talking about!" "Highway-robbers, thieves, . . ." she mentioned. "I defend myself with my knotted club and my friends. Polad, Seena, and Jamsheed may bring their herd for grazing too, so I will not be alone," he answered. Zareen-Geesoo said, "You are a little kid, it is too early for you. . . . Mahmud was a powerful man, and what if the thieves come?"

"Don't frighten me, Zareen-Geesoo. I can take care of myself. I have done it before. In addition, my dog Jalad, the executioner, is with me. He is a good dog." Now, Zareen-Geesoo sat in her bed and said, "Don't listen to Mother. She is always worried! Wait until the sun is out." Mohammad laughed. "Dear sister, taking this small number of livestock out for grazing is not a big deal!" He rubbed his eyes.

The smell of goat soup was slowly filling the room. Mehrana had already started preparing food for lunch. The large drops of rain were still falling. The village was getting ready for a long and gloomy winter ahead.

Most of the people of Vasemereed were poor peasants; only a few owned their farms, and some worked on government land. This village could not be called a place for living if it wasn't for its mosque and a *maktab*, religious school. It was just a combination of some mud huts. Not many people in this village knew the Andijani family well. Although they had lived here for seven years, they still were considered as outsiders. Throughout his time in Vasemereed, Professor Ahmad Andijani was mostly busy planting wheat, barley, cotton, and some vegetables.

The father of the household, Professor Ahmad Andijani, died three years ago of a heart attack. He was only forty-two years old. He was skinny. His face was yellow and sad, and he hardly smiled. He was a farmer, but he also wrote many things. He would write on fine Chinese paper. He was a carpenter too, and he was able to repair and fix many things, especially farming tools and doors and windows. He looked like a grave old man. He was dignified, revered, and serious. He was suffering from an internal pain not known to many people in the village.

He came to be known to the villagers as Professor Ahmad the astronomer. At night, he would talk to his children about the stars and would write strange equations and draw strange shapes and graphs. He would spend hours calculating mysterious equations and formulas. He would climb on the roof when the moon was shining and spend many hours observing the skies and the stars. Some of the people who did not like him at first used to think he was involved in witchcraft. But in a short time period, the villagers realized that he was a knowledgeable astronomer, a scientist, and a good man.

The village Mulla and teacher, Sheikh Mostafa Urganji, respected Professor Ahmad. Once in a while, the two would get together and discuss various topics. Professor Ahmad also had a little store where he would take orders for his carpentry jobs, write letters for illiterate people for a small fee, and he even would interpret people's dreams. Due to his wide encompassing knowledge and honesty, the villagers liked him. Professor Ahmad was also physically sick. He was coughing quite often. These coughs were continuous and painful. Twice a day he would go to the mosque to pray to Allah. He would not talk to anybody unless he was talked to. He became the most respected person in the village. His wife, Mehrana, too was well respected by the villagers.

Neither the menfolk nor the women in the village could find out more about this family. The villagers were wondering why this family had relocated to Vasemereed! What was the reason that they had to leave the city behind? Through the people who would go to the city more often, the villagers learned that Professor Ahmad had served as the court astronomer.

In the late tenth century C.E. the province of Khwarazm was ruled by an Iranian dynasty that spoke Persian. The region was under the domain of two amirs. To the east of Amu-Darya was the Amir of Kath and to the west the city Gurganj, or Organaj, was located. Amu-Darya is an Old Persian name for the river that empties its water into Lake Aral. The Greeks called this river the Oxus; the Arabs knew it as Jeyhoon. To the east of Amu-Darya there is another river called Sir-Darya. Both of these rivers have always been very significant to the local population. The word *Darya* is Persian, meaning the sea. Indeed, Persians call any large body of water the sea. Therefore, we know why the world's largest lake, the Caspian Sea, is known as a sea. Even Lake Aral is sometimes called the Aral Sea. The Old Persian name for the Nile River is the Nile Sea. (For a detailed geographical description of this region, please see Le Strange, 1905; Barthold, 1968; and Kamiar, 2006.)

Vasemereed was located on a caravan road. Many caravans moving between cities in the west and those in the east would stay in this village. South of this village there was a large desert called Beaban-e Ghuzz or the Ghuzz Desert. It is located east of the Caspian Sea in central Asia. Khwarazm was a fertile region. The inhabitants would grow grains and fruits of many kinds for export. Thanks to the water from the two rivers mentioned earlier, cotton could be cultivated in this dry region. The farmers and some nomads were involved in raising livestock too. Wool, dairy products, and meat were also produced. The margins of the desert provided a very good grazing area. The grasslands, steppes, of central Asia were really important for raising livestock.

Every year, merchants came to Khwarazm from as far as Eastern Europe and Russia. They would bring all types of fur and skin, including weasel, sable, beavers, squirrel, ermine, and mink, to be sold or traded with local products. Local workers would process the leather, skin, and fur. Local tailors and dressmakers would produce the best clothes for export. Other local commodities included fish and fish products, honey, hazelnuts, jujube, grapes, sesame, wooden boats, ambergris, box-wood, wax, swords, bows and arrows, chain mail, shields, rugs, and colored cotton and silk cloth.

Slaves, however, were the most important item of trade. These slaves came in many colors, shapes, ages, and cultural backgrounds but mostly were nonblacks. Stealing or just outright kidnapping of children from rural areas, migrating tribes, and even cities was very common. A poor family might sell some of their children to slave traders. The whole population of a village, city, or tribe could be taken as slaves if they were defeated in a conflict.

Young girls and boys were especially paraded in the slave bazaars. In Khwarazm there were some schools that trained slaves preparing them for serving in the courts of the ruling class or to become soldiers or sex objects. Some of these slaves became important political leaders. Many slave mothers, mostly concubines, gave birth to Caliphs, Kings, Khans, Amirs, and Shahs.

South of Vasemereed was this desert that had no boundary. It was home to a group of migrating Turkish tribes called the Ghuzz. They were involved in raising livestock, but the most important source of their income was stealing anything and everything, including kidnapping children for slavery. They would sell slaves as far as China to the east and Russia and Eastern Europe to the west.

Soon after his arrival in Vasemereed, Professor Ahmad Andijani began to look like the rest of the villagers. Like any other peasant, he would work on the farm according to the season. In the winter, he would work as a carpenter and only go to the mosque twice a day. Sometimes he would stay longer and listen to the preacher Sheikh Mostafa Urganji, who was also the teacher of their religious school, the *maktab*. The women of the village soon started to like Mehrana, Professor Ahmad's wife.

Mehrana was a very good midwife. She became the most reliable midwife, especially for complicated pregnancies and deliveries. She was also a very good stylist–cosmetologist. In the art of makeup and hair styling, nobody could compete with her. The village headman, Kadkhoda, was pretty sure now that Professor Ahmad was in the court of the Amir of Khwarazm and was an astronomer.

It was only a week after the death of Professor Ahmad that a representative of the court arrived in the village with several rolled-up papers that were given to Mehrana. The state accountant gave 140 gold dinars to Mehrana as compensation. Apparently, Professor Ahmad had been forgiven for his mistakes. Thus, Mehrana was able to buy two milking cows.

Although Mehrana had given birth to seven children and had a rough life, she still was very attractive. Mohammad was only six and a half when he began attending *maktab*, along with thirty other students. The children were taking basic education, especially reading the holy book of the Quran. They also learned Persian and Arabic. Mohammad had only four books. They were very old and almost torn apart because he had read them so many times. He could write everything in these books from memory. He was able to surprise everybody in the household and in school. Like the other shepherd boys, Mohammad carried a homemade flute. But he never learned to play it, because he had no time to practice. And whenever he did find the time, he would open a book and get lost in its pages and daydream.

CHAPTER TWO

Into the Darkness

The young boy slowly stood up. He was slim, with skin color like wheat. He had large, bright eyes. He was wearing an old white shirt, over which he wore a long cotton gown. He also was wearing a pair of baggy white trousers and a pair of woolen socks. He did not forget to wear a jacket over the gown and put his night cap on. Finally, he threw his white turban over his thick black hair. As he opened the door leading him toward the desert, the chilly air slapped his face. The sky was a dark, tar-like color, high and mysterious. Not even one bright light could be seen in the sky and it was biting cold.

He hated to go and did not want to work. But he loved his mother and knew well that if he did not take the livestock out for grazing, they would die of hunger. "Why are you waiting?" asked Mehrana of her son. "It is nasty weather and the rain is getting heavier," he replied. "But you know they have not had anything to eat for four days now, Mohammad." "Yes mother, you are right." "Please be careful so you do not catch a cold, and wear your scarf around your neck," she said. At last he had to go. Zareen-Geesoo opened her eyes and watched him as he left.

Mohammad went down the porch and washed his hands, arms, and face. As he was getting ready for his morning prayer, he could hear the call for prayer from afar. After praying to Allah, he opened the stable door. The animals were ready and they eagerly rushed toward the door. He picked up his knotted club. At the last moment, Mehrana handed her son a bundle of food that contained some salty cheese, walnuts, and bread. Mohammad followed his herd, with his dog Jalad following close by. He was not in any danger as long as he and his herd were within the walls of the village. The main threat came from the Turkish Ghuzz tribes in the desert south of the village. In their black tents, they sat waiting for their prey. At times, they would even attack settlements around the desert.

It had been four days since these animals had any food, Mohammad thought. But he knew margins of the desert still had some grass. After moving about one *farsang* away from the village, Mohammad was hoping to find a good grazing ground. His goal was to reach an area by some low-lying hills where some mausoleums, or graves, with some other old structures were located. Suddenly, he felt something touch his leg. It was his dog Jalad.

Mohammad began to feel worried now and said to himself, "Mother should not rush me through this. She thinks that since all of the shepherds are racing to take out their herds, there will be nothing left for our animals. She thinks everybody is going to 'the Black Hill.'" "Work and work from dawn to dusk," he muttered to himself. Then he thought somebody was after him. After looking carefully, he didn't see anything. He was getting the ominous feeling that somebody was hiding behind the big tree nearby! The rain was getting heavier all the while and he could sense a flash flood forming.

He checked his gown pocket to make sure he had brought a book along. As a shepherd boy he thought books were his best friend. Young Mohammad pressed the handle of his knotted club and felt ready to face any danger. He did think about the food in the bundle his mother had given him. As for the sheep and goats, they were able to find their way instinctively through the heavy rain. But Mohammad was stumbling into mud and shallow ponds. When he realized that he and his herd were getting away too far from the village, he felt a bit scared and started getting bad thoughts. He began thinking about hungry wolves and wild, uncivilized nomads. They would come on their running horses with their long machete-like swords and cut off the heads of defenseless people.

"Why so early," he grumbled, "not even dogs get out at this hour." As soon as he thought of dogs, he remembered that he had a good dog accompanying him. He remembered Jalad! In Persian, the word *jalad* means executioner. Mohammad chose this name for his dog after he saw how masterfully his dog had killed some foxes and jackals. Jalad was a wolf-dog with long hair and a very friendly look. Jalad was instantly at his feet when Mohammad called him, so he felt a little stronger. By a low, friendly whimper, Jalad showed his affection to his young master.

It had been three years since Mohammad has been using the area around the Black Hill as a grazing ground for his cattle. In addition to carrying his knotted club and having Jalad by his side, he usually would carry a whistle.

All these were for his personal safety. The whistle was a product of the city of Kath located toward the east. Another tool used by some of the shepherd boys was a kettledrum, or rather drums of any size. On seeing nomads coming from the south, they would beat the drums as loud as they could, and hearing the loud drumbeats everybody around would run toward the village, close the gates, climb the watchtowers, and get ready to defend their homes, their lives, and their property. The village defenders would use anything available to repel the invaders, including sickles, axes, knives, and rakes. In big pots, they immediately started to boil water or oil to be thrown over the invaders.

If the walls of a village were high and well defended, the invaders would be forced to leave, with no harm done. But if the village was not well fortified, the nomads would commit the worst crimes against the villagers. They would cut the throats or rip the stomachs of men, rape the young women, and kidnap those they could sell in the slave bazaars. If the villages put up a good defense and were brave, the nomads would shed more blood of the innocent people and those they held guilty of fighting them. Sometimes they would tie up the elderly men and women to their horses, where they would die a dreadful death. Other times, they would throw the babies high into the air and on coming down cut them into halves with their swords. In many cases, the nomads would pick up young children by one leg, swing them around, and hit their skulls on the ground or the walls! Merely for their sadistic pleasure, the invaders would commit all sorts of cruelties. Then they would take whatever they could carry. They were worse than animals; they smelled bad and had no mercy.

The rural people had to suffer at the hands of the harsh geography, ruthless nomads, and tax collectors. Summer heat, drought, and famine were common. Winters were no fun either: they were chilly and unbearable. The region also suffered from floods and earthquakes. During the seven years of exile in this little village, Professor Ahmad's family had seen many invasions by the desert nomads. They would enter the rooms on their horses looking for young girls or boys to be taken as slaves. They would burn down the houses and leave bloody corpses everywhere. Government tax collectors were no better either. They would come with armed men to collect taxes of all types. If a farmer was unable to pay his taxes in cash, his land and property would be put on sale at almost half the price. Many times, these tax collectors would take the children away to sell as slaves to make up for the unpaid taxes.

Mehrana had been very patient during these black and painful years. No incident could break her resolve for survival and raising her children. Whenever she went to the city of Khwarazm, she would come across men who would tease her that they wanted to marry her, with bystanders laughing at her. Ignoring everything, she would buy the needed materials and hurriedly head back home, tired and hopeless. In addition, she had to collect firewood all by herself from the desert margins.

CHAPTER THREE

Into Slavery

Mohammad brought down his knotted club and looked back. Silence and darkness covered everything. He damned the Satan! For a while he followed the herd, and then he heard someone whisper. Jalad suddenly turned back and started barking fiercely. Showing his bright sharp teeth, he was getting ready to jump. He was getting wild, and then all of a sudden he charged at something in the dark. Then Mohammad noticed two dark shadows appear from behind a tree and one of them hit Jalad's head with a club. Mohammad heard a painful howl. He ran toward Jalad, with his club ready to hit the dark thing. Jalad was dead already. Then all of a sudden, the other dark figure hit him with a club from behind. Mohammad fell to the ground near Jalad and he could feel blood pouring out of a wound from the back of his head. He tried to put his hand over it, but he was unable to move his hand. Around him, the morning twilight was mixed with the darkness of the night's ugly faces. A group of big men circled him. He could see the "white parts of their eyes," the only things visible in the darkness. The "Ghuzz!" he whispered to himself. He was unable to say another word out loud. Needless to say how deeply he hated this name in his heart, however. One of the men said to the others, "Hurry up, it is getting late." Another one shouted, "Cut his throat."

A powerful hand grabbed his neck. In between the conscious and unconscious worlds, he saw the bright blade of a long knife in front of his eyes. So, was this the end of his life? Was this where all of his hopes and wishes would come to end? What would happen to his brothers and sisters? What about his mother?

Then a ray of hope pushed the fear of death away. He heard the sound of horseshoes beating the bare ground. The thieves on foot were being attacked by others on horses. In a split second, the thief who was holding Mohammad's neck lost his head to the sword of a horseman. The horsemen were members of the Turkish tribe of Ghuzz too. The very loud outcry of the man as he lost his head broke the morning silence. Now Mohammad was almost fully drenched in his attacker's blood. The rest of the horsemen were quickly getting closer. There were no more than seven or eight and they were attacking the band of thieves on foot. The horsemen were the obvious winners, who claimed the herd as their own property and Mohammad as their slave.

Life's instinct encouraged Mohammad to roll away from the path of the horses. The sound of horses approaching frightened the herd of sheep and goats and they started running all around and making noise. Just then, Mohammad heard another loud outcry of a person. The second thief with no horse was killed too. The horseman pulled his bloody, long sword from the thief's chest. Mohammad was still lying on the ground, bleeding from the back of his head. The strike he received was too hard. He felt it might have broken his skull. Fortunately for him, the thick scarf that he had on saved him. He surely would have been dead without the scarf. He touched his neck. It was wet, and it was painful.

Mohammad sat down and untied his scarf and wrapped it over the wound. Bunches of his long hair were stuck together with the dried, jelly-like blood. One of the Ghuzz shouted, "Some of these animals are dying. In the dark we shot them." The leader of the horsemen said, "Cut their heads off, and let's carry their carcasses." They did so and hung the carcasses in front of them on the horses. "Ollan, what should we do with this half-dead boy?" "Finish him," said Ollan, the commander of the Ghuzz. One of the horsemen got off his horse, drew his dagger, and was about to finish him when Ollan said, "Let's take him too." "He is badly wounded and bleeding . . . ," said the horseman. "Carry him, he will live," said Ollan.

A faint hope of life grew in Mohammad's heart. One of the horsemen tied up his hands with a coarse rope and then tied the other end of the rope to the saddle of his horse. He kicked Mohammad and shouted in Turkish, "Run, you dirty dog." Mohammad got onto his knees. Being dragged by the horseman, he was struggling to keep pace with his trotting horse.

The horsemen, numbering eight, headed south. The scared sheep and goats were running along. Mohammad too had no choice but to catch up with the horsemen. It was obvious, Mohammad was thinking, that a miserable life was waiting for him. Children stolen by the Ghuzz would be raped and then sold into slavery. He remembered the three young boys who were stolen from his village. They never came back, and nobody heard of them again. For a long time, their mothers could be seen crying and waiting by the main road hoping they would return, but they never got to see their loved ones again. Mohammad began to cry, and tears rushed down his face.

The horsemen rode in the desert for a while. The Ghuzz who was dragging Mohammad slowed a bit, then stopped and ordered him to get on the horse and ride with him. "Hold me tight, don't fall, you have given enough headaches!" Mohammad got the ride not out of pity but because he was slowing the horsemen down. The Ghuzz liked to navigate the desert as fast as possible. It was dangerous to delay in this ocean of sand.

About noon, when the sun was in the middle of the sky, the horsemen stopped in the middle of the desert for a quick lunch. One of the Ghuzz skinned a sheep, emptied its stomach, and put the carcass over a fire made of the desert shrubs they had collected. Another Ghuzz got some salt out of a bag and spread it over the carcass. Yet another one got his drink from the back of his saddle. It was mare's milk kept in goatskin. The Ghuzz offered Mohammad some of this sour milk. It smelled and tasted bad. Soon after they ate the roasted meat they were on their way again. They repeated their festivity late in the afternoon again. The horsemen obviously wanted to reach their tents as soon as possible. Their main goal was to sell the surviving animals and process the carcasses of the dead ones. They would add salt to the meat and put it in the sun to dry. They would also process the skin. The Ghuzz used these skins for many purposes.

Even in the summer, the desert temperature at night is much lower than that during the day. Sometimes, water may turn to ice in the middle of the night. The heat of the day would nevertheless be unbearable. As for Mohammad, he still was bleeding. He was so weak he could not hold on to the horseman anymore and he fainted and fell to the ground. The Ghuzz then helped him get on the horse again. Soon they reached a little creek, where they took another break and made some kabob. Mohammad was given a few pieces of the leftovers.

Mohammad had never seen his animals butchered. Before, when they were full-grown, Mehrana would sell them to the village butcher. Mohammad loved his animals. Some of the lambs were so beautiful he gave them names. He called a ram Angry, another one Champion. He called an ewe Fawn, another one Royal Falcon, and yet another Petal, and a fourth as Lovely. Now they were being massacred right in front of his own eyes. The horsemen were getting rid of the animals, for they wanted to move faster. With innocent eyes, the sheep, goats, and lambs were witnessing each other's death. They would not struggle even when they felt the sharp knife slice through their throats. And Mohammad was unable to do anything for them. After two more hours of riding, they arrived at an old, partially ruined caravansarai. The Ghuzz decided to stay there for the night.

The rooms were dark and dirty and most of them had no roof. When they did, the ceilings were covered with a thick layer of black soot. The floor was filthy and full of garbage. The Ghuzz cleared the floor of a room and slept there. They covered their heads with their cloaks and within minutes started snoring. Mohammad's hands and feet were tied up and he was left alone in one corner. He was thinking about his *maktab*. If he had not had any problems with his new teacher, he would not have become a slave. He realized he was feeling very tired. After all, he had one of the most eventful days of his life. His eyelids were getting heavier, and in no time he was snoring too.

CHAPTER FOUR

Mulla Hassan

A few days before Mohammad was captured and was taken away as a slave, an unexpected event happened in the village of Vasemereed. A new teacher, Mulla Ghyasseldin Hassan Ashtiqhani, was appointed in place of the old one, Sheikh Mostafa, who had recently died. The new teacher was nothing like their previous teacher. Mulla Hassan was ill-tempered, bad-mannered, ill-humored, and ugly. He did not like Sheikh Mostafa's good students such as Mohammad, and he would get very impatient if any of them said something good about their late teacher.

On the third day of teaching, this new teacher slapped one of the students. Although a good student, his pronunciations of Arabic verbs were not according to what Mulla Hassan knew as correct but were based on the method taught by the late Sheikh. The new teacher insulted another student when he was a little late bringing water for him. He was a strange teacher and obviously not a good one.

The late Sheikh was a dignified teacher and a respected personality. He was loved by his pupils, although once in a while the Sheikh would punish them by flogging. He seemed like a serious father who loved his children. His students would do anything for him willingly. Unlike the late Sheikh, Mulla Hassan was foul-mouthed, scurrilous, and abusive. He seemed to enjoy beating the students without any reason. Since the beginning, hate was mutual between him and Mohammad. Neither did Mohammad like him nor did he like Mohammad.

The late Sheikh Mostafa was Vasemereed's only teacher. He was getting old and was more than sixty-five years of age. The previous summer, his wife, Beebee Rana, Venerable Lady the Beautiful, had suddenly died. Four months later he died too. It happened during the lunch hour. While drinking from a small bowl of milk, the Sheikh suddenly fell back against the wall. After hitting the wall, a small amount of white foam came out of his mouth. Although, there were twenty-four pupils present, only a few noticed this horrible event. It was Poolad, the oldest student, who first saw it and simply screamed. He was followed by Seena and Jamsheed. They thought that their teacher had just fainted and would be fine soon. As Poolad watched his teacher's body, he was thinking what would happen if he was dead! He had seen dead people before.

Mohammad was in school too on that day. Actually, he was daydreaming about the beautiful Gohar Taj, "Jeweled Crown," his one-time playmate in the palace of the ruler of Khwarazm. She was about his age. The last time he saw her was five years ago, two years after Mohammad's family had moved to Vasemereed from the city. Mohammad was with his father, Professor Ahmad, who was in the city to repay his debt to the brother of the ruler. Mohammad saw Gohar Taj, but she was sent away before he had a chance to talk to her.

Mohammad's dream was badly interrupted by Poolad's scream. Mohammad was so stunned he did not even move from the place he was sitting. He just sat there motionless as the rest of the students gathered around their beloved teacher. Without realizing, tears began to roll down his cheeks. He had a hard time understanding the situation. Especially after his father's death, Mohammad looked up to Sheikh Mostafa as a true father figure. He loved his teacher dearly, who was a real gentleman. The Sheikh always cared about him, because he considered Mohammad his best student. The Sheikh would listen to his questions very carefully because they were smart and difficult, and he always tried to answer them very carefully.

The village of Vasemereed was a remote place in the frontier. The villagers, like many other people in the country, wanted to make sure that they could find a good teacher for their children. A major force was the parents' interest to educate their children in religious sciences, especially reading and understanding the holy book in Arabic. From age six, every male child could attend the *maktab*. They would go to school until age fifteen. The teacher would be paid from the religious endowments (*awqaf*). If they were interested and could afford it, the students would go to larger cities to obtain higher education. Calligraphy, painting, ceramic tile making, and architecture were all related forms of arts that could become a source of income. In turn, some of these students became teachers.

In the eight years that Sheikh Mostafa was the village teacher, most students transformed from little children and became young men. When the number of students increased, the Sheikh hired a younger teacher named Sheikh Abbas to teach lower levels. Mohammad had had one year of schooling before his family was relocated to Vasemereed. He was a very smart and speedy learner and would attract the attention of his teachers.

In tenth-century Iran, some of the more well-off families would start training their children by the age of four so they would be ready to go to school. They would learn the alphabet first. Then they would begin reading and memorizing the holy book, Quran. In these traditional schools, students would learn about religious subjects, mathematics, letter writing, and Persian and Arabic grammar. Only four of Sheikh Mostafa's students, including Mohammad, were promoted to the higher level in school. Mohammad read almost every book available to him. Sheikh Mostafa also allowed him to borrow books from his own little library, which had about twenty books.

Happy times in school for Mohammad ended with Sheikh Mostafa's death. Mohammad was hoping that Sheikh Abbas might accept the job of teaching and stay in Vasemereed, but he was not willing to continue living in a remote village. He accepted a tutorial job in a rich household in the city, where for tutoring a few children he was offered thirty gold dinars. After all, he was a good teacher. After his departure, the school was closed for a few weeks until a new teacher named Mulla Hassan arrived. He was younger, less experienced, and less educated. He also had bad conduct and often misbehaved with the students. He could not stand anybody praising the late Sheikh Mostafa, who had attended institutions of higher education in Baghdad and several other cities. Mulla Hassan particularly disliked the fact that some of his students came to school late, some by up to a few hours. Mohammad was one of these students.

Mohammad arrived at school late only a few times. But Mulla Hassan got angry and insulted Mohammad. In rural areas, students had to help their families. After his father's death, his responsibilities had increased. He had to take care of the animals.

In addition to his salary, Mulla Hassan was expecting each student to bring him gifts, including eggs, milk, and honey, but he hardly received anything from the Andijani family. As soon as Mulla Hassan found out that Mohammad was Professor Ahmad's son, his behavior changed. He told the village headman that he knew Professor Ahmad. He called Professor Ahmad a mysterious person, someone who was thrown out of the ruler's palace because he could not predict the movement of Saturn and read the future, and so he and his family were exiled to Vasemereed.

The last time Mohammad was late, he was not allowed to enter and was expelled from the school by Mulla Hassan. If this had not occurred, Mohammad would still have been a student at his village instead of becoming a slave.

Mulla Hassan was so very different from Sheikh Mostafa. The villagers were surprised to find out that the new teacher was very greedy and materialistic. He was allured and fascinated by expensive things, especially Persian carpets. He was more than thrifty. Indeed, he was very cheap. He would borrow money and never repay. And in the school, the students did not like him at all. Instead of teaching school curriculum and subjects, he would mostly talk about limited experiences and trips or just things he had heard but not read about in books or learned in school. Most of the subjects he was dealing with could be generally labeled as superstitious and not based on facts. After all, Mohammad was the son of a mathematician-astronomer. He had learned from his father and Sheikh Mostafa to think logically and not accept anything without good reason. Therefore, Mohammad was the first to laugh and tell jokes about most of Mulla Hassan's topics that were based on superstitions. Most of the pupils would look at Mohammad and laugh too. Even after school, the older students would ridicule Mulla Hassan's lectures. Apparently, he was making a fool of himself.

One of the superstitious stories told by Mulla Hassan was that it would rain if a person could pound and smash garlic in a mortar on the top of a mountain in the province of Mazandaran, located southeast of the Caspian Sea. His reason was that the smashed garlic would cause humidity to condense, thus forming rain. Another story was about a natural spring in a cave called Asmandan in a chain of caves named after Solomon, son of David, in a mountain range called the Arch of Mazandaran in the above-mentioned province. He said it would rain whenever this spring is contaminated and that the runoff from the rain would then clean the spring.

According to Mulla Hassan, there was a mountain between the city of Herat and the province of Sistan in southeastern Iran that would protest if it was dirtied by animal or human refuse. He would say he has heard that in Egypt there was a large natural spring near a temple on the top of a mountain that if polluted by people becomes poisonous. He believed that blood would gush out from the feet of a person cutting trees such as pine, poplar, and sycamore. Thus, people should avoid cutting trees—which was not a bad idea for a region like central Asia. This belief might have had its origin in Zoroastrianism, the old religion of Persia that encourages planting and maintaining trees.

In the village of Vasemereed, however, the farmers had no choice but to cut down trees. They needed more land. They needed to make charcoal and needed wood for fuel. What about dried trees? Mohammad asked Mulla Hassan. "People need to cook and heat their houses in winter. They need to make doors, windows, furniture, and tools. Without using wood, the human civilization might collapse!" continued Mohammad. Mulla Hassan's ideas were not flexible. "You never cut a tree, dead or alive," he replied. Without providing any reason why, Mulla Hassan got very angry and shouted, "What do you know about our world, you stupid shepherd boy!" and threw a sharp writing tool made of reed that hit Mohammad on his face and cut the corner of his eye. Now, Mohammad was surprised because he honestly wanted to find out. Mulla Hassan cried out loud and said, "You just shut up. Do not disturb my lessons, and just do not say another word. I am telling you, you should not cut pine, poplar, and sycamore trees under any circumstances. Is that understood?" Some of the students thought he may be right and some were not sure, but most believed him anyway. Not Mohammad, of course. He could not accept an idea forced on him without explanation.

After school, he asked his mother whether he could cut down a tree that was dead. Actually, his mother liked the idea. She could use the wood for cooking. Mohammad picked up one of his father's saws and started cutting. He, under the spell of his teacher's superstitions, was afraid first and kept on constantly watching his feet. Then nothing happened. There was no blood after all! The next day in school, he narrated his experience to his close friends and they all laughed.

Mulla Hassan felt like a winner, at least in front of his students, in the case of cutting trees. Hence, he kept telling more superstitious stories. One was that it was inauspicious for a household if their rooster crowed in the evening. The owner of the rooster should kill it immediately. Although Mulla Hassan had barely any knowledge about astronomy, he never studied the subject; he loved to give astronomy lessons based on what he had heard, which was largely superstitious. He could not imagine that a shepherd boy would refute his stories.

One of Mulla Hassan's stories was that there was a star in the sky that looked like a scorpion. If one finds it at night and stares at it, that person would become immune from scorpion poison. Mohammad had some basic knowledge of astronomy. Therefore, when he heard Mulla Hassan saying that many devils and demons were living on the moon and a giant witch was living there too, he couldn't believe it. He went on to say that one could see her eyes, eyebrows, and nose on the full moon. Mohammad could not take it anymore. He, while shaking, politely asked, "In relation to your story about this witch, have you seen any references in the Greek, Chinese, or any other astronomy books?"

While unbelievably angry, Mulla Hassan tried hard to show he was not. He called Mohammad to the front of the class and made him kneel on the reed mat in front of him. And Mulla Hassan slapped the left side of his face. One could see the five finger marks on his face. He plugged his ears, preventing him from hearing. The mad teacher was shouting very loudly. "You dirty animal, what do you know about astronomy. You are no more than a stupid shepherd boy." Showing his big hand to the class, he said, "This is my reference, you better accept it." Mohammad swallowed his anger and said, "I still need the name of a book, sir." This made Mulla Hassan angrier and he continued slapping his student harder and harder. "Why don't you just shut up?" he screamed.

Well trained for most of their lives, these young students were unable to accept this kind of logic, especially at a time when there was a movement toward scientific experimentation in every corner of the empire. But Mulla Hassan had more baseless superstitious stories. One day he said that it was bad luck if a dog howled out loud at night. In order to stop the dog, the head of the household or anybody present should put all the shoes and sandals upside down. This would stop the dog's howling! Mohammad was probably the first, if not the only, student to try his teacher's approach to quiet a dog's howling. Of course, it did not work. Now the dogs' howling was more noticeable to the students, who would have all their shoes in front of the room upside down. They could hardly see any relationship between dogs howling and their shoes.

Another day Mulla Hassan said that snakes found inside one's house was a good omen. They are God-sent auspicious creatures that bless the home and bring riches. Therefore, if a snake is seen inside one's room one should not kill it!

It was unbelievably sad to learn that almost a week later a housewife saw a snake in her basement and was killed by it. She was told by her son, who was a student of Mulla Hassan, that if she sees a snake she should not try to kill it, or even run. The snake was a good omen for their home, according to him. In the evening, when the family members returned home, they found the poor woman's cold body lying on the floor, and the snake was still around. Without thinking too much they knew the source of this superstitious belief of not bothering snakes that have entered your homes. That evening the villagers found out and confronted Mulla Hassan for teaching such superstitious beliefs. Yet he did not stop telling more stories.

Once again, Mulla Hassan said that he has heard that Samanid Sultan Noah has received a strange horse as a gift from the king of the land of Apishab. This horse, according to Mulla Hassan, had two heads, two feet, and two wings. He said that he has heard the Sultan has flown this horse over the city of Bukhara. Then he continued with another story. "A witch put a spell on a horse and the riders and they turned into a copper statue and would wave at the passengers." His next story was about a beautiful, colorful rock in Tibet that has magical powers, and if people who are not native to the region happen to look at it, they will die while laughing.

This was the straw that broke the back of Mohammad's patience. He actually burst into a loud laughter. With him, the whole class started laughing boisterously. This made the teacher very mad. He shouted at Mohammad and said, "Be quiet, my lessons are not comic jokes, and why do you think they are funny?" Mohammad said, apologetically, that he was sorry because he could not control himself. "Dear teacher, please forgive me." He continued, "It is better dying while laughing than being bitten by poisonous snakes." This was just an innocent comment. He did not mean to ridicule his teacher's stories. Mulla Hassan went blue in the face; he was so mad he kicked a disk in front of him and with a clogged voice said, "Just get out of my *maktab*, you *darazgoosh* (donkey)." And Mohammad left quietly.

When Mohammad arrived at home and explained what happened in school, his mother became very upset. She said, "You are not allowed to quarrel with your teacher. You go to school to learn not to fight. You are becoming more mischievous, and let me remind you that you cannot give your sarcastic comments in the class anytime you want to." So she reprimanded and reproached her son: "You know, within ten *farsang*, we cannot find another *maktab*; thus, we have to be very careful with Mulla Hassan. I do not think you want to stay in this little village and become a farmer for the rest of your life," she commented.

Mohammad did not like rural life either. So when his mother reminded him that without education he will remain in the village as a poor peasant, he felt scared. He knew farmers as a very honorable group of people and had high respect for them, but he did not want to become one. Life in the village was very boring to him. Work was hard, weary, and monotonous. He knew it was almost impossible to raise animals and plants all his life. He really wanted to go to a large city and continue his education. Sheikh Mostafa had lent him some books that helped broadened his horizon. He wanted to become a physician, an astronomer, a sage, or a professor. He remembered his father working in the court of the ruler of Khwarazm. Therefore, he wanted to earn a salary from a government or a court of a ruler. After a short while, thinking about his comment in the class, he regretted what he had said. He went to his mother and asked if she could go to school the next day and visit Mulla Hassan. He wanted to tell him that he was sorry and sincerely wished he could excuse him.

Like everybody else at that time, Mulla Hassan had a nickname. It was Abu Hosham, but he was only known as Mulla Hassan. He liked to be addressed, however, by his full title, His Excellency Mulla Hassan Abu Hosham.

On the following day, Mehrana took some pure honey and a goatskin full of cheese and some goat meat to see Mulla Hassan. On arrival, the first thing she did was address him as Dear Abu Hosham and apologized for her son's behavior. She said she, as well as her son, was very sorry for his presumptuous comment. Mulla Hassan pretended that he was not willing to forgive Mohammad, but it was not easy to not accept an apology from a beautiful woman such as Mehrana. He looked at her beautiful black eyes and hair, and her round and gorgeous face reminded him of all the good things he had heard about her. She was known as the best housewife and mother. And Mulla Hassan was a bachelor. Moreover, she was the best cook in the village, and she knew how to sew and style hair. Furthermore, she was a midwife. If Mehrana agreed to marry him he would be more than willing to settle down.

Mulla Hassan had several other occupations in the past. He had been a soldier and a warrior and had fought against infidels. She was a widow, he thought, and he was ready to take a wife. To express his interest in marrying her, the first step was to have a friendly relationship with her son.

The next day Mulla Hassan went for a walk around the village. He ended up passing by Professor Ahmad's house and was delighted when he saw Mehrana. He thanked her for the honey and cheese and said they tasted very good. Mehrana asked him to enter the house and have some food. She was just finishing baking pita bread and some food for lunch. He was offered freshly baked bread and some mixture of smashed lamb meat and beans. They were really very delicious, wholesome, and agreeable to the taste. He stayed briefly. After thanking her for the food, he left.

They were not really rich, he thought, after observing the interior of Mehrana's house. But he saw a very expensive Persian-Khorasani woolen carpet. He estimated it to be worth at least 150 gold dinars. On the other hand, she was the master of three different trades. She was a midwife, a hairstylist, and knew sewing. He thought that she might be able to earn at least fifty dinars. Mulla Hassan's salary was twenty dinars. Together, they could have somewhat of a good living compared with other people in this village. He also thought about the fact that she was a widow and had several children. And it was still possible that she might reject his proposal for marriage. He was thinking that his enemies spread the rumor around that he was a mean and abusive person. But then he thought, by merely proposing, he had nothing to lose. A few days later, Mulla Hassan sent the village headman's wife to informally ask Mehrana whether she wanted to marry Mulla Hassan.

Mehrana explicitly rejected the idea, saying, "I do not want to remarry at all." This negative reply really surprised Mulla Hassan, but he was still hopeful that Mehrana might change her mind. So he asked the mother of one of his students who was a friend of Mehrana to repeat his request. The answer was still negative. This made Mulla Hassan mad, and he decided to get revenge. It was an insult for a man to be rejected by a woman. Now poor Mohammad was at the mercy of his angry and rejected teacher. When Mulla Hassan learned for the second time about Mehrana's negative response, he decided to expel Mohammad from school.

A couple of days later, Mulla Hassan came down with a bad cold and chest pains. He asked Mohammad to bring him some milk. The next day, Mohammad brought him some milk in a bowl and put it in front of his teacher. But Mulla Hassan, who was looking for a reason to show his disappointment, actually kicked his student—the son of the woman who rejected his marriage proposal. He picked up the bowl and tasted the milk. His facial expression changed into displeasure and he immediately wrinkled his eyebrows and asked, "What kind of milk is this? It tastes like water. Did your cheap mother mix it with water? After two months, your silly and greedy mother has sent me milk that tastes like water, for the teacher of her stupid son. You *daraz-goosh*, I told you to bring me milk but your mother earns many gold dinars from being a midwife and owns a Persian carpet. . . . Just get out of my school." Mohammad was listening to Mulla Hassan patiently. He said politely, "Your honor, you have been unkind to my mother by calling her these words. I know her. She would never mix milk with water. I believe that this was very good milk. Actually, I had some this morning and it tasted fine. If it tasted bad or like water it may be because you are sick." Mulla Hassan told him, "Just go away, and tell your mother that after forty-eight years of age I know the difference between real milk and that mixed with water."

The next day Mulla Hassan told Mohammad to ask his mother whether he could borrow their carpet for a short time. He said, "I am having some guests and want my room to look better." Mehrana said she had no problem, and so Mohammad took their only expensive item to school and gave it to his teacher. Unfortunately, they never got it back. Only for a few days, Mulla Hassan left the Andijanis alone. Then he told Mohammad that he still was sick. "Tell your mother to kill a chicken and make me some pottage," he said.

The following day, Mohammad brought roasted chicken and some pottage. This delicious pottage was in an expensive china bowl. He put it in front of his teacher in the room next to their class and waited to be dismissed. Mulla Hassan used his wooden spoon and the moment he tasted the pottage, he shouted, "What kind of food is this? I have never tasted anything like it before. It tastes like garbage." He angrily kicked the china bowl and broke it. The bowl was a gift from his father's astronomer friend from the city of Kashmar. Mohammad said, "You broke it!" The teacher replied, "So what? Why do I give a damn? The pottage tasted bad, anyway."

"Actually, I had some of it at home and it was very good, and you know my mother is the best cook around," said Mohammad. He swallowed his anger and took the broken pieces of the china bowl and went home.

The next day Mohammad was two hours late for school. He had to take the animals out for grazing. Mulla Hassan already had told the students to lock the *maktab*'s door so Mohammad could not enter. The following day, he showed up on time and there was no problem entering the school. But when he greeted Mulla Hassan, he said, "You showed up your ugly face!"

Mehrana told her son to be very careful and not to make Mulla Hassan angry for any reason. She hoped that he would not come up with any problems with her son. Unfortunately, Mulla Hassan was determined to get rid of Mohammad. Mohammad reminded him of his failed attempt to marry and settle down. "I thought you would not come to school today too," Mulla Hassan told Mohammad. "Dear Abu Hosham, I am sure you recognize that I love *maktab*, but it is my duty to help my mother. She is unable to take care of the animals, the farm, her own work, and raise seven children. I promise to be on time in the future," Mohammad replied. Mulla Hassan said, "You have missed so many classes, you are lagging behind, and I do not want other pupils to learn from you. Furthermore, I think you are becoming lazy too."

Mohammad said, "My dear teacher, I promise to be on time." Mulla Hassan shook his head in disgust and hatefully said, "You shepherd boy, you are simply wasting my time. Just leave me alone you *darazgoosh*, get out and just get lost." Mohammad asked, "Why do you call me by these words? I have not done anything wrong." Mulla Hassan said, "It was near noon that you came to school yesterday. School is not a barn that you can enter any time you wish to." Mohammad said, "Very early in the morning I have to take care of our animals, and my younger brothers or sisters come later to help me. That is the time I am released so I can come to school." Mulla Hassan said, "These are personal problems unrelated to me. I am not going to let you come to school anymore. You think I have forgotten your stupid comments about my lessons? You are not able to understand my knowledge about the pine, poplar, and sycamore trees; you are not able to digest the science that deals with snakes. It is a waste of our time." Mohammad had nothing to say. The teacher, however, was on a roll and kept talking. It seemed like Mohammad was the source of all his problems, failures, shortcomings, and disappointments. He stared at Mohammad with his mean, yellowish eyes and said, "You

do not have the potential to become a scientist and work for the government. You are better off continuing as a shepherd. I do not want to waste my
time anymore." Mohammad got upset, because even his family was not from
a rural area and his father's job was not related to farming. Mohammad said,
"My father was the court astronomer."

Mulla Hassan looked at Mohammad in contempt and said, "I do not think
this was an honor. I am glad you did not say that your father was the Grand
Vizier. You rude boy, get out of here. I know you, your father, and your
mother. I know your father Professor Ahmad Andijani. He was a poor man
and your poverty is well known in this village. He was afflicted with poverty.
Actually he was lucky to die young, so he did not have to suffer much. You
and your family members should suffer, because God does not like you."
Every word left a painful wound in Mohammad's heart and spirit. Mulla Hassan was done. Full of hatred, he was willing to lay the blame for all of his
problems on Mohammad. "God only may save you," said the teacher. "And
if it was not for this rich merchant's help, your family would break down. In
this store in the city, your mother sells her products, including herself."
When Mulla Hassan reached this point, Mohammad could not take it anymore. Mulla Hassan was accusing Mehrana in front of all of the students.
Mohammad, choking back tears, angrily said, "You have no right to accuse
my innocent mother; you are an ill-natured man. Be ashamed of yourself, and
you cannot charge anybody like this."

Mulla Hassan was a malicious, malignant person. He knew he should not
stay silent and let the young boy talk back to him. So he reached for the twig
of a pomegranate tree that he usually kept handy in a bucket of water for
punishing students. While he was shouting and beating Mohammad with
this wet twig full of knots, he kept on abusing him, "You are an ill-intended
boy. You are contaminating and tainting the spirit of my students. Just go
away, you *darazgoosh.*" Mohammad was badly beaten. He was bleeding from
several places, including his hands and face. Slowly, he made his way home.

The next day, Mohammad went to school with his mother. On hearing
Mehrana's complain Mulla Hassan said, "Your son mocks and holds everybody's ideas in contempt. Especially, he ridicules my stories. He is very picky
and bothers everybody. Because of his boldness and impudence, he does not
have a place in my school. I cannot allow your boy to have a bad influence
on my pupils. Your son only deserves to be a shepherd and no more."
Mehrana wanted to say something, but the angry teacher stopped her and
said, "Your struggle is useless, I am not going to let your son stay in my
school."

Mehrana too got very angry and said, "Dear Abu Hosham, why do you think you have inherited this school. It is not a family business." Mulla Hassan too raised his voice and said, "No, why do you think it is your husband's inheritance? Your husband was known for breach of trust, treachery, and dishonesty. He was kicked out of the court only to live in poverty in this remote village." Mehrana's face turned red with anger, and with a trembling voice, she replied, "You must be really low, dirty minded, and ignorant to insult my deceased husband." Mulla Hassan shouted back, "You lowly rude woman, get out of my school, or I will tell my students to throw you and your son out of here."

Before leaving, Mehrana said, "I feel sorry that you take advantage of your position and prevent my son from continuing his education." Mulla Hassan went as far as saying he doubted the religious beliefs of Professor Andijani's family.

Mehrana recognized that very instant it was useless, and she left. Unbelievably, Mulla Hassan still was hopeful that Mehrana might change her mind and accept to become his wife. So for the final time, he asked the miller's wife to go to Mehrana and repeat his request. She told Mehrana, "If you accept his proposal, Mohammad can return to school too." Mehrana said, "The answer was and still is no, and I do have an option for my son. He does not have to go to school here."

This conversation occurred just four days before that fateful morning when Mohammad was captured to be taken into slavery. Because he was not allowed to go to school for four days, Mohammad became a full-time shepherd. Mehrana was thinking about sending him to some school in the city. Although she was unable, financially speaking, to do so, maybe she was looking for a miracle to happen. Mohammad did not have any choice but to tend to their herd. He most often was thinking what if his older brother was not taken into the military . . . and many other what-ifs!

CHAPTER FIVE

The Ghuzz

If, instead of Mohammad, his sister Zareen-Geesoo took the herd of animals out for grazing, she would have been kidnapped by the Ghuzz. They would have been happier to take a girl into slavery. She would have been auctioned off in one of many slave markets for a larger sum of money than her brother. Although slavery was discouraged in Islam and slave owners were encouraged to free their slaves, it was accepted by all religions. During the zenith of international trade in slavery, many Muslim-Arab merchants were responsible for a systematic hunting of human beings in east Africa. As late as the 1950s, King Saud had several thousand personal slaves.

In the tenth century in Transoxania, the local amirs who had recently accepted Islam as their religion were more serious about preventing slavery, particularly female slavery. Kidnapping and trading Muslim girls by the Ghuzz would have been punished severely. But the Ghuzz did not need to sell their captured Muslim girls in the Muslim world. In the neighboring non-Muslim countries, the court of some rich individuals were willing to pay large amounts of money for Muslim girls. It was not uncommon for the local Muslim amirs and rich families to have slaves of many origins, both female and male. These slaves would have been used and abused for many purposes.

In the same manner, the Muslim armies would take many so-called infidels into slavery and keep them as personal slaves or auction them in the market. Non-Muslim armies, of course, would do the same. This was a common practice, by both sides, during the Crusades, for example. The difference, however, was that in Muslim societies after giving birth to a baby, especially a baby boy, the slave mother would receive her freedom, and in many cases she would become the first lady or the queen. In non-Islamic lands, this was not the case. Slaves were kept for labor and lust.

The Ghuzz tribes would take Muslim girls to surrounding countries, to be sold to Chinese merchants, Indian temples, or to the slave merchants from the Byzantine Empire. Slavery was a profitable trade for many Turkish tribes. Even the two Iranian dynasties of Samanids and Khwarazmids were mostly unable to curb slave trade by the Ghuzz. They were getting reckless and bolder every day. Not only the rural areas of the northeast, but most of eastern Iran was at their mercy. Even Sultan Mahmud and his son Sultan Masud did not achieve any major victory over the Ghuzz. In fact, Sultan Masud was defeated by them once. The Saljuq Dynasty also had a hard time fighting the Ghuzz. It was in 1153 C.E. that Sultan Sanjar, one of the most powerful kings of the Saljuq dynasty, was defeated and he, himself, was taken prisoner. Still the Ghuzz, mostly a group of nomadic people, had respect for his source of power and authority and, maybe because Sanjar was of Turkic origin, he was treated differently in his four years of captivity. According to some historians, the Ghuzz treated Sultan Sanjar with respect, although he was closely guarded. "It is being said that he sat on a throne by day but was placed in a cage at night" (Sykes, 1969, p. 51).

The sun was on the brink of dawn when the Ghuzz woke up. Mohammad was unable to sleep well due to the cold, rain, and wind. He was kicked most of the night by a Ghuzz. Mohammad just stayed put in his place. The Ghuzz had some churned sour milk and bread as breakfast. They took the road to the south accompanied by Professor Ahmad's sheep and goats.

Mohammad was behind a Ghuzz on a horse again. He had to put his hands around the Ghuzz because he had already fallen down several times. He was getting very weak from walking on foot in the desert, bleeding, and not eating well. Until noon, the horsemen were on the move without delay. Mohammad only saw some desert animals, including some snakes. Each time he fell, he would receive lashes from the Ghuzz. He was slowing them down and was becoming a burden for them.

Many Turkic tribes including the Ghuzz used to live in Mongolia and western China. For a long time, they had been fighting each other and the Chinese for grazing grounds. They were pushed out of China, and the Great Wall was built to prevent these tribes from invading China. In central Asia, including Transoxania, these Turkic tribes intermingled with the local population; thus new lineages and new tribes were formed by the sixth century C.E.

The Ghuzz used to live on the banks of Syr Darya and had expanded to the shores of Lake Aral and the Caspian Sea. The lower banks of the river were their winter quarters. In the summer, they migrated toward the upper banks in the direction of the mountains in Afghanistan. They were constantly in search of grazing grounds and water for their large herds of animals.

Eighty years before Mohammad was kidnapped by the Ghuzz, they were visited by an Arab traveler representing the Caliph in Baghdad, Ahmad Ibn Fadlan. The main goal was propaganda and conversion of the Turkic tribes into Islam. Ibn Fadlan, although sometimes unclear, has provided us with some information about the Ghuzz from the early tenth century. He wrote an account of his journeys to Khwarazm toward the northwest, Russia, and all the way to Bulgaria in 921 C.E.

He reported in his book that he and his team stayed in the city Gurganj for the winter of 921. In spring, after ice was broken in Amu Darya, with enough provisions, warm clothes, and few camels they entered the land of the Turks. He reported that the Ghuzz had a life full of hardship and misery. In spring, these Turks in tents were hardly safe from the snow, ice, and very harsh climate. According to him, the Ghuzz were pagans, but when dealing with Muslims, they used Allah's name very often. The Ghuzz called their leaders *arbab*, meaning the master or the lord. A common Ghuzz would consult their master for even trivial matters.

Ibn Fadlan wrote that the Ghuzz, in the case of unpleasant events, would look at the sky and say "Birtankary," which means the "Only God." He also reported that the Ghuzz did not wash their bodies, especially in the winter. The Ghuzz women, according to Ibn Fadlan, were careless about covering their bodies. They were not bothered about being seen by strangers. The adulterers, however, were dealt with severely. They would be cut into two halves. They would execute the adulterers by bending two nearby trees and then after tying the legs to the trees, they would release the trees.

Ibn Fadlan wrote that the Ghuzz liked to listen to and recite from the holy book. Anytime he or any one of his companions said a prayer or praised Allah, the Ghuzz would do the same. He reported that marriage conditions were very simple among the Ghuzz. Dowry usually included a couple of camels or horses or any other animals. It was the duty of the eldest son to marry his father's wife after the death of the father, if she was not his mother. The Ghuzz believed that submerging into water was a part of witchcraft. Thus, foreign merchants were not allowed to do so. The Ghuzz did not have a formal religious guide for slaughtering an animal. They would hit the head of the animals until it was dead. When receiving Muslim guests, the Ghuzz would invite them to slaughter the animal that would be used for food, according to Islamic traditions.

Ibn Fadlan believed that the Ghuzz were very honest and trustworthy people. If a person of Turkish origin died in the house of a Muslim friend, the Muslim friend should pay with his life according to the Ghuzz. If this Muslim friend did not submit himself to the Ghuzz, and if he passed through Ghuzz land, he would be taken captive and killed. Ibn Fadlan has mentioned the name of the leader of the Ghuzz at the time of his visit. He was called the Little Yanall. And although he accepted Islam, his tribe members objected. Thus, he returned to his old religion of worshipping many gods. Ibn Fadlan wrote that the Ghuzz would leave sick persons in a tent until they die. The Ghuzz would bury their dead in a large well along with their weapons, food, and wine. If the deceased was a rich person, they would kill up to a few hundred of his animals and hang the heads of these animals on the grave. The Ghuzz believed the deceased person will arrive in heaven on the back of his sacrificed animals. If a deceased Ghuzz had killed people in his life, the number will be indicated by woodcuts on his grave.

Ibn Fadlan's general observation was that the Ghuzz were much better off than other Turkic tribes. It was not unusual to find families raising herds of up to one hundred thousand animals. He reported that the sheep and goats would find grass in the snow and under ice. Using their hooves, these animals removed the snow to find grass. They even chewed ice and got very fat. He further reported that these animals got very skinny in the summer because they could not find ice. This was one of Ibn Fadlan's misconceptions, however.

The Bashgards, a subgroup of the Ghuzz, were the most uncivilized and the dirtiest of the desert people. They were able to kill human beings very easily. They would even kill each other without much reason. Their body hair, including their beards, was full of lice. They would pick the lice from their dirty, worn clothes and eat them. Each one would be carrying a sharp piece of wood, hung on their neck, for defensive purposes. They worshipped a multitude of gods, including the god of summer, god of winter, god of rain, god of wind, god of water, god of day, god of night, god of quail, and many more.

These were the people who had kidnapped Mohammad.

CHAPTER SIX

Yalldowz

The Ghuzz who was carrying Mohammad on his horse was getting tired of him because he was so weak and he fell several times already. Mohammad could not hold on. The Ghuzz called to the leader of his group by name and said, "Ollan, this boy is dying. It is useless to carry him any longer." The leader said, "Hold on to him. We are almost there. When we reach the black tents, we will sell everything, including the boy." On the other side of a hill they saw several black tents located in the middle of the desert where there was some grass growing, which was used as a grazing ground for sheep and goats. Next to the black tents, Mohammad saw a dried tree that gave him some hope, because the whole view was not unfamiliar. He was reminded of his own village.

A few dogs that looked more like wolves started barking, and then began to chase the riders. There were four in all, two black and two russets. They immediately attacked the horses. Ollan brought out his leather lash and hit the big black one. But instead of going away, this dog jumped and tried to bite Ollan's horse. From the back of the black tents an old man came out wearing a fur hat. The old man's name was Yalldowz. He called his dog by name and said, "Be quiet, Seechqan." In Turkish, this meant a mouse. In some communities people named their pets by opposite names. The dog called mouse was actually very big.

These black tents were very important dwelling units for many nomadic groups including the Ghuzz. They were made of goat hair. Because goat hair is oily, water from any type of precipitation cannot penetrate inside. Yet because of the porous nature of the material, smoke could get out easily. There was only a drinking-water well in the middle of the tents. Beside the well, a bucket attached to a rope could be seen. When Ollan saw the old man he said, "Hello old fox, hello Yalldowz." The old man rubbed his eyes and laughed and said, "Hello to Desert Wolf, hello Ollan and welcome. What have you got now? Have you stolen idols from Hindu temples or Chinese silk, dishes from Bukhara and Samarqand, or pearls from Kish and Seeraf from the Persian Gulf Region? What have you brought to be sold to me?

The Ghuzz dismounted from their horses. Only Ollan hugged and kissed the old man. Yalldowz was about sixty-five years old and had yellowish eyes like that of a tiger. He was tall and his face was full of wrinkles. He was one of the "Friendly Ghuzz." This meant that he was receiving salary and rations from the government in Khwarazm in order to defend the borders and help the caravans have a safe passage; he was paid especially to pass on information to the government about outlaws, thieves, and highway robbers. In truth, the friendly Ghuzz would spy on the caravans' dates of arrival and departure and inform the outlaws. They also would buy and trade the stolen materials and slaves from the thieves. Yalldowz calmed down his dogs, put them on leashes, and joined his newly arrived guests with their stolen materials.

Everybody followed Yalldowz. They entered the large tent and sat in a circle. Yalldowz left for a couple of minutes. When he came back, he was carrying a big linen tablecloth. He spread it on a big worn-out carpet. He then arranged some food on it, right on the floor, including some dried pita bread, a bowl of yogurt, and some wild acorn fruit. Then he brought the main entrée, which was preserved meat kept inside goatskin. Yalldowz put portions of this meat saturated with fat on several clay plates. Everyone got a plate. Without any delay, the Ghuzz hurried to devour the food.

While still eating, Ollan asked his host, "Dear Yalldowz, how is your new wife?" Ollan burst into a loud laugh, and looking at his friends, he said, "Every three or four years, Yalldowz marries a new wife among the northern Ghuzz, then gets rid of them and later he marries a new one." Ollan's comment was not baseless. Thus, Yalldowz smiled and said, "But my last wife, Tarllan, is an experienced she-wolf. We are a compatible pair. I don't have any plan to get rid of or to kill her. She has married twice and both of her husbands died." Then Ollan commented, "And she is the one that will bury you. She has done it twice before. We know any two becomes three."

Mohammad was able to understand the Turkish language spoken by the Ghuzz. He was astonished that they could talk about their wives in public. Although he was only fourteen years old, he knew that it was forbidden for the Muslim people to talk about their wives in front of strangers. But the Ghuzz would talk about their wives as if they were talking about horses, sheep, and goats. They, however, valued wives who were good housekeepers, especially if they knew how to weave carpets.

Trade negotiations started after they had some more milk. The two sides began bargaining about the stolen items, including Professor Ahmad's animals. Ollan and his men were also carrying some cloth, containers, scarves, and carpets stolen from other people. Negotiations went on for almost two hours. Yalldowz purchased everything. He paid a few golden, silver, and mixed coins as the price of the items. In addition, Yalldowz gave a bag of sugar, one candlestick made of silver, a pair of boots, four fur cloaks, and some buttons and beads. Finally, Ollan pointed at Mohammad and said, "Buy this boy too, he was a shepherd. He can take care of your animals." Yalldowz walked toward Mohammad, took his two ears and squeezed them. Then opened his mouth and checked his teeth, his neck, his chest, and feet. It was like he was inspecting an animal. After Yalldowz found out nothing wrong, he said, "Alright, I buy him too. How much would he cost me?" Ollan said, "I am asking three mirrors, a Toosi scarf, a full-piece cloth, and twenty silver coins."

Old Yalldowz said, "No, that is too expensive. He is sick and will die soon." Then he took Mohammad's pulse and counted. "He has fever, too," he commented. Ollan said, "You, Desert Fox, know that he is fine and you may be able to sell him to some Chinese slave merchant for fifty golden coins." Yalldowz stared at Mohammad more carefully. His face saddened. Ollan was surprised and asked, "What happened?" Yalldowz did not reply. It seemed he was out of this world. He could not lie to Ollan. Yalldowz was touched by Ollan. It was like he was awakened and said, "Nothing, nothing. What were you talking about?" Yalldowz said, "The Chinese slave merchants will not buy this skinny boy. He is worthless, he cannot fight in the wars, he cannot work on the farms, he cannot even be a good servant in the festivities of the courts." "You are trying to lower the price of my slave," said Ollan. "If he was without any defect, I would not have sold him at that price," said Ollan. Yalldowz gave it a serious thought and then said, "He is not even worthy to be sacrificed." Ollan laughed and did not think he was serious. Mohammad understood those words, but he did not think so, either. Yalldowz said, "I am still not sure why he is so weak and pale?" Mohammad knew why. It was Ollan who answered, "You see, he is wounded and was bleeding. He has lost most of his blood. That is why he is pale. I promise you, with the kind of food Tarllan makes, he will recuperate soon. Afterwards, he can both serve in the armies and in the courts." Yalldowz said, "He may die before recuperating." Ollan said, "Dear Yalldowz, this boy has suffered too much. He has not eaten for two days and he has been bleeding as well. I assure you he will be able to take care of your animals. You can even use him as the beast of burden and use him for plowing your lands. You just feed him and he will be fine."

Yalldowz shook his head to indicate his negative response. He said, "You are a lazy man. You do not invade into the northern villages. You just capture poor people like this boy. Instead of this dying boy, if you had a few good-looking girls or a few well-built farmer slaves, I would have made you rich. Thus far, I have no choice but to accept the price you are asking. In the future, however, I am not going to pay what you ask."

Yalldowz turned his head toward Mohammad and ordered him angrily, "Hey, little dumb boy, get up and go behind the arbor and say hello to the lady of the house. Ask her whether she needs you to do anything. You stupid boy, do not even think about escaping. You cannot cheat or deceive me." He continued, "From today until I change my mind, you are my servant and slave. Committing the smallest guilt or having any fault would make me cut your head off like a goat. I decide to keep or sell you. If I like you and you finish your work, I would sell you to noble and honorable people who are very fair and take care of orphans and poor children like you. But in case of any mischief, I will sell you to such people that you will regret a thousand times a day that you were born."

"In this house we feed you, and instead of what I paid Ollan, you have to work. God help you if you do not listen to orders carefully and not do what you are asked to. You will be punished if we are not satisfied," said Yalldowz. Mohammad went behind the arbor. Now he could walk freely because his feet were not tied up anymore. He looked around. He did not find anybody.

Yalldowz gave what he promised Ollan to buy Mohammad. In addition, he gave a goatskin full of churned sour milk. Ollan drank some and gave the rest to his friends. Ollan said, "Dear Yalldowz, the living conditions in Transoxania are deteriorating. On my way back, like last year, I promise to bring you twenty young girls and twenty worthy and working boy slaves you can sell at much higher prices. Yalldowz replied, "These are just empty promises. Show me in action." Ollan cried, "We will see, we will see." Then he and the seven other thieves mounted themselves on their horses and took to the road. Yalldowz called his wife, Tarllan.

She did not come but cried, "What do you want? I am busy washing the baby." Yalldowz looked at Mohammad angrily and said, "Go and say hello to the lady of the house. You are our slave. Until I sell you, you should do everything we tell you without any delay." Mohammad saw a man behind the arbor that was washing a baby. The baby was standing naked in the middle of a big wooden pan and was crying. When Mohammad got closer, the person washing the baby turned around. It was not a man. It was Tarllan, Yalldowz's wife. She was wearing men's clothes. She was tall, with broad shoulders, and looked strong and well built. She had the ugliest face that Mohammad had ever seen. Her face was yellowish and hairy and she had pocked skin, maybe due to smallpox, marked with long cuts of sharp objects. She had a big mouth, flat nose, and ugly eyes. She had a grim look that would disgust anyone who saw her. Just then, Yalldowz came from behind the arbor. He said, "This is the slave you wanted. He will help you with the work around the house." Tarllan looked at Mohammad heedlessly and said, "Oh, oh! This dying boy can help. We have to feed him. We do not even have enough food for ourselves. He will eat our food and will steal our stuff."

Yalldowz said, "Do not worry about him now. I will think of something. But before anything else, let's behead these animals and salt their meat and hide and put them out in the sun to dry. Tarllan said, "But winter is near. If we process and dry the hide, my brother will come this way in a month. We can sell him up to forty fur cloaks." Yalldowz said, "Your brother is cheap. I do not want to trade with him anymore. I want to sell my products to the Khazar tribe or the Russians." Tarllan replied, "Why would they buy your products when they have the best in the world?"

Yalldowz said, "Do not waste time. Let's start." His wife was not sure and said, "We should not . . . we are unable to process all of these animals. We will lose money." Yalldowz was afraid. He said, "These animals may have some brands. Their owners might inform the security forces. They might find out these were stolen and arrest us. Ollan is a careless thief. Somebody may be following him. He himself could report us to the authorities. We will then suffer." Tarllan laughed and said, "Who can find us in this huge desert among several thousand black tents?" Yalldowz said, "These animals could have some marks and this boy may report us." Tarllan did not say anything, because he was right. Then she said, "Let's kill the boy first. I do not like him."

Yalldowz said, "I will sell him. I have paid for him. There are some people who will be willing to pay and buy him." Tarllan answered, "He is about to die. Nobody will take him even for free. Who will pay to buy such an ugly slave?" Yalldowz said, "Do not worry. There is a tribe that has a celebration once a year when they sacrifice a young boy in order to satisfy their god." Tarllan said, "This is not practiced among the Ghuzz anymore." Yalldowz replied, "I have known this tribe for three years. You are right. They are not of the Ghuzz origin. They do their ceremonies in secrecy. I have been able to provide them with the slaves that were sacrificed the last three years. And more importantly, they pay good money." Tarllan said, "It is not a good idea to deal with such people. If the authorities find out about what you have done, they will punish you." Yalldowz said, "You knew those boys. One day they disappeared, and I did not tell you who the buyer was."

Tarllan said, "My baby Batoor is tired. Let me put him in bed, then I can help you." "Hurry up," said Yalldowz. "I am afraid of the authorities. She took the baby to his bed inside of the arbor. Their little house (arbor) was located in the middle of the black tents. It was a more permanent structure made of a few wooden poles covered by a felt made of animal hair. The floor of the arbor was covered by some old and cheap carpets. It had a dome-like roof also covered by felt. The entrance was rectangular. Another felt was hung over it, which was like a curtain and used only at night.

Although the Ghuzz believed in many gods, Yalldowz recited some prayers, sharpened his knife, and started to cut off the head of the stolen animals. He was actually enjoying what he was doing. Like an old and experienced butcher, he was cutting the throats of Professor Andijani's animals one by one. He would make a hole near the shank of each animal's legs and then he would blow into the hole in order to separate the skin from the body.

Mohammad's heart was filled with sorrow. He was unable to watch Yalldowz killing the animals. The ground was all bloody. The dogs could be seen waiting. Mohammad was thinking about the time and the effort he and his mother had put in to raise those beautiful animals. Two hours later, Tarllan made some goat soup. She poured some soup in a small copper bowl and put a wooden spoon in it and offered it to her slave. "You boy, come and eat." Mohammad was so depressed that he did not hear Tarllan. She, however, thought that he had ignored her; thus, she got angry and cursed him. He then picked up the soup and tasted it. It was dirty and tasted bad, and was very hot. He could see very big red peppers in the soup, which burnt his mouth so badly he jumped up to get some water. He had noticed the jar containing water was outside the arbor, so he rushed out the door toward it. But Tarllan thought he was trying to escape. Therefore, she followed him with a big tree stub. Hurriedly, Mohammad blurted out in Turkish, "I want some water!" She hit Mohammad's shoulder anyway. It was a painful blow and the bowl of soup dropped on the ground. She went on cursing nonetheless.

In the desert, autumn days are short. It was getting dark already by five o'clock. Yalldowz unleashed his dogs, who started running around the camp excitedly.

It was about an hour after the sunset that Yalldowz brought out a metal yoke that was attached to the end of a chain about five feet long. He put this yoke around Mohammad's neck. Mohammad was standing near the entrance of the arbor. After Yalldowz put the yoke around his neck, he had to sit down.

This was due to the weight of the chain, and it also shortened the distance between his neck and the other end of the chain. Yalldowz took that end inside the arbor and fastened it to the ground using a peg and a hammer. Like an animal, now Mohammad was on a leash. This was done to prevent him from running away.

This was the way the Ghuzz would treat their slaves. These captured individuals would be tied by a chain. The Ghuzz made the slaves sleep outside, while they would keep their goats and sheep inside tents. The slaves thus were less valuable than animals. Individuals captured by the Ghuzz would be sold and bought several times until they arrive at their final destinations. In most cases, they would remain slaves for the rest of their lives.

Yalldowz threw him an old blanket that was full of holes. This was his night cover. Nearby, Mohammad found a sun-dried brick and used it was a pillow. At least the ground was sandy. Yalldowz dropped the felt that like a curtain covered the entrance of the arbor. He turned off the lamp inside and in minutes began snoring.

This was Mohammad's first night that he had to sleep with an iron collar. It was a cold and windy night. The metal yoke around his neck was very tight and it soon got cold. The chain was kept very short so that his moves could be controlled by his master. He was lying on the bare ground with his head near the entrance. Anytime he turned and tossed, the chain would make a noise. So it was impossible to escape at night.

Most of the Turkish tribes of northeastern Iran were involved in robbery and catching poor people for slavery. This was going on for a long time; it was at least a thousand-year-old tradition. The Ghuzz, Aghuzz, Uzbeks, and many other tribes would invade Korasan, Kerman, all the way to the Caspian Sea province of Mazandaran and the southern province of Fars.

The seminomadic and semicivilized tribes created a painful saga in the history of Iran. They would rampage the eastern lands particularly when there was no powerful central government or when it was weak or badly divided. At the time of a powerful central government, the eastern frontiers were usually quiet. These tribes would not dare to invade. They would come, however, at the time of internal disturbances. Many Persian kings and sultans, including Cyrus the Great, Sanjar, Sultan Masud, and Nader Shah, had to fight, repel, and punish these tribes. These offensives were in reaction to the inconvenience created by trespassers and were defensive in nature rather than conquering. It was hard and very expensive to mobilize large armies to defend the eastern desert frontiers of the Persian Empire.

This is why history repeated itself so often. We do not have a scientific explanation for it. We know, however, the desert environment of central Asia was very poor in resources and the population was growing. In the open deserts, the horizon is never too far. Nomads would see rich land at hand. With the exception of river valleys, water shortage was a major problem for farming and animal husbandry. The soils were infertile and the rains very unreliable, grasslands were very limited, and no mineral resources were to be found. More importantly, how long could these poor people suffer? Therefore, the poor nomads would attack the poor farmers. This did not mean that the very rich people were safe. Sometimes, they too could lose everything to nomadic robbers.

The way Yalldowz and Tarllan treated Mohammad was very common among the Ghuzz. Yalldowz and Tarllan both had Turani blood. Mohammad, on the other hand, was Irani. Even in the legends, these two nations had always been enemies. The legendary book of poems by Ferdosi (935–1020 C.E.), called *Shahnamah*, or the "Book of Kings," is based on the continuous struggle between good Iranis and bad Turanis. The nomadic people of Turan have invaded Iran in legendary accounts as well as in real history.

Whenever Tarllan would beat up a slave with the big tree stub that she kept, she had no fear or feelings. Sometimes, she would hit slaves more severely than she would any animal. She seemed to have no sentiments or feelings when she heard these slaves cry out because of the tormenting and painful blows they received from her. It did not make any difference to her whether these slaves survived or died.

Love, passion, sentiments, and feelings are associated with different levels of civilization and continuation of human history. In more advanced societies, these feelings become more tender. In more advanced civilizations, human beings would understand love, affection, and happiness or sadness and hopelessness better than less civilized societies. Central Asia's infertile land and harsh nature was represented by the couple that kept Mohammad in a yoke. The people from the barren lands of central Asia were jealous of the mainland Iranian people. The hard-working people of Iran found water underground on the Iranian plateau. By means of the *qanat* system, they produced many products on the farm and raised many animals. By the next century, however, the Turkic tribes became so powerful they defeated Sultan Masud and imprisoned Sultan Sanjar.

The night was windy and cold. And Mohammad trembled all night long, with his yoke chained to the ground. The blanket was quite small, so however he tried either his head or his feet were exposed. It was a stormy night, and it had been raining too. The clouds were loaded, and it seemed like it was raining from all directions. Mohammad could not sleep, although he was very tired. Reduced to a tormented slave, he began to wonder why some people have such fates. He wished he was home, although it was not an easy life.

It was only three days ago that his biggest problem was his bad teacher. When alone, sometimes he would complain to himself about the hard work and the endless chores. He would ask, "Why should I be doing all the work? I have to take the animals for grazing early in the morning, work on the farm, milk the cows, and still help mother. . . . I am only fourteen years old, and yet I have so many responsibilities. The work never ends." But until three days ago, he had a roof over his head. The food was always ready at mealtimes and tasted good too. He had a real pillow under his head and a quilt to cover his body. He had a loving mother whose love and affection was unlimited. He had brothers and sisters too. Every evening after dinner, they would talk, laugh, and have fun together. His biggest problem then was his teacher. Now, life itself was a problem.

Mohammad began to cry. His tears got mixed with the raindrops and were washed away in no time. He could see no hope in his life. He was in pain but he was thinking about the kind of pain his mother would have felt after her son and animals disappeared altogether. He got calm after crying for the longest time in his short life. At the bottom of his heart, there was some hope. Then he heard a mysterious voice from afar, mixed with the rain and wind, saying, "Dear Mohammad, do not worry. You will live. You will get out of this dreadful and hideous situation. Do not be hopeless and disappointed. Just do not despair. You will be having a long and prosperous life."

In those painful moments, suddenly Mohammad was feeling better. Although seemingly unlikely, he believed every word he just heard. He felt he was not alone anymore. He was thinking maybe this was one way to greatness. By now, his cover was completely wet. Anytime he covered his head, his feet were out and when he covered his feet with this felt full of holes, his head was out and at the mercy of the elements.

Yalldowz and Tarllan at least could have roomed him with the animals in one of the black tents. The reason they did not put him in a tent was that they looked at all Iranians as their enemies. This feeling had its roots all the way to the time of Cyrus the Great. In reality, however, the couple were afraid of the Iranians, which was totally unlike their attitude toward others of their tribe. They were afraid to put Mohammad in a tent because they believed that the Iranians were very smart and even had magical powers, which they could use to easily get out of any hardship. Thus, they suspected Mohammad might run away. Even a boy of his age could be crafty, tricky, and deceitful, with magical powers. Therefore, they thought he might escape if left alone in the tents at the back and so they put him in chains and tethered him to the ground at their threshold.

The couple got out of their hut at sunrise. When Yalldowz saw Mohammad all wet and cold, he said, "If you forget about running away, I will let you sleep in the black tent tonight." Mohammad could not respond. Yalldowz removed his iron collar and Mohammad began to rub his neck. He could feel the place where the yoke was on his muscle. Then he heard the baby crying, who too had woken up. Mohammad sat in the sun all day long. The chill of the night had made him sick. But the sun warmed him up and relieved the pain in his muscles and bones.

By noon, Tarllan gave him some watery soup with no meat and a dried piece of pita bread. He cut the bread into smaller pieces and dumped them in his soup to be soaked. The dogs also got the same kind and amount of food as Mohammad. That night he was allowed to sleep in the black tent. Yalldowz thought one night at his doorway was enough to teach him a lesson. He had to learn to obey and forget about escaping. These black tents were old and weather-worn. Although he was safe from rain, it was another chilly night.

In this way, six weeks passed. Only a few times the thieves brought their commodities to be sold to Yalldowz. A few days later, in return, Yalldowz would take the commodities to be sold in nearby cities. Mohammad's apparent obedience caused Yalldowz to allow him to take the animals to graze near a hill not too far from his camp. Mohammad was a hard-working person and he carried out all of his tasks efficiently. He was a worthy slave and Yalldowz was getting to like him. But Tarllan now was getting jealous of him and she complained continuously. She even said that they did not have food for him and that, more importantly, the government soldiers or *jandars* may pass by and see him and ask who he was. She suggested many times to her husband to get rid of him as soon as possible.

Mohammad would walk around the camp in chains. The sound of the chains would indicate that he was still nearby. Yalldowz, who himself was once jailed, had run away with such chains. So Mohammad was being watched at all times. He had to wake up early, milk the goats and sheep, and take them for grazing. Yalldowz would watch him from a nearby hill. More importantly, the dogs were observing and watching him all the time. These dogs were very clever too. Under their watchful eyes, he could not make any wrong moves. It seemed at all times they were waiting for a chance to jump on him and get him by his throat.

He tried many times to win their friendship but was unsuccessful. The reason was that he did not have anything to feed them. Yalldowz and Tarllan were poor. Even bread was rarely available. She would bake some every other week only. Mohammad and the dogs would eat the same food. However, anytime Yalldowz killed an animal, the dogs would have more to eat than Mohammad. They would eat most of the stomach contents and intestines and other by-products that would be thrown away by Yalldowz. Sometimes, Yalldowz would save these by-products for the next days in a secret place so neither Mohammad nor the dogs could find them. To ensure his dogs do not lose their killing instinct and hunting abilities, whenever Yalldowz had a lamb or a kid that was dying, he would set his dogs on the animal, who would tear it apart and eat it. So the dogs were never hungry.

Little by little, Mohammad was allowed to take the animals away from the camp for grazing. Slowly he noticed there was a vague and ambiguous sound coming from the distance. Especially, when the desert was quiet, he felt the sand flowed like water. The sound was clearer at night.

Soon winter arrived and the whole area was covered by snow. The snow was powdery and the wind would carry it everywhere. The silence of the desert hardly would be broken by the cry of wild animals. Life too was more miserable for him in the winter. When the spring rains arrived and the snow started melting, he could hear the sound of the river more clearly. The sound would give him some far-reaching hope and calmness. Now he was sure. He could hear the sound getting louder in the daytime. This was the time he started to seriously think about running away. He noticed that Yalldowz was waiting for a special customer. A few days earlier, Mohammad heard Yalldowz saying to his wife, "This boy is so weak that nobody would buy him for work. He is only good to be used for sacrifice."

Mohammad thought that maybe Yalldowz was joking and not really serious. Where could Yalldowz find people to purchase him for the sake of sacrificing him? In the following days, Yalldowz asked him many questions. Mohammad felt that he may have influenced Yalldowz not to sell him to that special customer who was coming in late March.

Late one afternoon, three months and six days after Mohammad was captured and put into slavery, he saw a column of dust rising in the northern side of the camp. He could see a few riders on their horses coming toward them. In a reddish horizon in the outset of that evening, they were galloping in the direction of the black tents. Yalldowz noticed them, too, because the dogs started barking and were becoming very agitated. Yalldowz stared at these riders and rubbed his eyes.

It was raining gently. He smelled the air. His nostrils were expanding. It seemed like he was trying to find out who the riders were from their odor. Yalldowz was a very experienced hunter, and thus had a very strong sense of smell. Most often he could recognize the identity of people from a distance from the odor of their bodies. Actually, it was easier to recognize riders coming from the north, in the direction of the wind. He knew that the Ghuzz hardly washed their bodies. Consequently, they would stink and he could tell whether the riders were friends or foes. In addition, most often the Ghuzz would carry raw meat under their saddles when hungry, and they would eat the raw meat while riding on their horsebacks. This gave them a characteristic smell.

Yalldowz was able to smell the odor coming from the north. He could tell it was distinct from the usual stinking odor typical of his people. If they were not among the Ghuzz, then who were they? The closer the riders got to the camp, the more certain he felt about the identity of the riders. Coming from the north, in the direction of the capital city, for sure they were not friends. They were the *jandars*, members of the government security forces responsible for roads, caravans, and rural areas—similar to gendarmes.

"They are *jandars* of the Amir of Khwarazm," Yalldowz shouted while jumping in the air. He called his wife and said, "Hurry, hide the boy. If they see anything, they would punish us very badly. You know how ruthless these soldiers are." Tarllan said, "Instead of hiding him, let's kill him. We can get rid of his body easily." Yalldowz said, "You dumb woman, they are about to reach us. We have no time to kill him."

Tarllan stared at the road while combing her hair. Her husband was right. She stopped combing as soon as she had begun. The riders were too near. The wind was blowing their blue cloaks as they were spurring their horses on. For the last time, Yalldowz almost shouted at Tarllan and said, "Get the boy and hide him among the sick animals and the milking ewes in the far side of the black tents." Mohammad was inside the arbor. His hands were tied up by a rope. She took him to the last black tent and in a friendly voice told him, "Just lie down and shut up. The riders coming in our direction are thieves and murderers. If they find you here, they will kill you. Do not make any noise. If you keep quiet, I will set you free."

Mohammad, after spending three months and six days in captivity, was much weaker than before. He just looked at Tarllan with his big black eyes. He was too frightened to say anything.

The riders included a captain and four *jandars*. They were mounted on well-groomed big horses with saddles having silver rivets. They were armed with bows and arrows, spears, swords, and shields. They slowed down their big horses near the camp. The captain shouted, "Who is the owner of this camp? Where are you, man? You dirty animal, come and put your dogs on a leash and quiet them."

Yalldowz was hiding behind the arbor and watching the riders carefully. He saw and recognized the riders as *jandars* of the Amir of Khwarazm. They were all young, well groomed, and well built. They had very beautiful cloaks on and their boots and helmets were shining, indicating they were all well paid. It was the duty of the *jandars* to ensure safety and security in the countryside. They would inspect the camps and black tents once in a while. They would also bring food and weapons to so-called friendly tribes that had converted to Islam.

The *jandars* dismounted themselves near the camp. Their horses and weapons were making a lot of noise. The horses were scratching the sand; they were thirsty. The captain of the group touched his long and hanging mustache and cried, "Who is the owner of this camp?" He was new in the force. He was not too well informed about this region.

The captain ordered one of the *jandars* to get some water for the horses. He used a bucket attached to a long rope to get water from the well located in the middle of the camp. It was at this very time that Yalldowz showed up from the back of the arbor. He said "Hello" flatteringly, while rubbing his hands together. He immediately ran toward the dogs, put them on a leash, and took them to the back of the black tent. The captain asked him, "Tell me, nomad, what's new?" While smiling, Yalldowz replied, "My dear Amir, in this huge desert hardly anything changes. What we have here is heat of the day, cold of the night, snakes, roaches, lizards, and scorpions." "Alright," said the captain. "Get me a cold drink, kill a lamb and make some kabob." Yalldowz shook his head sadly and said, "My dear Amir, these domestic animals belong to somebody else, and I am not allowed to kill any, but we have cold sour milk." Then he handed a goatskin full of sour milk to the captain.

The captain asked him whether he had purchased or sold any slaves recently. This time Yalldowz bowed humbly and said, "My dear Amir, I am a Muslim now and I am not involved in trading humans anymore." At that very moment, Tarllan put a handkerchief in Mohammad's mouth because he was trying to stand up and say something. "What is in there?" asked one of the officers pointing at the farthest black tent. He thought he heard something. "Nothing important! That is the tent where we keep sick animals and the milking ewes," said Yalldowz, while the color of his face was fading. The captain said, "Maybe you are keeping stolen materials you usually purchase from thieves." "No sir, actually, I was expelled from my tribe because I accepted Islam and they will kill me if they find me. My earlobe will become the largest part of my body. Furthermore, I am a Muslim now, and I am not involved in anything that is against my religion," answered Yalldowz. "So, you are a Muslim?" asked the captain. "Yes, Sir," responded Yalldowz. Yet the captain slapped Yalldowz. "Father dog . . . , bastard, liar, if you are a Muslim what is this?" the captain said angrily pointing to the bronze statue of a quail that hung on the arbor. The quail was among the gods worshipped by the Ghuzz, indicating that Yalldowz was not a Muslim.

The captain said, "You dirty thief-murderer. You started lying to me. . . . We have traced some thieves' paths coming toward your camp. Unfortunately, we lost their course. Where are they?" He hit Yalldowz again. Yalldowz cleared the blood coming out of his mouth and said humbly, "I swear to Allah that I am not an idol worshipper. My stupid wife forgot to remove that statue. God damn her." The captain took the quail idol from the arbor and threw it toward one of his officers and said, "Let's go and inspect the black tents." It was getting dark. They just walked in front of the tents and looked inside the tent where Mohammad and Tarllan were lying in the middle of the animals. Mohammad moved a bit but was pressed down by Tarllan. His mouth was covered, and there was no way he could scream.

"Go get a lamb and fix us some food," ordered the captain. "I will carry out your orders, sir, but my animals are sick and their meat is contaminated with a strange disease, probably with anthrax. Now, you decide. I do not want to endanger your life," replied Yalldowz. "Are all of your animals sick?" asked the captain. "Yes, sir, this disease is killing my entire herd. My dear Amir, just look behind the black tents, you will see at least ten to fifteen carcasses. The disease is frightening. It not only kills animals, I am sure it is dangerous to humans too. I do not even skin the carcasses. I am afraid to do so," pleaded Yalldowz. The captain said, "I do not believe you. You are a liar. I have no reason to trust you." "Let's take to the road before it is too late," he ordered his men. It had started raining. The *jandars* got on their horses, made a lot of noise, and galloped away spurring their horses.

When the *jandars* reached a certain distance, Yalldowz started laughing loudly and called his wife. She released Mohammad and came out of the tent. "Dear husband, you are making a mistake by keeping this boy alive. You do not know when your so-called customers will come to buy him. The *jandars* will come back. Do you know how they punish the Ghuzz trading Muslim slaves? My father had told me a story of such a Ghuzz who was burned alive." "Why don't you do it yourself?" argued Yalldowz. "The infidels that sacrifice human beings may show up late and by then the *jandars* may catch us." "I have never killed anything or anybody. You do it. You kill so many animals so easily. You kill him," said Tarllan.

Yalldowz said that he was unable to kill an innocent person. He said he had never killed a child. "When I look at Mohammad, he reminds me of a son I had by the name of Toghan when I was very young. He died of an unknown disease."

Mohammad had been listening to the couple. He knew Turkish and was able to understand what they were talking about.

CHAPTER SEVEN

The Escape

Tarllan picked up a tree stump and a long knife that still had some dried blood from being used to behead animals. She went toward the black tent where Mohammad was lying on his back and his hands were still tied up. He was ready for that moment. As the Ghuzz woman stepped inside, he hit her with his feet using all his strength. She was not ready for such a strong blow. As she fell to the ground she cried from the pain in her stomach where Mohammad kicked her. The brawl was so loud Yalldowz heard her and ran toward the tent where they had kept Mohammad captive. At this very minute, lightning brightened the sky and thunder shook the ground. A bolt of lightning hit the dried tree by the camp and it caught fire. These natural elements together had the Ghuzz couple very frightened. Even Yalldowz cried out loud.

Mohammad sprang up and jumped out of the black tent. He began running toward the hill in the west of the camp with all his might. Fortunately for Mohammad, as was ordered by the *jandars*, Yalldowz had his four dogs on leashes tied to the ground. Otherwise, the dogs would have caught him in no time before he reached too far.

Yalldowz inspected the black tent and saw his wife lying flat on the ground groaning from the pain in her stomach. She said in a tone full of hatred and disgust, "I have told you many times, just kill this wicked rascal, go and get him. If you do not kill him, I will kill you. I hope this time you do it." Yalldowz said, "Now, I go after him." But the Ghuzz did not know, of course, that in Mohammad's native village of Vasemereed, he was the fastest runner and he could outrun everybody. Had he known this, Yalldowz would have started the chase without wasting any time. Moreover, Tarllan's painful yell woke her son up sleeping in the hammock, and he began to cry.

In addition, the natural elements provided Mohammad with a few minutes' head start. He was running in the rain with his hands tied with rope. Anytime the ground and sky was lit up by the flashes of lightning, he would become more frightened that he may be killed by it or seen by the Ghuzz. It was unclear why Yalldowz did not go after his slave immediately.

In about fifteen minutes, Mohammad reached a wide river. He stumbled into the water. Fortunately for him again, the river was not too deep. When he reached the middle of the river, the water was up to his chest. Now he could hear the dogs following his footsteps. They were barking very loudly and coming in his direction. But in the darkness of the night in the middle of the river, Mohammad knew the dogs would lose his scent and thus be unable to catch him. He was taking very careful steps. He did not want to drown in the river.

Apparently, Yalldowz had called off the chase by now, Mohammad thought, because the dogs' noise was getting further away from the river. Yalldowz probably knew it was useless to search for his slave at that time of the night, because the dogs were unable to help either, after they reached the river. The Ghuzz might have been thinking of going after him in the morning in the light of the sun. The Ghuzz was an experienced hunter. He knew his slave could not go very far. The Ghuzz Desert was featureless. He was confident he would be able to catch him the next day. Once Mohammad reached the opposite side of the river, silence fell on the land. He could not hear the dogs anymore.

Mohammad had difficulty climbing the bank of the river. It was muddy, wet, and steep. When he finally made it, he was cold and he was tired. He sat down for a few seconds to catch his breath. Then he tried to find a way to untie his hands. As he was walking, he stumbled on a rock with a sharp edge. He cut the rope and freed his hands using that sharp edge. Although, it was cold and raining, he cried happily and jumped into the air. He was free after all. The hope of living filled him with renewed energy. Even though his main food at the camp throughout his captivity was millet soup and a goat dish without the meat, he felt like he had lots of energy. He could walk fast with long steps. In a short while, he reached a caravan road. He guessed it might be in the south–north direction. Although he knew some astronomy, he was unsure about the direction of that road, because it was raining and the sky was covered with clouds. This meant he was unable to put his knowledge of the stars to use for deciding which direction to take. However, he knew that he must go in the opposite direction of the Ghuzz campground. And he walked in that direction until morning.

Without taking any break, he kept walking away after the sunrise. He felt he was getting hungry. It had been hours since he had any food. He could not remember the last time he had any good food recently. He walked another three hours until he saw a camp belonging to another Ghuzz. They were the only residents of the desert after all. So he turned and walked in a different direction. It was too easy for the Ghuzz to identify Muslim people. The Ghuzz and many other Turkic tribes would not circumcise their male offspring. Thus, Mohammad knew for sure on being captured, inspected, and recognized as a Muslim, he would be returned into slavery. He would be returned to Yalldowz.

He walked for nearly two more hours, when he reached a hill. He saw an arbor with nobody around. He also saw a pot on the fire. He walked closer cautiously. He realized that residents of the camp were away on their business of hunting or attacking the caravans passing by. He also recognized that they must not be too far because the food was almost ready. It had been twenty-four hours since he had any food, and the food over the fire was smelling really good. He took the last step uneasily. There was absolutely nobody around. He quickly removed the cap and the piece of white cloth that covered the food and found out that it was a type of Turkish food (nowadays called Istanbully *polow* or Istanbully rice dish in Iran) made with rice, meat, carrots, onions, green beans, oil, and salt. (The recipe for this dish probably came from the city of Istanbul, Turkey.)

He became very happy on finding such heavenly food in the desert. He took the pot off the fire and took some of the food with his dirty finger and put it in his mouth. It was a delicacy compared with the food made by Tarllan. It was something so luxurious and pleasing that he decided to take a break and enjoy the food. He saw a bucket attached to a rope by the water well. He dropped the bucket into the well to draw some water so he could wash his dirty hands. He used the white cloth covering the rice to wipe his hands dry. Then he noticed some onions that were hung by the door. He took one and smashed it using the palms of his hands. He sat down to eat with a full appetite and had about one third of the contents of the pot. This rice dish and the fresh onion tasted exceptionally good. The smell of the food was so good that after a short pause, he started eating again. About half of the food was still in the pot. Mohammad took the pot and put it back on the fire, which was dying out.

He walked around the desert for an additional three days and three nights. He saw some low-lying hills and another river. He felt he was walking in a southerly direction. By noon, on the fourth day of his escape, he saw a hill. When he climbed it, he saw a camp consisting of an arbor and three black tents. He also saw a man and a woman fetching water from the well. At that very moment a big wagon became visible to him. It was being pulled by six black and white oxen. Four men were sitting on the wagon. Mohammad was extremely happy on sighting the wagon.

He had seen this kind of wagon before. Old merchants, mostly of Chinese origin, would use this type of wagon. He decided to go and ask them for help to be taken to Kath, the capital city of Khwarazm. Before taking another step, he had a good look at the camp one more time.

CHAPTER EIGHT

Yalldowz Again

This camp was very similar to that of Yalldowz. Mohammad felt somewhat surprised and remembered the few months of wicked life before his escape. Remembering that bitter and evil experience, he thought the view was very similar indeed. But when he was first brought to Yalldowz's camp by Ollan, it was autumn. Now it was the beginning of spring and the land was covered by flowers and grass.

He still was wondering where he was that moment when someone tapped him on the shoulder and then began yelling, "Got him. Dear Yalldowz, I found your slave. He came back by his own feet." It was like he had woken up from a bad dream. He tried to run away, but the man put both of his arms around Mohammad and stopped him. It was impossible to free himself from those strong hands clutching him hard. The man dragged Mohammad down the hill all the way to the next camp.

When Yalldowz saw Mohammad at hand, he started laughing madly and slapped him on the face. Tarllan too arrived with a little sharp sickle determined to kill him. But she was stopped by Yalldowz when he heard the bells clanging around the oxen pulling that huge wagon. Yalldowz said happily, "These are the ones that I have been waiting for. Last year, I had promised to find them another young boy for this year's sacrifice. Now we can get rid of this rascal."

Yalldowz was still unsure that he would not escape again. So he picked up a big piece of wood and hit Mohammad on the head. Mohammad fell to the ground.

During his escape and travels in the desert, Mohammad was not certain in what direction he was going. The night of his escape it was raining and cloudy. Hence, after a few days and nights of aimless walking, he returned to Yalldowz's camp unknowingly. Traversing the featureless desert is not an easy job. Only very experienced individuals and those who know the stars' configurations can make it. Although he had spent most of his life in a rural area, he had no experience navigating the desert. On that dark night he was unable to find his way out of the desert. He therefore came back to the place that he had escaped from. On the night when Mohammad ran away, Yalldowz and his dogs lost him in the night after Mohammad crossed the river. Yalldowz thought he could find him easily the next day and when his neighbors heard that his slave had escaped, they all got on their horses and searched most of the surrounding areas, but no one found him.

Arvaj, one of the Ghuzz, told Yalldowz that there was a camp belonging to the Lorians about six *farsangs* (thirty-six kilometers) away and Mohammad may have found refuge with them. The Lorians were a group of Hindu musicians invited to Iran by Bahram the Zebra Hunter of the Sasanid Dynasty to entertain people. They numbered about three thousand. Arvaj believed that Mohammad was with them. However, when the Ghuzz inspected the Lorians' camp he found no trace of Mohammad.

When Yalldowz and Arvaj were talking about what to do next to Mohammad, they heard the big bells and Yalldowz recognized the wagon that was being hauled by six oxen. After Yalldowz heard the wagon's bells, he shook his head and said, "They are coming to buy a slave from me for their annual sacrifice and I have none." Arvaj asked, "What did you say and who are those people?" Yalldowz said, "They call themselves the Tammami people and say they serve sick and needy people. They have a temple that is located at some distance from here by a high mountain range where the people with leprosy live in caves. These sick people are apparently being helped by the Tammamis, who gave them food, fruits, and medicine. In that big temple, every year on the twenty-eighth day of spring, the Tammamis have an important celebration." Arvaj commented that he was unaware of the temple nearby. Yalldowz said he had not seen the temple by himself but had heard about it from a friend who had spoken to a person with leprosy living in the caves. Yalldowz added that this temple had been around at least for a thousand years and that the Muslims had once destroyed it. Just then Yalldowz's talk was interrupted by another Ghuzz called Orghon, who said he saw somebody behind the hill and would go see who he was after giving his horse some water to drink. Arvaj said, "Do not rush, I will go." The wagon was approaching Yalldowz's camp and Mohammad was approaching the wagon to ask for help while Arvaj was behind him. Mohammad was taken back into slavery so easily, this time by Arvaj, Yalldowz's neighbor.

Yalldowz walked toward the wagon humbly and bowed. There were a total of four people on the wagon. The person in charge, it seemed, was probably fifty years old. He had a face dark brown in color, burned by the sun, shaggy eyebrows, and a grim look on his face. He politely responded to Yalldowz's greetings. Talking to Yalldowz, he asked, "Do you remember your promise?" Yalldowz replied, "Yes, Sir. One of the Ghuzz that deals with me has found you a slave. You can see him. Right there on the ground."

The grim-faced man jumped off the wagon and walked toward Mohammad. Before bending, he said, "But he is dead! I am not going to buy a corpse from you." Yalldowz said, "No Sir, he is not dead. He is only unconscious. I had to hit him to keep him from running away. When conscious and on his feet, he is very quick and agile. He might even escape again." The grim-faced man came back to his wagon and said something in an unknown tongue to a fat man with a reddish face still on the wagon. The fat man and the grim-faced man then walked together toward Mohammad. The fat man put his thumb on Mohammad's pulse and started counting. He also listened to Mohammad's heart beat and put a little mirror in front of his mouth and said, "Dear Bargozeeda, this young boy is alive, but unconscious." Bargozeeda said, "Dear Shenavanda, please give him some medicine and bring him back to life." The fat man acting like a doctor was called Shenavanda. These two names meaning the Chosen and the Listener were common names among followers of the ancient religion of Persia, Zoroastrianism, or fire-worshippers.

Shenavanda, the fat man, the Listener, got a leather bag from the wagon. From this bag he got a small bottle out, removed its cap and put it in front of Mohammad's nose. Mohammad sneezed first and then he opened his eyes. Shenavanda said, "The pain in his head will be gone in minutes." Bargozeeda ordered Shenavanda, "Untie his hands." The fat man did so and helped Mohammad stand on his feet. Bargozeeda ordered Shenavanda again saying, "Give the boy some *whoma*." This was the name for a potion or elixir. It was a sweet cure-all potion used for curing the sick. The fat doctor put some drops of *whoma* in Mohammad's mouth. It was a very powerful medicine. Mohammad seemed to receive a lot of energy and felt light and happy, forgetting all his pains.

Shenavanda petted Mohammad on the head and said, "From your eyes, I can recognize that you are a very smart kid. I can see that you are a bright boy, maybe taken from a nice family. We will help you to end your painful life." Mohammad stared at Shenavanda and asked, "Who are you?" Shenavanda replied, "We are very good people, we help the poor, the sick, and people like yourself. Please trust us." Shenavanda then helped Mohammad get on the wagon. Although he felt less pain after drinking *whoma*, now he was feeling numb and weakened. He felt dizzy and his eyelids were getting heavy. Shenavanda asked him whether he was alright. Mohammad somehow opened his eyes and said, "Yes." Then Shenavanda asked him what his name was. Mohammad said, "I do not remember." Shenavanda asked, "What were you doing among the Ghuzz?" Mohammad answered, "I do not know." Shenavanda further asked, "What do you wish to do?" Mohammad answered, "I wish to take a nap!" He was in deep sleep before the wagon took to the road again.

The wagon was moving slowly when Bargozeeda threw a small bag of gold coins toward Yalldowz and said, "We would like to depart. We'll come back next year same time for another young man." Yalldowz rubbed his hands together and said flatteringly, "Dear sir, would you like me to bring you some water or food or anything? Bargozeeda replied, "No thank you." His feet were still hanging out of the wagon and Yalldowz was holding on to the fence-like metallic edge, up to one meter high, of the wagon and kept asking questions. "Is it true that you really sacrifice the young boys you buy from me?" Bargozeeda put his right index finger over his lips and gently said, "Quiet, he is sleeping." Shenavanda said, "Do not worry. He will not wake up. The potion will keep him numb for hours." With a look full of hatred, Bargozeeda said, "Such a foolish and inappropriate question!" "The reason I asked you this question was that I provide you with these young boys; however, their life is so miserable, they are better off dead than alive," said Yalldowz. "We are followers of Tammami. Sacrificing a young boy on the day when our prophet Zakarya Tammami died is an important good deed and has very high rewards," advised Bargozeeda.

Yalldowz said, "Then, give me a promise." "What promise are you nomadic Ghuzz asking?" replied Bargozeeda. Yalldowz asked, "When you sacrifice this boy, is it possible to make it less painful? I have heard that some tribes such as the Khazar and Atils do have sacrificing traditions. Upon the death of a rich and powerful man, his servants would be sacrificed and buried with him. I also heard that the heads of these poor people would be smashed. It sounds horrifying! I feel bad. He reminds me of my son." Bargozeeda and Shenavanda exchanged a quick look and simultaneously said, "No, we cannot promise!"

"Why you good people do not promise," asked Yalldowz. "How do you know we are good people?" asked Bargozeeda. He asked this question with wide, penetrating, and angry eyes. He wanted to see how honest the Ghuzz was in his statement.

Yalldowz repeated, "How do I know you are good people? I do not need to explain. I am an old man. Half of my teeth have fallen. I eat dishes filled with meat and shish-kabob, but you eat only millet, beans, lentils, and peas." Bargozeeda smiled.

Yalldowz was thinking that at least he could get a promise that Mohammad's death would be less painful. Thus, he repeated his question as to why they would not promise him to kill Mohammad less painfully.

Bargozeeda shook his head and said slowly and clearly, "Because a painful death is ordered by our prophet. If a person being sacrificed dies under pain and torture, our reward and servitude is much higher and more worthy. But the person being sacrificed without pain is not any different from anybody else dying. It would be like a quick death with no rewards for us. That is, the suffering of the person being sacrificed increases our spiritual rewards." The Ghuzz continued, "I feel really bad, from the bottom of my heart. He looks like my son." The wagon was hardly moving. Yalldowz sat down on the ground and said, "Your gold coins are so bright and attractive. I am just a poor nomad. Since my younger years, I have known only daggers, swords, and blood, attacking villages and stealing their animals. I have been associated with the Uross people, who never wash their bodies and put their own refuse on their wounds to heal. I have dealt with the Khazar tribe, the Turks from the other side of the river, and even the Romans. I have beheaded sixty people with my own hands. But now I feel upset. For the first time in my life, I feel pain in my heart for somebody else's life. I think I like him. I cannot ignore him and his bright eyes. One night he talked to me about the different stars in the sky. He even knew their names."

Bargozeeda put another five gold coins in Yalldowz's hand and said, "Take this, and do not ask the impossible." "Go. Do what suits you, because . . ." Yalldowz began but he was interrupted by Bargozeeda, who said, "You talk too much and you are taking our time. You have sold the boy to us. It is none of your business what we do to him. How many times have you thought about the fate of the slaves you sell? Go to your camp. Count the gold coins and give them to your wife. You have no right to ask us about what you have sold us. He is now our property."

Yalldowz got angry and said, "But you are ruthless and foolish." Bargozeeda approached his curved Arabian sword that was inside its black sheath decorated with three large diamonds and said, "Keep your tongue inside your stinky mouth and say no more." Shenavanda continued by saying, "You are becoming rude to us. If you go on like this, we will have no choice but to send somebody to eliminate you altogether." Bargozeeda's look frightened Yalldowz. He felt powerless and under Bargozeeda's spell. Yalldowz was scared.

The mysterious, sad look on the faces of the people on the wagon was filled with trouble. These are the people that come from afar in their oxen-driven wagon covered with animal hide to purchase slaves from him. Unlike his usual trade partners, the people of Tammami never ate his food, never bargained, and paid cash. He was speechless. He compared them with his usual trade partners, mostly of Ghuzz origin, who were thieves, ate and drank greedily, and looked at his wife strangely. The people of Tammami wore clean white clothes and were fluent in Persian and Turkish but spoke in a different tongue with each other. They were calm and gentle, but with their stern faces appeared mysterious. Their coins were minted in Bukhara, Baghdad, or Khwarazm. They sometimes would give him coins of unknown origin. Yalldowz showed one of these coins to a jeweler. He thought it was of Chinese origin, but it was pure and authentic.

Yalldowz was very much afraid of Bargozeeda. His skinny face was like that of a skeleton. His face was long and similar to a horse's. He had two small mysterious eyes. His cheekbones stuck out and his complexion was grim and sad-looking. Yalldowz thought that he might be a grave digger who lived among the dead.

The oxen took few faster steps. Bargozeeda said, "We need five young boys for next year. It is the twelfth revolution of the solar system. We need to sacrifice five young boys. We need their blood to make the great elixir." Yalldowz kept talking, almost bragging that he did not know the boys would be killed. Bargozeeda was listening. Then he asked authoritatively, "Are you done?" The Ghuzz replied, "Yes."

Bargozeeda said, "I forgive you for being less polite to us. We are men of logic. But you are just a naïve nomad. You continue your trade and do not get inquisitive. There were people like you in Egypt who complained about sacrificing human beings during the flood of the Nile. Did the Arabs regret sacrificing their camels for the idols before Islam? You are like the Greek philosophers who ridiculed the Cartagian people for sacrificing their children." Yalldowz was surprised by Bargozeeda's rich knowledge and said, "I am sorry, I just felt bad for the killing of this innocent boy."

Bargozeeda's final words concluded that he did not lay the foundation of these ceremonies and he could not remove them. "There were thousands of people with leprosy who were anxiously waiting for the potion produced with the blood of these young boys. And if you feel bad, why do you sell these young boys to us anyway?"

The Ghuzz did not have an answer. The wagon was moving faster. When he took his first step toward his camp, the sound of the gold coins made him forget about the slave boy. He thought the amount of gold in this little bag was equal to one year of his total income. There was no better job than slave trade.

CHAPTER NINE

The People of Tammami

The white-dressed people of Tammami were traveling northward on a wagon pulled by six powerful oxen. They were on the road for eleven days suffering at the hands of the burning sun in the day and the biting cold at night. Who were these white-dressed people of Tammami? Where did they come from? and What was their goal in life?

Among the many religious, racial, and cultural groups from the medieval world, the people of Tammami, about whom we have very limited information, are shrouded in mystery. But they have a special place in the history of the Middle East. Carrying out the strange old ceremony of sacrificing human beings with pain and suffering is not new in our world. This was seen among some remote tribes in Africa and Oceania until the twentieth century. Only the expansion of civilization and mass media prevented it from being continued. The white-dressed people of Tammami found their way into Ghuzz lands in search of slaves to be sacrificed in ultimate pain.

Mohammad was in a deep sleep. He was actually in a semiconscious state, unaware of what was going on around him. The *whoma* potion was intoxicating him. He was lying flat in the middle of the wagon. The caravans of *jandarans* passing by would not notice anything strange and would not know what was really going on. The white-dressed people were reading books and reciting some strange words continually. At times they would stare at Mohammad's innocent face and maybe feel a sense of pity.

The people of Tammami reached the end of the road on the flatland. From now on the road was twisting and winding over mountains. They stopped for the night at the first caravansarai, but they stayed on their wagon. They only asked for some water and ice or snow, and barely looked at the *tanoor* where fresh bread was being baked and chicken being roasted. They parked their wagon in the yard. Early in the morning next day, they paid a few copper coins to the innkeeper before they left. The mountainous road was not very long, and soon they got on to a flat road. The desert was huge, with no end in sight. It was dry, barren, desolate, and uninhabited. The air too was dry and the unforgiving, burning sun was making it unbearable. Nothing seemed likely to stop the people of Tammami, who were moving northward slowly but relentlessly.

The four men in white driving continued on their way without much talk with each other or the people passing by. In the rain and even at night, they were on the move. Their food consisted of some beans, baked and dried and kept in a bag. They also had a clay jar filled with water. Mohammad woke up only a couple of times. One of the men would pour some of the thick *whoma* potion into his mouth. He would then go back to a deep sleep.

The *whoma* potion was the wonder drug of the Middle Ages. It was considered to be a cure-all by the Persians. It was formulated by a Zoroastrian priest in Iran and its ingredients kept secret for many centuries. It was used on people with mental problems and psychics. More commonly it was used as a pain reliever and used for putting patients to sleep.

By evening of the eleventh day of their journey, the white-dressed people of Tammami reached a high mountain range. Immediately on arriving on the mountain road, they heard a loud owl-like call, which was repeated a few more times. It seemed to be a secret code for the people of Tammami. When Bargozeeda became certain that it was a true code, he ordered Shenavanda, "You go to the tower of the people with leprosy and tell them to come to the temple for our ceremony. Tell them we've got a cure for their disease." Shenavanda climbed the mountain and Bargozeeda loosened the leash of the oxen, who continued to haul on the steep road.

The more they advanced on this mountainous road, the louder the owl's outcry became. The sound was so loud it finally woke up Mohammad. He saw many white-dressed people around the wagon and their number was increasing. All were wearing white mantles and long white hats. They were coming down from the mountain to accompany the wagon and its valuable cargo. Then the distant sound of a kettledrum was heard and was slowly approaching the wagon. Bargozeeda was reciting strange prayer words and carefully watching his followers. The newly arrived white-dressed people even looked more mysterious under their white long hats that covered their faces. They could see through two holes made in the hat. Bargozeeda called upon them and said, "Come, you miserable people, come and join us. We have a cure for you."

Bargozeeda was surprised by the number of the white-dressed people that still was increasing. He said to Shenavanda, "Their number is increasing every year." Shenavanda replied, "Yes sir, although leprosy is a fatal disease, they come here in the hope of finding a cure. The pure blood of the person being tortured and sacrificed may be a very important part of that cure." Bargozeeda said, "If we find the cure, in a short time the news of it will reach the whole world. It will be a renowned miracle and its fame will bring more followers to our prophet and more fortune for us. In a short time we will rule over the whole world." "It is true," said Shenavanda. He added, "I know you. You are a great chemist. With your knowledge, you could be the king of the world."

They finally reached a semiruined village. Outside, there was an abandoned *stwodone*, "the tower of silence." Bargozeeda commented, "I am glad that this village is isolated and is far from the caravan road. I have selected the *stwodone* as the place for carrying out our sacrifice." *Stwodones* were seen as a temporary intermediary place between death and resurrection by the Zoroastrians. It was a place where they left their dead to rot and be eaten by birds and other animals.

Bargozeeda said, "It is a good place. Nobody can bother us. We will carry on our religious duties in two days after we see the full moon."

In Zoroastrianism, the ancient religion of Persia, a waiting place for the bodies of dead people to decompose was called *stwodone* or the tower of silence. It was the intermediary place between death and resurrection. Literally, it meant a place of waiting, or a place of "standing." *Stwodones* were built on the top of some hills surrounded by gardens, mostly near large urban areas, all over the Persian Empire. Please notice the similarity between the Persian word *estadan* and *standing*, both meaning the same thing. The followers of the prophet Zoroaster, sometimes called the fire-worshippers, would leave their dead in the *stwodones* with their backs against the wall, standing on platforms and exposed to the natural elements. With help from the sun, rain or snow, wind, and scavengers, both animals and birds, including vultures, the flesh of the dead bodies would be gone. Slowly, only the skeletons or the bones would remain. At this time, the relatives of the dead come back for a true burial. They put the skeletons in white shrouds or big jars and bury them or leave bags full of bones in chambers deep in the basement of the *stwodones*, called *dakhma*. Most often the entrance doors to these basements would be closed up. Thus, this would become the final resting place for the dead.

After Islam penetrated and was accepted by the majority of the people, the number of *stwodones* decreased. Only a few in operation remained in the areas where Zoroastrianism was practiced. By the early years of the twentieth century, some *stwodones* were still functioning in the central part of Iran and in Transoxania. A few are found around the cities of Yazd and Kerman in central and southeastern Iran and in western India, where most Zoroastrians live.

The *stwodone* to which Mohammad was taken to be sacrificed was not in use anymore. After the Zoroastrians converted to Islam or left the region, this *stwodone* was used by the Buddhist monks for a long time. They set up a few idols and statues but did not succeed in recruiting new converts. Therefore, they too abandoned the *stwodone*. Then in the tenth century, the white-dressed people of Tammami arrived here.

They were a strange kind of people, with a different and unique behavior. They were involved in magic and sorcery and would undergo rigorous mortifications. For example, they would avoid eating or go on fasting for a long period of time or they would isolate themselves from the rest of the society. In addition, they would study a lot. And they would sacrifice human beings, young boys that is, on the day when their prophet was killed. They believed it would bring them the ultimate reward.

The *stwodone* that Mohammad was taken to was two stories high and had an elaborate basement with many chambers, *dakhmas*, housing thousands of clay jars filled with human bones. The whole building had a circular shape. On the lower level, it had a big circular hall that was used to carry out the main event, the sacrifice. The "standing" halls, the waiting rooms where the Zoroastrians would leave their dead, were located on the second floor. The building was made of rock, stone, and mortar. It was well built so it could endure the elements. Most of the walls, columns, and the ceiling of the first floor were made of marble stones of different colors. An iron coffin, a torch, iron brazier, a container that looked like a funnel, some big clay jars, and a statue of the Buddha were found in the basement.

The ancient people would bury their dead in different ways. Some of the earliest settled tribes would bury their dead inside their houses. In this way, they believed they were keeping all the members of the family together in one place. Cemeteries were located relatively far from urban areas during the time of the Median and the Persian dynasties. Cemeteries were called "cities of the dead." The Elamites, who had developed an important civilization in southwestern Iran, would put their dead children in pots that they used for cooking and put grown-ups in coffins made of clay. The dead would be in a sitting position, very similar to the position they had in their mothers' wombs. For the rich men, they would build *dakhmas*, or mausoleums. For some, they would make a face similar to the dead person's out of clay or carve it out of stone and put it on the coffin. Many followers of Zoroaster and Buddha used large jars to bury their dead. The white-dressed people of Tammami had the utmost re-spect for these jars, which contained their ancestors' remains.

In the middle of the roof of the *stwodon*, there was a square hole over-looking the first floor. The people with leprosy would stand around this hole and watch the sacrificial ceremony. The big hall was the place where the people of Tammami would torture and kill a young boy every year on the twenty-eighth day of spring when their prophet was killed. Some of the blood would be taken to be poured on his grave. The remaining blood would be given to the sick people to rub on their wounds hoping that the blood would cure them.

During a full moon, two nights after their arrival from the Ghuzz Desert, the sacrificial procession started. Mohammad was being carried on a stretcher that was followed by the four men who had purchased him along with an-other two hundred men, women, and children with leprosy. Mohammad was not intoxicated anymore. He was well aware of what was going on but was wondering whether he was dreaming.

Upon their arrival at the *stwodone*, Bargozeeda offered Mohammad a bowl full of sweet drink and said, "Drink it, so you get some energy." This drink was made of pure sugar from sugarcane grown mostly in southwest Iran in the province of Khuzestan. Sugar was not available to the general public at low prices at that time. Only very rich families and members of the royal courts could afford it. Mohammad had tasted that drink several times before when much younger, in the court of Khwarazm where his father was an astronomer. For about two hours he was ordered to sit on a black marble platform. Dur-ing this time, the white-dressed people of Tammami and the people with lep-rosy were dancing and singing around him. When the night arrived, Bar-gozeeda ordered twelve torches to be brought that would fully brighten the *stwodone*. After this, Bargozeeda took Mohammad's shirt off. Thus, he was sitting on this black marble platform half naked. Three hours through the night, the people in the *stwodone* were still dancing and singing and their numbers were increasing. More sick people were showing up. By now there were at least 250 people inside the *stwodone*. Most of them were sick, hoping to get cured on that fateful night. Although Bargozeeda could not wait to carry out the sacrifice as soon as possible, reciting all the prayers and songs required a lot of time. Thus he had to postpone the time of the sacrifice. The reason he was trying to wind up the ceremonies was that the beautiful spring sky was changing. Dark clouds were appearing one after the other and it could rain soon. Finally, the sacrificial ceremonies started.

Two white-dressed people held Mohammad down and another two tied his hands on his back and laid him down on a rectangular platform between big jars and coffins. One of them then poured a black liquid in the brazier and using two pieces of flint, lit it up, creating reddish-yellow flames. It was a frightening and strange sight, full of witchcraft and sorcery.

Bargozeeda put a hot, spicy, potion under Mohammad's nose. He sneezed and got back to his senses. In a joyful voice, Bargozeeda said, "About fifty-five years ago, our prophet was martyred. He had ordered his followers to sacrifice a child on the day that his soul ascended. We should cut and empty the stomach and then fill it with wine, resin, myrtle, and spearmint. We then swear and renew our loyalty to our prophet in front of a big fire."

Suddenly, the white-dressed people took off their hoods, showing their very old wrinkled, damaged faces. Their faces had specific deep and ugly features. It seemed the disease was eating out and carving their flesh. The look of what remained of their faces, after what was taken away by leprosy, was simply frightening. Mohammad's heart had almost stopped. He thought to himself, "That's why they cover their faces." He felt pain in every part of his body. It seemed like every cell in his body was trembling.

The white-dressed people were still dancing and singing around Mohammad. But he could not understand any of their strange words. These terrible people who were obligated to sacrifice a human being every year would hide in the caves and mountains. They were able to isolate themselves from the rest of society for more than a hundred years and avoid being prosecuted by Islamic laws.

Under the watchful eyes of 250 people, Bargozeeda exclaimed, "Now, in the name of our lord, Ibn Zakarya, we sacrifice this child. We hope that his pure blood that will be poured on our prophet's tomb will put an end to your pain and suffering. Yes, his fresh blood will shorten the time of the return of our lord. My friends and partners, this young boy is going to be sacrificed in this blessed place. He was an unfortunate boy. He was stolen by the Ghuzz and sold as a slave. His life was full of hardship and misery. He even was used as a beast of burden and for pulling the plow. At night, he had to sleep with a blanket full of holes outside at the mercy of the natural elements. We want to shorten a life that has been full of pain. This way, we send his soul to paradise and help his soul to leave his obliterated and tired body. My dear friends, on this holy night we sacrifice this young person with torture and torment to increase our rewards. We send him to the other world to visit with our prophet. As required by our tradition, we are blessed to have the gift of blood from this person. I am more than hopeful that the blood of this person will cure your problems. He is a pilgrim who will see our lord and you are lucky to be here to have a medicine for your sickness."

Bargozeeda stopped for a few seconds to observe the influence of his statements, and then with a voice vibrating with anxiety, he continued, "One of you sick people told me that this sacrifice is no more than murder. You do not like the idea although you might be cured. But I tell you, in our holy tradition it is a must to sacrifice. You needy people, I am telling you that I have researched enough about the life of this boy. He was an orphan and his family was very poor. He was stolen and sold as a slave. He had virtually no hope in his life. He had also told his owner that he was expelled from school before he was stolen. Dear brothers, the soul of this boy will fly high to meet our lord in paradise." Bargozeeda put his right hand on Mohammad's forehead and recited some strange prayer words while holding an empty container that looked like an alembic in his other hand.

Bargozeeda acted like an executioner. He shouted, "Right in front of your eyes, I will first cut the boy's jugular vein and count twenty-five drops of blood pouring into the alembic, which we will send to the graveside of our lord prophet. I assure you that this will shorten the time of his return to guide us again!" Bargozeeda stopped one more time. Then he and three other white-dressed people began humming more prayer songs. The words were a mixture of Sanskrit, Chinese, Arabic, Persian, and Turkish.

With fear, Mohammad was watching what was going on. He knew well what Bargozeeda was talking about. He saw his own death coming. He closed his eyes and recited a Quranic verse from memory: "We all are from Allah and return to him." He was certain that he was going to be killed. He had no doubt in his mind that those zealous people would murder him and his dead body would be on display in the butcher shop in the village of the people with leprosy.

There are records of human flesh being sold in Iran in the medieval age. This was done by the enemies of the central government to frighten the public. Some criminals would kill humans and offer their bodies to butcher shops and even cookeries. This method of scaring the public was done a few times during the Saljuq Dynasty by an Ismaili sect. It is also possible that the central authorities had done the same and blamed it on their enemies.

The tradition of human sacrifice has been recorded in some societies. In Egypt, for example, young girls would be thrown into the flooded Nile to satisfy the gods. In Carthage, sacrificing children was a part of religious duty. People accepted Iran's authority and stopped this practice when the Iranian navy, led by Darius the Great of the Achaemenid Dynasty, reached Carthage. Darius, in a letter to the government of Carthage, forbade human sacrifice. We know that although Carthage did not stay under Persian control for a long time, human sacrifice was discontinued in Carthage and most of North

Africa. Human sacrifice was never practiced in Iran openly, but invading tribes brought this custom to Iran. For instance, before the Mongols accepted Islam as their religion, after an important person died, they would kill all his wives, faithful servants, and maids and bury them all in one big grave. And in the Arabian Peninsula, in pre-Islamic times, some tribes practiced female infanticide.

The magical incantation, singing, praying, and dancing continued for three hours. It was getting darker and darker. Bargozeeda ordered more torches. Twenty-four more torches were brought in. In the early spring season, it was not uncommon to witness repeated thunder and sparks of lightning. Within minutes, a heavy rain started that killed some of the torches. Bargozeeda, in command of the operations, said, "We wait for some time and hope the rain stops. Then we continue the holy ceremonies . . ." At this very moment, a huge sound of thunder interrupted him. It was so loud that the people inside the *stwodone* were shaken with fear. While crying, most of them moved back from the main platform. The next clap of thunder was even louder and the accompanying lightning bigger. The unfortunate sick people got scared and rushed toward the stairways.

Bargozeeda got angry and shouted at the fleeing crowd, "You fools, stop! Let us continue our ceremonies. The blood of this child should cure your wounds." He waited for a few seconds and continued by saying, "The thunder and lightning are symbols of our lord's grace and blessing. They indicate our lord's happiness." Although it still was raining heavily, the sick people stopped in their tracks, seemingly accepting Bargozeeda's explanation, and began to return while bowing and raising their heads toward the sky to praise their lord. Mohammad lost all hope and started reciting Quranic verses out loud.

Bargozeeda removed his own curved Arabian sword and put it on the platform and borrowed Shenavanda's wider, longer one that looked more like a very sharp machete. Bargozeeda raised this big machete and said, "Now I am going to sacrifice this young boy. We have to torture and kill him with much pain in order to have high rewards. Therefore, I cut off his hands first, then his chest, and finally his legs." Once more huge thunder and lightning shook the *stwodone*. At this very moment a very loud, rough human voice penetrated the air, "Drop your weapon and do not move." Bargozeeda turned toward the sound. He was so astonished his machete dropped from his hand.

Up on the stairway, connecting the first floor to the roof, there were five men standing. Their turbans and mantles were all wet and with their swords drawn were ready to attack the white-dressed people of Tammami. The order came from the leader of the group, Abu Nasr Mansur.

CHAPTER TEN

Abu Nasr Mansur

Mohammad could hardly turn around and watch the newly arrived people. Fortunately, however, he was able to see more in the consecutive lightning that would light up the whole *stwodone*. The leader of the newly arrived people, a young man with battle-worn face, standing in front of four other men, had his long and sharp sword drawn and ready. When he saw the crowd amazed and in silence, he shouted, "You fools are becoming toys in the hands of these beasts that have lost their human compassion. If you do not disperse in minutes, I will punish you all. Caution . . . caution . . . you have been deceived by magicians. You are not allowed to kill an innocent human being for any reason. You should ask remedy for your wounds from Allah and nobody else!"

Bargozeeda, with eyes that looked like a pair of fireballs, stared at the leader and with a sound that was like an order said, "You, Abu Nasr Mansur Ibn Ali Arraq . . . just look at me." The young man looked into Bargozeeda's eyes, but he quickly realized those eyes were too powerful for him. Bargozeeda was known as a magician with extraordinary powers. The common people were afraid of him. Young Abu Nasr, leader of the four soldiers, was unsure whether he could resist the powerful magician. Thus, he looked at the ground and said, "Take away those hellish eyes from me or I swear to Allah, if you use your magical power, I'll order my devoted soldiers to send their javelins through your dirty chest and relieve the world of your devilish works."

Bargozeeda bowed strangely. It seemed the two knew each other. They must have had an encounter in the past, for they seemed to be aware of each other's abilities. In some kind of merciful tone, Bargozeeda said, "My Amir . . . you better leave us alone please and go back to town. I am sure you are busy too and have many other problems to take care of. Just run along and think about your own entanglements." Mohammad was thinking about those names. He was asking himself questions such as "Who is Bargozeeda? Who is Abu Nasr?" Then he would say, "Dear God, please help me." It seemed that these two knew each other well. Mohammad was thinking, in fact, that "all that rain accompanied by repeated thunder and lightning was sent by Allah to keep me alive." His little contemplation was interrupted by Shenavanda, who suddenly cried out loud, addressing the crowd, "Brothers . . . kill these fools. Kill your enemies that want to prevent your well-being. They do not want us to find you a cure for your wounds." The crowd was ready to attack.

Abu Nasr and the four *jannesars* were ready to defend themselves. Abu Nasr had his sword ready; he was not that afraid and with a rough voice, calmly said, "Just disperse." But the crowd did not move and started to murmur. Minute by minute, the crowd was getting louder and louder and was moving slowly toward Abu Nasr and his soldiers. A member of the crowd stepped on a corner of the floor of the *stwodone* and a large amount of rubble stones came loose. Some in the crowd picked the stones up and started throwing them at Abu Nasr and his men. The four soldiers used their shields to protect themselves. Abu Nasr was not carrying a shield; therefore, he received some wounds on his upper body and face. But he kept moving forward, ready to attack the stone-throwing people with his sword. They got scared and took a few steps backward. Then Bargozeeda ordered Shenavanda to snatch Abu Nasr's sword out of his hand.

Shenavanda took a few steps toward Abu Nasr, and without any fear caught hold of Abu Nasr's sharp sword with his bare hands. Although his hands began to bleed, it was as if he was not feeling any pain. Suddenly, he hit Abu Nasr's face with his forehand. It was a very painful blow that made Abu Nasr let go of his sword. Shenavanda now had the sword in his hands and held it between both his hands. The handle of the sword was in his right hand and the sharp tip in his left, and then bending it against his right knee he broke it into two pieces.

Another order came from Bargozeeda. He shouted to Shenavanda, "Now that you have broken his sword, I want you to break his neck too!" Shenavanda was a big and powerful man. He opened his arms with blood coming out of the palms of his hands, and he looked like he was going to hug Abu Nasr. Now, Abu Nasr took a few steps back, when one of his soldiers passed him a mace. Compared with Shenavanda, Abu Nasr was a little man. However, he was a trained warrior and an experienced one as well. He had led men in a few major wars.

A mace could be a fatal weapon in the hands of an experienced warrior. Abu Nasr aimed it at Shenavanda's head. But Shenavanda moved, and so he escaped getting hit. He got hold of Abu Nasr's neck with his right hand and hit his stomach with his right leg and seemed to be overpowering him. As ordered by Bargozeeda, Shenavanda was attempting to break his neck. At this very minute, one of Abu Nasr's soldiers, who was getting impatient, got close to Shenavanda and with great skill inflicted a deep cut on the left side of his upper body. This was a big and fatal wound. Just then, another solider hit Shenavanda on the head with his mace. A large amount of blood was oozing out of Shenavanda's side and probably his skull was badly damaged. He took a few steps backward and fell to the ground. That was the end of his life.

Bargozeeda meanwhile was watching this frightening scene all the while. And as soon as he saw that Shenavanda was dead, he called upon his followers by crying out, "Dear people of Tammami, take these five people, cut them into pieces alive and eat them!" Abu Nasr knew that Bargozeeda really meant what he ordered. He knew that he and his four soldiers were no match for a crowd of nearly three hundred. Therefore, he was trying to lead his soldiers out of the *stwodone*. Bargozeeda ordered the crowd to follow them. Abu Nasr had to order one of the soldiers to kill Bargozeeda with an arrow. This soldier was a master archer and his arrow cut Bargozeeda's throat. There was blood everywhere, with Bargozeeda bleeding profusely from the throat and mouth, and he too simply fell to the ground right where he was standing.

Mohammad was still thinking about the name Abu Nasr, which sounded so familiar. He could not remember when or where he had heard that name though. He then was approached by two of the soldiers and released from the sacrificial platform. In the confused outcry of the crowd, they were able to make it out of the *stwodone*. Outside, Mohammad saw an old man of oriental origin with slanted eyes and yellowish skin waiting with six horses. These Arabian horses were in excellent shape. It was clear the old man with the horses was waiting for Abu Nasr and his men.

The old man was speaking to Abu Nasr in a strange language. Immediately, the old man got a bag from the back of one of the horses, opened it, and took out a jar less than two feet tall with a wick sticking out of it. Abu Nasr took out two flint stones and lit the wick, that is, the fuse. Then the old man, in cold blood, threw the jaw into the crowd from the *stwodone* that had followed Abu Nasr and his men. The jar exploded with a huge sound and created a big fire.

One of Bargozeeda's bodyguards was approaching the old man with his sword ready. The old man took out a piece of reed and blew into it. Something flew out of the reed and hit the bodyguard in the throat and instantly immobilized him. The bodyguard's eyes bulged out and he touched his throat. Just before dying he seemed paralyzed and fell on his knees to the ground. Abu Nasr shouted happily, "Well done! Van Sho, use another one of your mysterious jars!"

Van Sho, the old man, took out another one of his secret weapons and lighting the fuse threw it at the crowd, killing most of them. Abu Nasr and his men took advantage of that moment and jumped on their horses and took off. Mohammad was riding with Abu Nasr. They were heading toward the city of Kath. After reaching a safe distance away from the *stwodone*, Abu Nasr untied his turban. Mohammad saw that part of his head was covered with dried blood. Abu Nasr talked to Van Sho in the same strange tongue that nobody else understood. Van Sho stopped his horse and so did everyone else. The sky was clearing up, and the full moon brightened all places. Van Sho got off his horse and brought out a bag, from which he took out a little bottle covered in leather. This bottle contained a kind of black oil. He poured some of the oil onto the tip of his index finger and rubbed it on Abu Nasr's wounds.

"If it was not for Van Sho, the people of Tammami would have sacrificed five more people for their false prophet," said Abu Nasr while laughing like a crazy person. They got on their horses again. Abu Nasr addressed one of his men and asked, "Do you remember what Bargozeeda ordered right before he was killed?" The soldier, Ali Oskafi, replied, "Yes, my amir, but I did not know what he meant by saying 'cut them into pieces alive and eat them'!" Abu Nasr replied, "That was exactly what he meant. The victim is to be cut into pieces while alive, and the victim's flesh would be eaten right in front of his or her eyes."

Ali Oskafi asked Abu Nasr whether there were tribes that practiced that kind of ceremony anywhere in the world. Abu Nasr asked back, "But what do you mean by the word *world?*" "The known world," he answered. Abu Nasr said, "My dear friend, our world is much larger than what we have learned about so far. The more we seek, the more surprised we get."

The wolves were howling and could be heard from afar. The men were all quiet, thinking about how large the world was, and began to trot faster. Sometime after midnight, they arrived at a caravansarai by the road. Abu Nasr knocked on the main door at the entrance. Someone shouted back, "Who the hell are you at this time of night?" Abu Nasr said, "It is me and my men, Khalil, please open the door." Khalil recognized Abu Nasr's voice. He removed the bolt behind the door and let the guests in. "Please fix us some food. We have no time and we must take a nap too," said Abu Nasr.

Khalil first apologized for being a little late in opening the door. He said because of the wolves and the thieves he had to be very careful. Abu Nasr said, "What about the security forces responsible for the safety of the roads? Apparently they are not doing their job properly." "You are right, my Amir," responded Khalil. Abu Nasr then asked, "What kind of food have you got?" Khalil responded, "We have some fresh eggs, fresh pita bread, and honey."

The scrambled eggs covered with some good honey were very delicious. Abu Nasr put his hand on Mohammad's right shoulder and said, "It is good to stay alive rather than being eaten alive. Sit down with friends and enjoy good food. What is your name anyway?"

"I am Mohammad Ibn Ahmad Andijani, my Amir. I am very fortunate to meet you and be saved by you," replied Mohammad.

Biruni, later in his book *Chronology of Ancient Nations*, wrote about the white-dressed people of Tammami. He wrote that Ibn Zakarya Tammami was a corrupt and vicious slave who claimed himself as a prophet in 933. He wrote that his followers had annual sacrificial ceremonies. After slaying their victims, they would empty their victims' stomachs and fill them with wine and some other ingredients. Biruni called the followers of Tammami as the *mobayza*, meaning the "whites," in Arabic, thus a reference to the "white-dressed" people of Tammami.

The Great Sultani School in the city of Kath was located in the eastern corner of a square or *maydone* called *kahferooshan*, or the "straw sellers." It was a place for selling fodder, including hay, barley, and dried wheat stems, meant for domestic animals. The main entrance of the school was domed and there was a little creek flowing in front of the wooden door. Fodder sellers had their stores around this square. There was a small shop where an old man whose art was calligraphy as well as penmanship took orders of letter writing. He would write in ink with a reed pen on yellowish paper. In the next corner not far from the school, there was a pond with running water for ablution, that is, for washing one's faces, hands, and feet, before the daily prayers. This square also had an ironsmith's shop, and regardless of the season, there was always some smoke coming out. By midday, the students would come out of their classes in groups of six or seven escorting their teachers. These teachers in their clean and expensive cloaks, big turbans, and loose white pants looked very serious and dignified. They usually would be accompanied by their students for a certain distance from the school. Sometimes, discussions of important subjects would continue for a farther distance and a long time.

At noon, one could hear the call for prayer from the minaret: "Hurry, Allah's worshippers, and hurry to pray. Dear Muslim people, rush for prayer." Most people, including students between twelve and twenty years of age, would line up to get ready for their prayer. They had to wash up first. After washing their faces, they would wash their hands and arms.

Mohammad now was attending this Sultani School in the city of Gorganj. Usually, he would go for prayers with his close friend Beejan Tabarestani. After completing their religious duties, they would eat lunch together. During summer months their food included bread, cheese, and grapes. It was a few days before the autumn equinox that Beejan looked at Mohammad's lunch and saw the same items as the day before, so he said, "You live in Abu Nasr's house. Is that what you eat every day?" Mohammad understood Beejan's sarcasm and said, "You are from a very rich family, and is that what you eat everyday?" Both laughed and said, "It is student life anyway!"

"I have heard from my professor that a stuffed stomach and soft bed are in contradiction with the quest for knowledge. A rich individual with a stomach filled with the best food resting over a silk mattress would not enjoy learning," said Mohammad. Beejan replied, "What kind of joy is it, suffering from hunger and living in isolation?" Mohammad responded by saying, "Yes, it is real joy and delight for me. You have not suffered, and what do you know about enjoyment? It is not possible to really have one without the other. You have not been stolen and taken as a slave one morning while you were still sleepy. Your faithful dog has not been brutally killed in front of your eyes. Your sheep and lambs have not been slaughtered one after another. You have not even seen bloody knives and swords. Have you ever slept outside in the cold desert rain in the mud, wishing you were treated like their domestic animals and kept inside a tent? These are only some of the painful moments I have seen in my short life! What do you know about suffering and pain?"

Beejan then apologized. Next Friday, Mohammad's food changed, at least one day in a long time. It included some small meatballs, radishes, and some bread. Beejan's food, on the other hand, included a baked fish, rice, some lima beans, and a large amount of raw garlic. Beejan was enjoying his dish of fish and rice with a full appetite. He would make a little ball out of the steamed rice and after adding a piece of fish to it, put the ball in his mouth and enjoy its taste. Then he would pick up a clove of peeled garlic and slowly chew on it. As for drinking water, they would use the fresh water that was transported from the mountains near the city in wooden pipes.

Mohammad now was eighteen years old. He had a medium height. Unlike Beejan, Mohammad was a very humble young man. His eyes showed him to be very smart and he behaved like an old, experienced person. Beejan, on the other hand, was a proud, even snobbish, young man who was tall, strong, and filled with a sense of self-reliance. These two were always together. So in the Great Sultani School, they were seen as a pair of good students and great friends.

Mohammad was one of the twenty-eight students supported by Abu Nasr. He paid for their food, rent, and clothing. Actually, Abu Nasr was the director of the royal observatory of Khwarazm in the city of Kath.

Mohammad, Beejan, and another student by the name of Abdulmalek Qazvini were roommates. A few minutes after their meal, when Abdulmalek joined the two, Beejan asked him, "Any news from home?" Abdulmalek answered, "Yes, my older brother got married and the younger one is sick. My father too is sick with asthma. My mother and two sisters have to take care of the farm. And, more importantly, it has been six months that I have not received money from home. But, fortunately, I received some yesterday."

"Really!" said Beejan. "Why didn't you ask me for money if you needed any?" Abdulmalek responded, "I know you are a very helpful friend, but I can do with little resources and I did not want to bother you until the situation was too bad! A few days ago, I sold my copper bowl and my knife and thus barely survived." Beejan said, "Anytime you need to borrow money, please do not hesitate to ask."

CHAPTER ELEVEN

The Andalusians

Mohammad and Beejan were busy eating when a servant came running and said, "The Amir had ordered all students to gather in the hall of the observatory. A very important matter has come up. Presence of all students is required." The servant hurriedly left to tell the others. Mohammad got apprehensive and asked, "What has happened that Abu Nasr has ordered everybody to go to . . . ?" Beejan too seemed astonished, "I am surprised too. . . . Until now we have not had the permission to enter the great hall of the observatory. Abu Nasr is requiring even the freshmen to attend this important meeting. The door of the hall is usually locked. It is a mysterious place for us. In fact, not many people are allowed to go there. And I wonder why he is asking for everybody now." Beejan continued, "Maybe it has something to do with this rumor spreading in the city!"

"Which rumor?" asked Mohammad.

"The rumor about the appearance of a comet in the sky that could collide with the Earth."

"Abdulmalek was talking about the same thing!" said Mohammad.

"When did you hear this rumor first? What was the source of this news?"

"I heard that the Indian astronomers have predicted this."

"Nonsense, there has been several other predictions of this sort that our planet will be destroyed by a comet."

The great hall of the observatory was circular in shape and was domed. This big dome made of green topaz stone could be seen from everywhere in the city of Kath and even from outside the walls of the city. The most interesting thing about this dome was that a part of it could be removed using levers of different sizes. At night, the astronomers could look at the sky by removing only a part of the dome. This was one of Abu Nasr's inventions that made the observatory at Khwarazm famous. This observatory's fame had reached Baghdad, Cairo, and Constantinople.

Mohammad and Beejan arrived in the great hall together. They saw a very conspicuous scene. They saw that Abu Nasr and Sheikh Abulfazl Khwarazmi, the school president, and three strangers were sitting on wooden chairs and right in front of them was Abdulmalek Qazvini, their own roommate. His hands were tied with a rope and one end of it was in the hands of a security guard. Abdulmalek was being interrogated! There were at least thirty students present.

After Mohammad and Beejan entered and were looking for a place to sit, Abu Nasr called them both and said, "You two come here and stand near your roommate." They stood next to Abdulmalek. Beejan murmured, "I hope Professor Abu Nasr does not ask me any questions face-to-face." Mohammad asked, "Why?" Beejan replied in a low tone, "He hates the smell of garlic and I had a lot of it today. I am afraid he may even kick me out of the school."

They were interrogated by Abu Nasr, who in a polite but commanding tone asked Mohammad, "Dear Ibn Ahmad, who came to your dorm room last Friday?" After a little thinking, Mohammad remembered last Friday and said, "Your honor, a woman and two men. They all had violet mantles over their clothes. The woman, the woman I remember, was wearing a very nice perfume. Even an hour after their departure, one could smell that perfume. The men had turbans with strange paintings on them. All three were wearing boots. I noticed this because I was afraid that the bottom of their boots might have been dirty and thus soil our rug that once in a while we pray on. After I told them, they took their boots off." "Then what happened?" asked Abu Nasr. "I was introduced to those strangers by Abdulmalek."

"I remember vividly," said Mohammad. "Abdulmalek introduced me as Mohammad Ibn Ahmad and he said that I am called Biruni, because I was born "outside" the city of Khwarazm and *birun* in Persian means outside. More importantly, the woman repeated my last name twice with some kind of strange accent and was laughing." "Then what happened," asked Abu Nasr. "Your honor, I remember more about this woman. She was wearing a pearl necklace. She showed Abdulmalek a piece of skin she got out of her big bag. Then Adbulmalek told me to leave them alone, because he wanted to talk to his cousin. Therefore, I left the room."

"Was she his cousin?"

"I do not know! I was not sure, because her clothes were not like other Persian women. She was wearing boots too. That is not common in Iran either. Moreover, she was speaking in Arabic! And her Arabic was different too. It did not sound like the proper Arabic spoken in Baghdad. It was a special type of Arabic that I have never heard before."

"Where did you learn proper Arabic, Ibn Ahmad?"

"Your honor, my father was a court astronomer and when sometimes I accompanied him we would meet several representatives from Baghdad. So I remember this accent."

"What did you see later?"

"I did not really see a lot, but while stepping out of our room, I heard her say that they were from Valen-sa or something like that! But I did not hear the name clearly. By that time, I was already outside my room."

"Dear Ibn Ahmad, was it not strange to see a woman and two men in our school?"

"Yes it was! It has never happened before."

"Did you report it to the president of the school?"

"Your honor, I thought why do Abdulmalek's relatives come from an unknown Arab land instead of Qazveen, but I did not get suspicious. Because I trust my roommates and I was busy with my own duties about school matters."

Abu Nasr, addressing the school president, said, "It was after this strange meeting on Monday that you noticed three very valuable books and some surveying tools and astrolabes were stolen from our observatory." Sheikh Abulfazl said, "Yes, my Amir, this was why I came to your house in person, but you were out hunting. Today as soon as I found you were back, I reported to you what has happened. I am sorry I troubled you. We needed you to take care of this important matter. Of course, I have already reported this to the chief of the police, because the Khwarazm observatory is not just like any other one. It has three hundred years of existence. You yourself, my Amir, have spent most of your wealth for this place. Finally, after our investigation we arrested this student. He has to give us information on the thieves, and then he himself should be severely punished."

Abu Nasr asked Abdulmalek, "Who recommended you to enter our school?"

"Salar Marzban, he is one of your cousins who is the governor of Gilan."

"Do you come from Roodbar in the province of Gilan?"

"No sir, I am from Qazveen. My father's name is Ghayasodin and my mother was a slave from Slavonia."

"Strange, very strange!"

Then Sheikh Abulfazl, the president of the school, started his interrogation by asking Abdulmalek whether he would confess or not.

"Do you admit that you have stolen three books and some tools from our observatory?"

Abdulmalek was silent. He did not respond.

The Sheik got angry and shouted at Abdulmalek and said, "Are you dumb, can't you speak? You know in this city the guilty people will be sent to jail, and under the torture of the executioners they would confess quickly. It is easy for my Amir and I to send you to jail. It is only because of our Amir's generosity and his compassion for students that we are not sending you to the officials. Let me ask you this question. "Do you admit that last Friday you met with the three strangers?"

"Yes, I do!"

"Where did they come from?"

"I do not remember!"

"You do not remember, yet you want to study astronomy and mathematics here with this type of brain! You are acting up. Feigning ignorance and you think we believe you?"

"It was a hard name and honestly I have forgotten!"

"After you receive fifty whips, you will remember that name."

Abu Nasr said, "He is not really able to remember."

Abu Nasr asked more questions, not from Abdulmalek but from Mohammad.

"Do you remember what those three people were saying?"

"I had left the room. Thus, I was not there to hear what they were talking about, your honor." Abu Nasr then asked Abdulmalek, "What type of business did they have with you?" He was silent again. The Sheikh raised the tone of his voice and said, "Do you want us to send you to the chief of the police? We want to keep the respect and reputation of our school; otherwise, we will."

Abdulmalek's face got red and he said, "I really do not have a lot to say. Those three people came from a very faraway land to bring me a letter from my uncle whom we were assuming was dead many years ago."

"What was in that letter?" asked Abu Nasr.

Abdulmalek did not answer this question, which made the Sheikh angry. He shouted, "You animal, why are you silent?" Abu Nasr said, "Please do not get abusive and try not to get angry."

"Where was your uncle sailing?" asked Abu Nasr.

"In the Mid-White Sea, but I am not sure."

Mohammad added, "That sea is also called the Sea of Rome."

"Why do you think I am guilty, if my lost uncle has written me a letter?"

"Where is the letter?" asked Abu Nasr.

"They took it back," answered Abdulmalek.

The Sheikh said, "You are lying. I do not believe you. Why did you give the letter back to them. They probably ordered you to steal the books and . . ." Abu Nasr said, "We are trying to find out what actually happened. He is innocent until found guilty. And we have no proof that he has taken anything from the observatory. Abu Nasr deliberately used the word "taken" instead of "stolen."

The Sheikh threatened Abdulmalek that he will be sent to the city officials if he did not confess. Abu Nasr said, "You do not have to confess. But if we decide to send you to jail, I cannot intervene and lower your punishment. Here, I am the guardian of the school and I can be somewhat forgiving. We do not have very harsh punishments here."

Mohammad was thinking how nice this man was. Abu Nasr was a national hero, a champion, and a very generous man. He had pure Persian blood in his body. He was trying to find a way not to damage the future of his student. He was the founder of the Sultani School and he loved the place. He even did not want to punish a guilty student. Abu Nasr was an honorable man, proud and with high morals. He did not want to send a student from his school to jail to be treated like a common criminal. Unlike the Sheikh's abusive, insulting, and angry words, Abu Nasr's nicely put advice to Abdulmalek worked. He kneeled in front of Abu Nasr and held his robe and started crying out loud and said, "Your honor, my Amir, I am not a thief. Please do not send me to the city police. They will cut off my hand." Abu Nasr took Abdulmalek's shoulders and said, "Yes, my son, as long as you are inside this school under my jurisdiction, I decide your punishment. I can call your crime a bad mistake. You will be receiving no more than ten whips and three days with no food and you'll have to wash your classmates' dishes for three days." Abdulmalek asked, "If I explain everything that I know, will you expel me from school?"

The Sheikh was ready to respond. But Abu Nasr pressed his arm and said, "If Abdulmalek promises not to repeat his mistake, I feel he has repented and is honest." At this very moment one of the teachers entered the hall and gave a letter to the Sheikh. He said that the letter was from the chief of police. The Sheikh read the letter and told Abu Nasr that the chief reports to us that one of our students was seen with three strangers who were wearing violet mantles who entered the Shrine of Baba Rustam on Friday. The only thing that attracted the attention of the police was the presence of a young woman. After they were found to be foreigners they were released. This report was sent to the police chief because the two men were armed.

Abu Nasr looked at Abdulmalek and asked, "Tell me what this meeting was about. I promise to keep you safe, if you explain everything." Abdulmalek said, "In this case, I will tell you everything." Abu Nasr said, "Yes, my son, please tell everything."

"They come from a faraway land, beyond the White Sea," said Abdulmalek. Everybody was listening curiously. Then he stopped. Abu Nasr asked, "Why did you stop?" Abdulmalek replied, "What else do you want?" Sheikh Abulfazl got angry and abusive again and said, "You are a malicious person, why can't you just tell everything!"

"They were carrying a letter from my uncle. He lives in Andalusia and he is a court minister of one of the Caliphs." Sheikh Abulfazl got upset and said, "This means you are following the Caliph of Andalusia instead of the Caliph of Baghdad!" Abu Nasr looked at the Sheikh angrily and said, "You are not helping." Then he asked Abdulmalek to explain what the letter was about.

Abdulmalek said, "My uncle's letter was about a book written by a magician. He asked me to send him that book with the three individuals that met me." Abu Nasr said, "But this is not an important request and was not a secret. What was the reason to go to the Shrine of Baba Rustam to meet the three people? Now tell me the name of that magician and when and where he was living?" Abdulmalek replied, "He lived about two centuries ago in Turkistan and had killed himself in nitric acid." Abu Nasr said impatiently, "Are you talking about the masked man of Khurasan? The three people that met you came from the other side of the world just to get a book?" "Yes, my Amir," answered Abdulmalek.

Abu Nasr said, "I am curious how it can be possible that the fame of a magician has reached Europe and encourages three people to come here to find his book." Abdulmalek commented, "They were not interested about the masked man himself. They wanted to learn about his magic acts and inventions." Abu Nasr asked, "What inventions?" Abdulmalek answered, "They told me that in the Royal Library of Khwarazm there was a book explaining how the masked man made a fireball like the moon that every night would come out of a well, stay in the middle of the sky, and brighten everywhere like daytime. I learned this from Maria." "Who is Maria?" asked Abu Nasr. "She is the woman that accompanied the two men from Andalusia," replied Abdulmalek.

"Maria was a scientist and astronomer. She told me about that book. She actually gave me the call number of that book. I went to the Royal Library shortly after midnight. I found all three books that Maria asked for very easily. I also took two astrolabes and a few other surveying tools. I met the three in the Shrine of Baba Rustam the following night and gave them what they asked for," admitted Abdulmalek. Abu Nasr was listening with sadness. Then he said, "You have a fairy tale, young man. It is hard to believe that your uncle survived the storm and reached Andalusia on the other side of the Sea of Rome. It is even more surprising that your uncle knew that you are studying in the city of Khwarazm to send his people to steal books from our Royal Library. I think you just came up with such a story. You could be a spy who came here as a student to get hold of those valuable books and send them to Andalusia."

Abdulmalek stared at Abu Nasr and said, "I swear that I am not a spy and had no idea that my uncle was still alive. I have lived in Khwarazm for three years. I remember, however, almost two years ago, right in the beginning of autumn, there was a gathering of many scientists and travelers from all over the Muslim world. Among them, there were two from Andalusia. They may have found out about those books and reported back to someone in their country." Abu Nasr looked directly into Abdulmalek's eyes and said, "Yes, I believe you. I even remember that meeting. They visited our library and were surprised to find out that we had two hundred thousand books." Sheikh Abulfazl was getting tired now. He asked Abu Nasr, "What should we do with this boy?" Abu Nasr replied, "Unfortunately, he has stolen three of the rarest books in the world and some other valuable tools and given them to foreigners. But I have promised him that he will not be punished physically. Moreover, I myself will be in trouble if I do not punish him. He has to be expelled from the Sultani School."

Abdulmalek was happy; at least his hand was saved. Yet he began crying. He tried to get some mercy from Abu Nasr. But nobody paid attention to his tears. Now, Abu Nasr was very angry for losing a few of the most valuable books they had. The three well-dressed strangers sitting in wooden chairs watching this interrogation until then stood up, and one of them said, "We will send our *jandarans* after them." This man was the Royal Minister. Abu Nasr said, "It is a good idea, but it seems almost impossible to find them. By now, they might be in the province of Gilan, which is not far from Azerbaijan. From there, the three thieves will go to Byzantine and then sail west to Andalusia." The Grand Minister said, "We, however, will try our best." Abu Nasr commented, "Unfortunately, the world of Islam is divided into many rival feudal kingdoms. If it was during the Old Persian kingdoms, with well-fortified borders, these foreign thieves could not have got away with those valuable books."

Abu Nasr said, "We will expel this young man from our school. He has lost his honor and title as a student." He asked Abdulmalek whether he has received any money from those thieves. He did not respond. But one of the teachers said, "My Amir, we have learned that he has received one hundred gold coins from those strangers. We found a bag containing coins under some bricks inside his room." Then the teacher gave the bag to Abu Nasr. The bag was dark green, and it smelled of perfume. Probably, it was kept with Maria's perfume. Abu Nasr took out one of the gold coins and from its weight he felt it was pure gold. On one side of the coin a Quranic verse was inscribed. On the other side, there was the face of a man in Arabic costume. It was minted in Cordova. Abu Nasr was fascinated by the quality of the coin. He could not read the inscription, so he asked Mohammad to see whether he could make something out of it. He could not either. But Mohammad apologized for being naive and leaving his room and not being a little more inquisitive when Abdulmalek asked him to go because he wanted to talk with his cousin! "I did not know my roommate was not a trustworthy person."

The interrogation was over. Everybody, including Abdulmalek, was gone. Mohammad, however, was still standing in the corner of the hall staring at the floor. He was thinking about how he was rescued by Abu Nasr and was treated like a family member. Moreover, he was recommended by Abu Nasr to attend the Sultani School, one of the best in the world. Now he was ashamed that his roommate had done something wrong. To Mohammad, who loved books, especially those rare and very valuable books, stealing them and giving them over to foreigners was the crime of the century. At this moment, Abu Nasr touched his shoulder and said, "What are you thinking about?" Mohammad responded, "I am thinking about what kind of low-life people come from a faraway land to steal our books?" Abu Nasr said, "Actually I admire their determination. The fact is that they are searching for a very significant matter. The magician that Abdulmalek mentioned was a great man of science and a very important inventor. He was the first person in the world who sent a heavy object into the sky and into the atmosphere. I know well those books that were stolen. One of them was written by the so-called magician and was called the *Book of Mercury*. There were only four copies of it kept in libraries around the world, in Baghdad, Cairo, Constantinople, and of course our own copy that was stolen. Dear Ibn Ahmad, if everything written in this book could be understood and practically carried out, it would revolutionize the world. This book was written in codes and with our limited knowledge, we cannot understand it."

Mohammad asked Abu Nasr whether the masked man of Khurasan himself wrote that book. Abu Nasr replied, "No, my son, he did not. Actually the basic information was gathered by a group of scientists during the Sasanid Dynasty, in particular, during the thirty-year war between the Persian and Roman empires. Much of the basic information was gathered from Roman prisoners of war and was recorded in that book by Persian scientists, of course, in codes. Later, the masked man of Khurasan got a copy of the book. He spent many years of his life trying to understand and decipher the books. Then he was able to send his fireball, named the Moon of Nakhshab, into the sky at night. This fireball would brighten the sky for about a month. Nights were as bright as days. I have been fascinated by his inventions. I believe it was like a miracle. I know that the masked man was a very important scientist. He was the most knowledgeable person about the science of matter and chemistry. Laymen thought he was a prophet. He was able to defy the Caliph's army several times. He resisted for about twenty years. When finally defeated, he submerged himself in a big jar filled with nitric acid, and thus disappeared. His followers believed that he flew to heaven. Laymen are not able to understand that harnessing and utilizing natural forces is like a miracle."

Mohammad was silent. He was in his own world. He too was now fascinated by the story of the masked man of Khurasan. He had many questions in his mind; most started with "what-ifs."

Abu Nasr broke the silence and said, "I wish our security forces could arrest Maria, who is from Valencia in Andalusia."

"What would you do with her, if she is arrested," asked Mohammad.

"Such a scientist woman is one of a kind in the world. If I see her, first I would pay homage and bow in front of her. Then I would ask her to marry me. It is true, together we can decipher the *Book of Mercury* and change the world into a better place. I know, unfortunately, I am unable to see her. She is now hundreds of *farsangs* away from here going toward the land of the west, Andalusia. I am even sure that she is not a follower of Islam. Her name is really Mariam. She and many other Christians pretend to be Muslims in order to get close to the Muslim government of Andalusia."

"It is also very sad that the Muslim government of Andalusia is so badly divided among the many little feudal uncles, cousins, and nephews. They are isolated from the rest of the Muslim world. They even do not have any relationships with Baghdad. They are surrounded by many enemies. They have a minor connection with North Africa, via the strait of Gibraltar. The Christian scientists pretend they are Muslims to save their lives and make a living. But in reality, they want to discover and learn from the Muslim achievements in science and technology. They know that sooner or later the Caliph of Andalusia will fall to the Christian forces. It is very obvious. Scientists like Maria know they will benefit by learning from Muslim achievements," lectured Abu Nasr.

CHAPTER TWELVE

Debates

The city of Gurganj, called Jurjaniyya by the Arabs, was as famous as Khwarazm. It was the economic center of the Khwarazm region and for a long time also functioned as the political capital of that territory. It was located to the west of the lowest reaches of the Amu Darya River (Oxus). The city, whose age is not known, was captured by the Arabs in 712 C.E. They decided to replace the city of Gurganj by building a new city called Fil (Fir). However, the new Arab city was destroyed by the river.

To maintain their control over Khwarazm, which was an area at that time on the frontier of the world of Islam, the Arabs divided the region into two parts. The native dynasty, entitled the Khwarazmshahian, Kings of Khwarazm, was allowed to retain the northern part, with the city of Kath as their capital city. But Gurganj became the residence of an Arab Amir who controlled the southwest. This arrangement lasted through the next two centuries. During that time, the Arab Amir, Mamun Ibn Muhammad, was able to get rid of the native dynasty and reunite the whole of Khwarazm under his rule and he took the ancient title of Khwarazmshah.

The city of Gurganj was captured by the Saljuqs in 1043 C.E. and once more became a major city of Khwarazm, which excelled Kath in importance. It was in this century that the city of Gurganj grew rapidly, and by the thirteenth century it became one of the most prosperous cities of the Muslim world. Unfortunately, like many other cities, Gurganj was captured by the Mongols in 1221 C.E. and razed to the ground. The Mongols flooded the city by diverting the river. Ten years later, a new town was built on a new site farther away from the river, called "Little Gurganj," as the capital city of the region. Later it became known as Gurganj again. Today the city of Gurganj, spelled "Urganch" by the Russians, is located in the modern country of Uzbekistan.

The city of Kath, on the other hand, was the ancient capital of Khwarazm. It was situated on the east bank of the main channel of the Amu Darya River, at a short distance from the modern city of Khiva. The location of Kath was highly affected by changes in the channels of the river. Therefore, it was accordingly moved at various times. Little information is available about the city's pre-Islamic period. At the time of the Arab invasion in 712 C.E., led by Qutaiba Ibn Muslim, the city of Kath was the center of the old Khwarazm civilization that was impaired by the destruction of the invaders. Biruni himself, many years later, wrote that Qutaiba had destroyed the ancient civilization of the region. And, of course, we know that Biruni was born near the city of Kath.

By the end of the tenth century, the city of Kath revived itself and actually started competing against Gurganj. The end of Kath's prosperous times as the political center of Khwarazm came in 995 C.E. when Mamun Ibn Mohammad took over the city. Kath became a subordinate of Gurganj. The native ancient dynasty that survived two Arab invasions of Transoxania was called Al-e Araq and Family of Araq, centered in the city of Kath. They used the Khwarazmshah title.

Almost a month after the *Book of Mercury* was stolen by the three people from Andalusia, on a Friday morning at the end of summer of the year 990 C.E., the Khwarazmshah, King Abu Abdulla, threw a magnificent party in the "Garden of Joy" that was situated near the Amu Darya River in his capital city of Kath. King Abu Abdulla was an able man and controlled a large portion of Transoxania. This party and gathering was an annual tradition when on the first Friday after the end of Ramazan (Ramadan), the month of fasting, all famous scholars would meet. It was a scientific gathering of some sort. In the middle of the Garden of Joy, a big and beautiful pool house with a big hall was recently built for these annual meetings of scholars who came from all over the Muslim world. Scientists, writers, authors, astronomers, and many others would be invited to come to the Garden of Joy to debate the topics of metaphysics, religion, poetry, art, history, and geography. This meeting and debate would then be repeated a week later.

Topics of discussion and debates would be recorded by scribes. Everything said in those gatherings would be written on Chinese paper, bonded, and kept in the Royal Library of Khwarazm for future reference, thus adding to the number of books in this library, making it one of the largest in the world.

This gathering and debate was really sponsored by the queen, Zar-Afshan, the Gold Scatterer. She actually owned the Garden of Joy. Queen Zar-Afshan and her two young and beautiful daughters Gohar Afshan, the Gem Scatterer, and Gohar Aeen, the Gem Mannered, and hundreds of noble women would sit behind a curtain and participate in these meetings. Queen Zar-Afshan, indeed, was the hostess of these gatherings. Although she was a learned woman and owned the Garden of Joy, her main reason for having those meetings was to compete against two other more famous ladies of the royal families. Zar-Afshan was throwing these parties in rivalry with the daughter of the Caliph of Baghdad, Shajarot al-Dor (Tree of Pear), and Azarmidoukht-e Grangoushvar (Daughter of Fire with Expensive Earrings), daughter of King Qabus of the Zyari Dynasty in Tabarestan, southeast of the Caspian Sea.

Shajarot al-Dor and Azarmidoukht would sponsor similar annual scholarly gatherings. These gatherings laid the foundation of scientific research. Especially, if these debates were kept in the written form in the libraries, these books transferred knowledge from one generation to the next. The royal families used these gatherings as a means of propaganda, particularly; poets would praise the generosity of these royal families. The hidden agenda, however, was that now many scholars would attend each of those meetings. The larger the number and the larger the prize, the more important the royal family would become. This was the basic reason for competition between the three women of that time late in the tenth century.

Poetry reading was not common in ancient Persia. It was more of an Arabic tradition, especially before Islam. The city of Mecca was the main center for annual poetry reading. The winners, the best poems, would be hung in the city and copies would be sent to even other parts of the Middle East. It is not certain whether the Persian poets learned the art of poetry from Arabs, but we know that some famous Arab poets were Iranian by origin or education. Some actually were well-versed in both languages.

Arabic poetry mostly had simple meanings based on the Bedouin life of limited circumstances, dealing with bygone lovers in camel-litters, campfires, low-lying hills, twinkling stars, clear skies, and tribal warfares. Iranian poetry, on the other hand, dealt with deeper and wider content, including philosophy, logic, and mysticism. In the pagan times, Arab poetry dealt with simple natural forces, the Arabian Desert, poisonous winds, and sad evenings. Animals such as camels, horses, cows, and lizards were described.

Yet Iranian poets were influenced by a much diversified environment and geography that was rich and meaningful. The Persian poets were able to see four seasons, and on top of the plateau, or down in the river basins, they witnessed many flowers, birds, and butterflies and could write poems that were innovative and rare.

This national treasury is not found in any other language in the world. Thus, when Edward Fitzgerald translated Khayyam's *Rubaiyat*, not only men and women of letter but British laymen also enjoyed it. It is still a mystery how a Persian poet of the twelfth century could captivate the minds and hearts of modern European people.

King Abu Abdulla was willing to open his royal court to many learned people annually. Whenever the gatherings were small, he would become very upset and would complain to his vizier saying, "Why do not they come? Maybe my prizes are smaller than those of the Caliph of Baghdad and Qabus Ibn Washmgir of the Ziyarid family." Then he would say, "But Qabus is drunk most of the year." The Ziyarid king, Qabus, and his courtesans did enjoy drinking wine, and they served it during those scholarly meetings too.

Actually, Khwarazmshah was not being fair to himself. His court was visited by many learned individuals. Moreover, he had pure Persian blood and his ancestors originally came from the province of Gilan in the southwest of the Caspian plain. In addition to competition by the queen against the ladies of other royal courts and propaganda, the Khwarazm court's main goal for these annual gatherings was seeking knowledge. He remembered vividly that Mamun, Caliph in Baghdad from 813 to 833 C.E. and the son of the famous Harun al-Rashid of the *Arabian Nights*, was the first to organize such gatherings of scholars of every kind.

Mamun sponsored these meetings to have a fair debate among scientists from many nations. His mother, who was an Iranian and well educated, did attend most of those gatherings. He also ordered the translation of many Greek, Persian, Syrian, and some Hindu books into Arabic. To do so, he hired Jewish, Christian, and Iranian scholars. These important translations were copied in Baghdad and widely distributed throughout the Muslim world.

In the history of the Middle East, it is not surprising to see kings' mothers, wives, daughters, and sisters being concerned about knowledge. Mamun himself and his mother would listen to debates among Muslims, Christians, and Jewish scholars and reward them equally. These meetings would take place in Baghdad, the capital city of the Abbasid Caliphate. Baghdad was a preeminent city with the largest number of educational facilities, hospitals, and libraries in the world. After the Renaissance, these books were translated into European languages. Therefore, Mamun saved many ancient books. What he did in the early ninth century was very important for Europe of the fifteenth century.

As usual, the 990 C.E. annual meetings were held in the Garden of Joy in a house called House of Seven Domes. This house had four big doors for air circulation. The big hall was somewhat cool in the early autumn morning. Little wooden windows at the base of the domes also would help to refresh the air inside the big hall. This building had a Sassanid style of architecture. Those sitting on the stairways would see a large pool, with many goldfish and a large fountain in the middle. It was believed that when someone stepped inside the Garden of Joy, at any time of the year, his or her heart would be saturated with joy and pleasure. Every season, especially in the spring, there were thousands of nightingales, canaries, and many unknown birds singing. The garden's air was always filled with the lovely fragrance of many different flowers. The building was surrounded by four pools of water containing different kinds of fish and a couple of swans, moving slowly in dignified circles.

As soon as everybody was at the place of their rank and order, the young male slaves or servants would serve the audience little cups of mocha coffee, known as Arabic coffee, which was imported from Yemen. Although coffee was introduced into Europe in the 1500s, dark Arabic or Turkish coffee was common in the Muslim world much earlier.

On the first Friday after the end of the month of Ramazan in the year 990, Abu Nasr, the nephew of the Khwarazmshah, had an important role. He was the organizer and introducer of the prominent guests. Every individual scholar would be greeted by him. He would shake their hands and would hug and kiss the ones he knew personally. Every guest then would be guided to their proper places according to age and their level of knowledge and wealth. Abu Nasr, although not very old, was a famous scholar himself. He was a famous mathematician, astronomer, and historian-scientist. His fame had reached beyond the Khwarazm borders. The topic of the first discussion on that Friday was about recent travel around the world. These travels into the unknown were very interesting to the royal families as well as to the scholars of the day.

Recent travels and new discoveries were significant for three reasons. The first two reasons were related to expansion of Islam as a religion and increase in trade. The other reason was related to the fact that these travels and discoveries would change the science of geography. Therefore, these stories were very popular in the royal courts and scientific gatherings. Traveling and exploration around the world was like an occupation. There were adventurous people who would go into unknown places. Even merchants came back with their own stories about strange places, animals, plants, and people. Many manuscripts would be written by scribes, and copies would be made to send to libraries around the world.

It was about midmorning that the first person got permission from the Khwarazmshah to speak. He was an Arab traveler from the city of Basra in southern Iraq. His name was Abul Abbas Nurodin Ibn Muhammad Basri. He claimed that he had sailed into the Dark Ocean and of course made it back alive. He had already been to several royal courts in several capital cities. His talks had many audiences in the world of Islam.

Khwarazmshah asked Abu Abbas, "Please tell us about your observations in the Dark Ocean and what surprised you on your voyage?" Abu Abbas said, "My dear Sultan, my observations hardly can be understood, and I hardly can explain everything!" Khwarazmshah said, "Try your best. We want you to explain everything in detail. Please do not leave out anything. And if we find your story believable, we will honor you with an important prize."

The man from Basra explained that the Dark Ocean was located beyond the Indian Sea toward the south. "As soon as our ship entered the Dark Ocean, the color of the water changed." Khwarazmshah asked, "What color did it change to?" The explorer said, "It changed to red, like the color of fire and blood." Abu Nasr did not let the explorer continue by asking him a question about stars in the southern sky.

The explorer replied, "We saw the constellation of the Bear." While looking at Mohammad Ibn Ahmad, Abu Nasr said, "Pardon me, but the stars in the southern sky should not be the same as what we have in our sky!" The explorer said, "That is not the case. You young scholars read about these things only in your books. But I have seen those stars with my own eyes." Abu Nasr pointed at Mohammad, by putting his index finger on his lips, to say nothing at that moment. Then, addressing the king and with his permission, Abu Nasr asked the man from Basra, "Thus, anywhere in the world we see the same stars at night." The man's response was affirmative. The explorer continued by saying, "We sailed until the edge of the Dark Ocean and we saw the Qaaf Mountains that like a very high wall surrounded the world." Abu Nasr asked impatiently, "What shape did they have?" The explorer answered, "They were shaped like a rectangular cube." Abu Nasr then asked, "For the moment, let's ignore the whole world including the solar system and the universe. Just looking at our own planet, what is the shape of the Earth?" The explorer answered while laughing, "You, yourself know the answer! What kind of inquiring questions is this? Of course, our planet is flat and is surrounded by the Qaaf Mountains. These mountains are at least thirty thousand zar'a tall. (Zar'a was a unit of measurement of length in Iran, before the introduction of the metric system. It was about 104 centimeters, amazingly very close to one meter.) The explorer even claimed that he has heard the legendary bird Simurgh. The water of the ocean became agitated and stormy whenever this bird roared. While smiling, he looked at Mohammad and then stared at the king.

Khwarazmshah asked Abu Nasr, "Dear nephew, what do you think about all these? That man has reached the end of the world. Do you think he deserves to receive our grand prize or not?" Without waiting for Abu Nasr's response, Khwarazmshah asked the man from Basra, "Do you have more interesting stories?" The man said, "Yes, your honor, many more." The explorer continued, "We actually first reached the land of Hindustan. This country has a very large population. Here, it never rains. All of the needed water is taken from the two rivers of Sind (Indus) and the Ganges. People in Hindustan are very healthy. They age more than 120 and up to 200 years. They never get sick. They have never had any experiences with pain, aching, or ailment. In Hindustan, we saw a tribe called Seenolfan. The members of this tribe had hands and tails like dogs and hairy bodies. We saw another tribe of giants that were very tall, reaching more than forty zar'a and some up to a hundred zar'a. They had only one eye. In Hindustan, there is a region that is very barren, almost nothing grows in it. But this desert is full of gold. Here, from afar, we saw very large ants, about the size of a fox, that would separate the gold from sand and make high hills. The local people ride on camels that have just given birth, and take some gold. These camels run very fast for the sake of their babies. The giant ants cannot reach those camels. In Hindustan, we saw another group of people that had eight fingers and toes on each hand and each foot. The same people had very, very large ears. Their ears were so large that they would reach up to the middle of their bodies. The Hindu people have a tradition to put a dagger in the ground at the time of thunder and lightning. By doing this, the thunder and lightning would stop. On the coast of Africa, we saw a tribe of people whose faces were like humans but their bodies were covered by wool. They were mostly females. We captured some of them, but they made so much loud noise, we had to kill and skin them."

The more the man from Basra talked, the more the audience was attracted to his tales. The king of Khwarazm himself was fascinated by those strange stories. He was probably thinking about women with wooly bodies and deserts filled with gold. . . . The explorer from Basra was finally done. After a long bow, he sat in his place.

At this time, Abu Nasr said, "Dear uncle, let's listen to the next explorer, then we could decide who deserves to receive your grand prize." Khwarazmshah said, "But dear nephew, I want to see what the audience thinks about the first speaker." The oldest scholar in the hall said, "Your honor, we mostly are library and book users. We hardly have the time or money to take such dangerous voyages. However, if he claims that he has been to Hindustan, visited Africa, and seen the Dark Ocean and the end of the world, we accept his claims. The reason is that he had so much detailed information about those places. In addition, his observations about our planet being flat confirm Ptolemy's ideas. Thus, we have no reason to doubt his claims." Khwarazmshah commented that the explorer from Basra was telling the truth and he deserved to receive the grand prize.

Abu Nasr was insisting to at least ask a few questions to the second traveler. The Shah said while smiling, "We can ask him some questions, but he will not receive any prize from us." With the Shah's smile, the audience started laughing. Khwarazmshah asked Abu Nasr, "Anything else, my dear nephew?"

Abu Nasr waited for a moment. His angry and loud voice broke the silence. He said, "Dear Khwarazmshah, I reject all of this man's claims. I strongly believe that he has not reached the Indian Ocean. Whoever accepts his claims is either a fool or is spiteful and has no idea about scientific research."

It was a frightening moment. Nobody in the hall seemed to be breathing or moving. All eyes were focused on Khwarazmshah. He too was wondering what to say to his beloved nephew, who was a knowledgeable scholar. Everybody was waiting until a female voice from behind the curtain was heard saying, "Alas, Abu Nasr, how could you accuse all of the scholars in this gathering and call them fools." It was the voice of Gohar Afshan, Khwarazmshah's daughter, defending the explorer from Basra.

The mufti, expounder of the religious laws of Khwarazm who was sitting in the front row, commented, "We cannot say that Abu Nasr accused all of the scholars here, because having doubt and debating important matters will bring out facts, reasoning, and understanding." Gohar Afshan was heard again saying, "But it's my father's decision to give the grand prize to whomever he wants. Yet, my cousin calls everybody uninformed fools." Abu Nasr answered, "But I called only the man from Basra a liar and nobody else. We, as a society of scholars, should not accept this man's claims so easily. This man is making up all these stories. Ants, the size of fox, nonsense! His stories are baseless. He has been to the Dark Ocean in his dreams only!"

Khwarazmshah appeared to be somewhat upset, he shouted at the woman behind the curtain. He said, "All of you women, including my own daughter, must be reminded that strangers should not hear your voice. If you have any questions or comment, just write them down on a piece of paper and we will take care of them. And I ask my nephew not to submit to anger but to use reasoning and logic to deal with this issue. Before anything else, let me ask the audience whether anybody wants to make a comment or not?"

The leader of the learned association of Khwarazm stood up, looked around the hall, and said, "Dear great king of Khwarazm, I believe in our gathering today, you are the most knowledgeable and learned person. We agree with your decisions. I believe that kings are like shepherds for the common people. It is the king who is responsible for the safety of the nation in the case of earthquakes, floods, drought, famine, epidemics, and invasion of enemies. Therefore, here we submit and obey your orders. My dear king, you have the experience and wisdom to decide in this matter."

The king was not really listening to him. He had heard this kind of advice hundreds of times before. He was actually thinking about how to deal with Abu Nasr. He was quiet for a few minutes. Another deadly silent moment passed. Then Khwarazmshah stared at Abu Nasr with a reproaching look and said, "I am sure my nephew did not mean to be rude to us. He just lost his temper. If he has any strong reason to reject this explorer's claims, I would like to hear him out. But I am aware that scholars present in our gathering today will condemn him. My reason is that not even a single soul agrees with Abu Nasr. Therefore, he is making a mistake challenging the explorer. We have more than five hundred people in this hall, and nobody has supported Abu Nasr."

"But I know that at least one individual agrees with me, one hundred percent," said Abu Nasr. The king and everybody in the hall looked around to see who would be brave enough to support Abu Nasr. Murmuring started. Nobody stood up or said anything. "Who agrees with my nephew's weak arguments?" asked the Shah, ridiculing. A young, shy, and weak voice came from the side of the hall saying, "I do." The murmur of the audience got louder. Everybody turned toward the voice that came from the left side of the big hall. Khwarazmshah asked, with a loud voice mixed with anger, "Who was that. I cannot see you. Stand up!" In the farthest southwestern side of the hall, a young man rose, and stood up without bowing, which was mandatory in front of the shah. Khwarazmshah saw a very young man of barely eighteen years of age. He looked frightened by the crowd. His face was pale, with a pair of worried eyes. Khwarazmshah asked, "Who allowed this boy to attend our meeting? I made myself clear when I ordered that nobody under the age of twenty be allowed to sit in our gatherings!" The commander of the *jandars* was surprised as to who might have let this boy sit on this type of high-caliber meeting and who has ignored the Shah's orders.

With a specific proud manner of his own, Abu Nasr answered, "I did my Lord. I invited him to attend this gathering." "Why? He is just a boy," asked Khwarazmshah.

"But he is not just a usual boy. He is one of our time's rarities. Yes, he is only eighteen. He has mastered philosophy, mathematics, geometry, metaphysics, astronomy, geography, and many other sciences, and he is a good physician too. He knows more about medicine than anybody else in this hall," responded Abu Nasr.

One of the audience members commented jokingly, "Therefore, he might be the reincarnation of Socrates, Aristotle, Plato, Euclid, and Ptolemy all in one." Another said, "Unbelievable, it is a miracle." Abu Nasr said slowly, "Listen, it is not a miracle. He has searched and learned knowledge." Khwarazmshah asked Mohammad with his hand to come to him. Mohammad walked toward a king for the first time in his life, very slowly. He was almost unable to take his steps. He made it. Now he was right in front of Khwarazmshah and everybody could see him.

Khwarazmshah asked, "Young man, what is your name?"

"I am Mohammad, son of Ahmad."

"Where are you from?"

"I am from the village Vasemereed."

"How and why did you come to Kath?"

It is a long story, your honor." But Abu Nasr added, "I rescued him from the white-dressed people of Tammami. They were going to sacrifice him. He has been living in my household since then."

"How old are you?" asked the Shah.

"I am eighteen years old. I was born on September 4, 973 C.E.

"Where were your born?"

"In the suburb of Kath."

"So, you are not born to a peasant family. I am surprised!"

"No, your majesty."

"What was your father's full name?"

"Ahmad Andijani."

"What was his occupation?"

"Astronomer."

"Andijani, Andijani, I have heard this name!"

"Yes, he was a state accountant and astronomer."

Khwarazmshah closed his eyes to remember the name, the man called Andijani.

"I remember him. He was working in our Treasury Department. He was accused of stealing money."

Even Abu Nasr was surprised. "Later, we found out that Mr. Andijani did not commit a breach of trust. He had never betrayed us. He was innocent. What a pity, I did not have a chance to apologize personally," said the king.

Now, the tone of Khwarazmshah's voice was mixed with compassion and re-morse and he asked, "Oh, Mohammad, son of Ahmad Andijani, tell me why do you think that the man from Basra is lying?"

Mohammad answered, "Great king of Khwarazm, this man said that the color of the water in the Dark Ocean was red. If the ocean is dark, how could he tell the color red? If we have another ocean, its color must not be differ-ent from those that we have discovered already. Secondly, he said that he has seen the constellation of Bear in the southern hemisphere. It is not true. The stars in the northern sky cannot be seen in the south. The southern sky has its own stars and planets. This explorer claims that he has seen the Qaaf Mountains and heard the bird Simurgh. He says he has seen one-eyed giants, fox-size ants, deserts filled with gold, wooly women. . . . These are all lies. These are myths, imaginary fiction, and nonsense. He probably heard of such stories in the coffee shops of Baghdad."

Khwarazmshah asked impatiently, "You mean his statements about the Desert of Gold, large ants, wooly women, one-eyed giants are all lies?" "Yes, your majesty, yes. Let me repeat my answer, they are all lies," said Mohammad.

For the first time in his life, Abu Abbas, a man of fifty-five years was be-ing challenged badly by a boy of only eighteen. Abu Abbas Basri was filled with anger. If it was proven that he was lying, he could be punished badly, even executed. He almost roared, "You impudent, rude boy, that is a serious accusation. I do not think you could prove me wrong."

Khwarazmshah was calm now. He invited the explorer to be quiet and re-spond when he is asked to do so. Then he asked Mohammad, "How will you prove your claims, young man?" Mohammad answered, "Your majesty, this world that is occupied by mankind is subject to certain complex laws, and there is nothing that cannot be explained logically. However, I heard the man had very few facts." The Shah asked, "For example?" Mohammad an-swered, "Remember the man's statement about people in Hindustan putting their daggers in the ground in order to stop lightning. It is because any metal would redirect the lightning away from striking. But it becomes a big lie when he says that daggers stop thunder and lightning."

The king of Khwarazm was unsure about the very high mountains around the world. Therefore, he asked Mohammad, "If our world is not surrounded by the Qaaf, what does?" Mohammad answered, "I have read that our world is surrounded by bodies of water. Our planet is like a full moon. It is a sphere in shape. It rotates around itself to create day and night and goes around the Sun, which results in having seasons. Our planet is in the air."

Khwarazmshah has never heard of such bold statements in his life. He got angry and shouted, "This is not acceptable. You are rejecting even Ptolemy's ideas! This is blasphemy. You must be a fool to believe in nonsense." A few of the audience members that disliked Abu Nasr said, "Yes, yes, he is cursing and rejecting every sacred belief that we have."

The explorer from Basra took advantage of the moment and shouted, while shaking, "This boy is a liar!" He was extending his hands toward the audience for pity. He continued, "Now, you know who is telling the truth. I swear to Allah, with my own eyes I saw . . . yet, this boy is accusing me of lying."

Although he was scared and his face was pale, Mohammad said calmly, "It does not matter how many times you swear to Allah. You are still lying. Those wooly women that you think you saw are some African monkeys that look like humans. Of course, if you catch them and put them in cages, they make too much noise. And you killed those innocent monkeys."

Khwarazmshah interrupted Mohammad. He still was angry with a red face. He invited Mohammad to be quiet and listen. He said, "The explorer's stories are not important to me anymore. But I want you to prove to us that the Earth is like a sphere in shape and rotates and goes around the Sun." This time Abu Nasr answered, "Dear uncle, this needs many years of research. I myself have written a treatise about his matter. I am willing to present it to you in another gathering of the scholars here."

At this time, the majordomo, chief of the table, arrived and announced that dinner was being served. Everybody left the hall. The king of Khwarazm was able to feed, with the best food available, a crowd of more than five hundred people very easily.

On the very next day after the great gathering in the Garden of Joy, Khwarazmshah called upon Abu Nasr and reminded him of his promise to present his treatise in defense of Mohammad Ibn Ahmad. Abu Nasr was ready. He had his treatise in scroll form ready. He addressed the king by saying, "This is a summary of the last few centuries of research by scholars who believed that our planet was spherical in shape. But practical application and proving their argument is not so easy. We need more time to do so." Khwarazmshah said, "Never mind that. We do not want to wait." So, Abu Nasr went ahead. He rolled out his scroll and started reading it.

"We have references in a book called *Virtues of Abu Hanifa*, written by Al-Movafaq. A contemporary of Mansour of Abbasid (754–775 C.E.), Caliph of Baghdad, Abu Hanifa was once asked an important question in a scientific gathering. He was asked, 'Where was the middle of the world?' His answer was plain and simple. Abu Hanifa's answer was 'In the place that you are sitting!' This answer indicated that he hypothesized that our world was spherical.

"When Ptolemy's book was translated into Arabic (during Mamun of Abassid Dynasty, Caliph of Baghdad, 813–833 C.E.), the Muslim geographers did not accept Ptolemy's idea that the Earth was flat. They virtually ignored Ptolemy's idea and went on trying to prove that our world was global in shape.

"Ibn Rustam, a Muslim scholar, said that our world is spherical in shape. The reason is that on our planets, the sun, the moon, and the stars do not rise at the same time. In the eastern part, they rise earlier than in the west. They set in the eastern regions earlier than the western regions. He also believed that the Earth looks like a ball and the sky surrounds it on all sides. He compared the Earth to the yoke of an egg and believes that the air around it should be compared to the white part of the egg.

"Ibn Algha too believed that the Earth is a sphere in shape. In a boat sailing toward the coast, first the top of mountains and higher grounds and trees can be seen. And the reverse happens sailing away from the coast. Ibn Khurdadbih, an Iranian geographer, wrote that the Earth is covered on all sides by air. He wrote, almost 150 years ago, that on the equator, the circumference of the Earth is equal to 360 degrees. He believed that each degree is equal to 25 *farsangs*. Thus, he calculated the Earth's circumference to be about 8,000 *farsangs* (32,000 km). Ibn Khurdadbih talked about two poles located at the distance of 90 degrees from the equator.

"Ali Ibn Husain Masudi argued that the land masses are located between China and the Fortune Islands in the western ocean. The distance between the two, according to him, was twelve hours of the sun's movement. He said, when the sun sets over the Fortune Islands, it rises over China.

"We have records of travelers who have been to the extreme north and south of our planet. In those two polar areas we have six months of day and six months of night. These two areas are cold year around.

"Our planet is like a ball. We can prove this in astronomy. Assume we have three volunteers. Assume we ask one of them to stay where he or she is. We ask the second person to move eastward and the third person to move westward. Those moving in different directions come back to the first person, but in opposite directions. The one who went east comes back from the west and vice versa. It is also very important to know that the person who moved toward the east when he comes back will be one day older than the one who stayed. The person who moved westward, however, will be one day younger than the first person. Let us assume one more time that we could go around the world and come back in the opposite direction in one week. For example, let us use the same three volunteers. Ask the first person to stay in the city of Kath. Ask the second person to go out of town from the east gate and continue going around the world. Upon arrival, he will enter the city from the west gate. It will take him eight days to finish his journey. The third person goes out of town from the west gate, goes around the world, and enters the city on his way back, from the east gate. It will take him six days to finish his journey around the world. The time passed for the person who stayed in the city of Kath is only, of course, one week."

"Dear Khwarazmshah, dear uncle," Abu Nasr raised his head from the scroll for the first time, "We are beginning to put these little pieces of information together. We will have a better understanding of the complex law of nature in the future. We, Mohammad and I, do not accept any unfounded claims such as those stories we heard yesterday in the Garden of Joy."

After the first grand meeting of scholars in the Garden of Joy, and when Abu Nasr presented his treatise to Khwarazmshah, Mohammad and Abu Nasr participated in several more. Mohammad became the talk of the town, especially on account of his age. Everybody was talking about this very young scholar. Anytime Mohammad participated in those meetings, the older scholars found out how keen and how smart he was and how knowledgeable a person of that age could be. He was reaching the highest stage in acquiring knowledge.

When Mohammad was brought to the city of Kath, he was reaching his fifteenth birthday. He still was a young boy. Children of the members of the royal family and government officials would ridicule and belittle him because he was seen as a person from rural areas. He still was wearing baggy pants and light cotton summer shoes instead of boots. His clothes were old and dirty and worn out. He most often felt he was carrying the smell of the Ghuzz tents. But at that age, he was a fully mature person. The pains of slavery taught him to be tough, never give up, and work harder. And because he was very smart, he had the ability to comprehend subjects of study very easily. Abu Nasr encouraged him. He was taken to the grand meeting of the scholars in the Garden of Joy on purpose. Abu Nasr wanted him to see for himself how hot and hard those debates would get. Abu Nasr deliberately wanted Mohammad to reject the explorer's claim. This was a part of his training. Mohammad had learned in four years in Kath what a student learns in sixteen years of education from elementary school through college. After a short time in the Sultani School the sons of the high government officials would not laugh at him any more. First, because he was associated with Abu Nasr and, second, because he was smart and most often helped them with their assignments.

Abu Nasr took Mohammad home. He got his own room in the exterior section of the house. He was treated as a relative of Abu Nasr, not as a poor student and apprentice. The most important part of Mohammad's daily life was to use Abu Nasr's large and one-of-a-kind library. The man himself, Abu Nasr, was one of a kind, one of rarity. In the old times, men were divided into two groups; men of arms and men of books. There was no mixture of the two. But Abu Nasr was exceptional. He was a brave man of arms and a very knowledgeable scholar. He knew more mathematics, algebra, trigonometry, astronomy, and physics than anybody else at that time. And Mohammad was fortunate to be associated with him. Abu Nasr looked at Mohammad as younger brother he never had. Mohammad became his most trusted person and confidant. After a short while, Mohammad moved from the exterior to the interior of Abu Nasr's house. Until recently, most of the houses in Muslim countries had two sections. The exterior part was used for men not related to the family by blood or marriage. The interior was occupied by female members of the household. The interior was called the *harem*. Therefore, Abu Nasr must have trusted Mohammad very much to allow him to stay in the interior of his house.

Abu Nasr was a perfect scientist ten centuries ago. He never used his knowledge of astronomy for fortune telling. For a long time astronomy, and especially astrology, was more than pure science. The astrologer would study the divination of the supposed influence of the stars upon human affairs and terrestrial events by their position and aspects in the sky. A star twinkling or falling would indicate the end of somebody's life. Astrology was mixed with superstition and myth. Astrologers were reduced to fortune tellers. Every royal family had a few astrologers. They not only studied the position of the stars, they also interpreted dreams. If they were good in the interpretations, they would be rewarded handsomely. If they were unable to explain dreams, they most often would lose their life or be expelled. Mohammad's fate changed altogether because his father could not or did not want to interpret the king's dreams.

This tradition has continued into the twentieth century. Nowadays, although science and technology have evolved so much, yet superstition is alive and well. Tens of thousands of fortune tellers work in the cities of London and New York. Most magazines and newspapers publish a horoscope section. Hitler had his own astrologer and based most of his decisions on what his fortune teller said. In the 1980s it was well known that Nancy Reagan had her own private astrologer.

Abu Nasr saw astronomy as pure science. He never used this as an occupation. His belief was against fortune telling. Mohammad too had learned from his teacher and mentor not to use astronomy for the interpretation of dreams or fortune telling.

Mohammad was very thankful, not only because his life was saved but because his fortune was secured by being associated with Abu Nasr. He was the most knowledgeable man of his time and the most famous scholar. This made him a target for those people who did not want to see such a man. Abu Nasr was accused of being involved in witchcraft, and some called him a crazy scholar. There were hundreds of people who were envious of him living in the capital city. Fortunately, he was among some real scholars who laid the foundations of progress in Iran ten centuries ago. He was one of the stars of poetry, literature, science, and knowledge that brightened the sky of the country. The tenth century was a time of metamorphism. The creativity of the Iranian element in science and civilization led to the growth of the Islamic Empire. This slowly crystallized and spread and became an eminent leader for the whole world.

Many times, Abu Nasr would invite Mohammad to join him to watch the stars on the roof of his house. They would gaze at the sky for hours together. He most often would ask Mohammad many questions. "What do you really know about the world? Do you know that our knowledge about our own world is too small? Do you know that we are fools enough not to recognize how uninformed we are? We believe that we are the most knowledgeable and wisest individuals in the world, yet we really know very little!" And Mohammad would say, "I agree!"

Abu Nasr would say, still on the roof, "Do you know that the most powerful people are so belittled in front of the secrets of life. The most powerful kings can be seen as nobodies when it comes to the understanding of the universe. We are born, we grow up, try to enjoy the best of everything, we develop feelings for those we love, we ride in golden litters, sleep in silk sheets, we go to the sea, we travel one end to the other end of the world, but when we think of our world, we have no idea where we are coming from or where we are going. We even cannot expect tomorrow. Today is tomorrow, and it becomes yesterday. Tomorrow, we will still be in search of the truth." "Yes, my Amir, I agree," said Mohammad.

"Have you been to the sea?" asked Abu Nasr.

"No, never. I have not seen the sea."

"If you sail, you think that the sea has no end. But dear Mohammad, you should know that the sea has its own end. You do reach the other coast. Sailing is necessary for you. At the sea, you feel so lonely and you think a lot. Thus, I would send you sailing."

"Dear Amir, what are we? Why do we come to this world? Where are we going? When will this world end?"

"Don't be so simpleminded! Do you think I have answers to those questions? Those are my own questions that I have no answers for."

"Why do you watch the stars?"

"Out of curiosity. I try to find some clues to my questions."

"What do you see, when looking at the sky?"

"I find out how ignorant I am!"

"What is the purpose of life?"

"To help other people. To be beneficial to other people."

"How can one be helpful to others?"

"Informing people is the best method of helping them. Unfortunately, our world is filled with poverty, misery, and ignorance."

"I agree, my Amir. What do you mean by saying ignorant people?"

"I can give examples. In Egypt, Rome, and even in our own country, it was common for brothers and sisters to marry. It was done to keep the blood pure and wealth in the family. Some of the Arab tribes were the most uncivilized in the world, before Islam. Some tribes even buried their female babies alive. In their cities, they had a number of whorehouses with red flags identifying them. They learned this from the Romans. But I am very angry at them, because when the Muslim armies defeated Iran, they burned the largest number of books. Of course, you have read about the fact that in Egypt and India there are girls who have dedicated their bodies to many temples."

"Yes, my Amir."

Abu Nasr was an unmatched and unparalleled person in history. Most of the royal family members were just having a good time. Very few of them worked hard or made sure to learn some of the available knowledge. It was impossible to find any amir like him who mastered so many subjects, including mathematics, astronomy, trigonometry, philosophy, and many others. He even did not care to put his own name on the many books he wrote. He was an unselfish person with nobility of feelings and generosity of mind. With such a high aspiration, he did not care about his own name. In his books later Mohammad admitted that Abu Nasr used his own name as the author of some of his books.

CHAPTER THIRTEEN

Lady Rayhana (Sweet Basil)

After that fateful day of debate in the Garden of Joy, Mohammad's star of fortune brightened in the sky of Khwarazm. Even Abu Nasr got closer to Khwarazmshah. In a short time, Mohammad showed more talents, one after another. Astronomy, as we know by now, had two aspects:

1. A scientific and research-related aspect that would attract real scholars only.
2. A superstitious aspect that would attract royal families, or even laypeople, for fortune telling and prediction.

In the tenth century, human beings were unable to explain many natural phenomena. Thus astronomy, by studying the location of the stars, sought to explain the present and predict the future. Kings and even religious leaders, who most often were the same, were not certain about their future. In order to prevent undesirable events, these princes and priests wanted to have some ideas about the future.

Abu Nasr was a scholar-prince. He was respected by the Khwarazmshah. Abu Nasr knew the minute points of astronomy and astrology. But he was probably the first scholar who differentiated between the scientific and superstitious sides. Mohammad, similar to his teacher and mentor, never developed a taste for fortune telling. During his residency in the city of Kath, Mohammad, our young scholar, became the most knowledgeable person dealing with mathematical, geometrical, and astronomical problems. He spent most of his time in the great hall of the observatory and the library of the city of Kath established by Abu Nasr.

In those years, Lady Rayhana, Abu Nasr's younger sister, developed an interest in learning scientific subjects. *Rayhan* means "Sweet Basil" and *Rayhana* is a feminine version of the name. At this time, Princess Rayhana was only fifteen years old. She was one of the most beautiful and well-versed girls in town and probably the whole nation. She was very smart. Most often, she was attending classes taught by her brother. She would sit in the class like any other regular student to learn mathematics, astronomy, and many other subjects. The Lady Princess Rayhana, as she was called, had big black eyes, slender nose and mouth, and uniform bright, white teeth. With her long black hair, she had a beautiful and joyful face. Mohammad and Lady Rayhana were living in the same household. Mohammad was treated as a very close relative by Rayhana. Thus, Princess Rayhana would not cover her face when talking with Mohammad.

Lady Rayhana was growing up as a princess. She acted and looked like ancient Persian royal family members. Like young men of her age, she was interested in horseback riding, polo, archery, and hunting. She had learned the art of hunting from her brother. Riding a horse with a helmet over her head, she had hunted a few deer and wild boars. She was healthy and happy. She acted and looked younger than her age, while Mohammad looked and acted older than his.

On reaching age eighteen, Princess Rayhana's future became the talk of the town. The rumor was that she was getting married to her father's cousin, the son of the governor of Gurganj. Mohammad heard this several times but never paid much attention to the story. He would look at Princess Rayhana as just another classmate, a good friend, a younger sister, or even as a daughter. Due to the fact that she would ask many questions from Mohammad that she did not want to ask her brother, Mohammad felt he was her teacher. She was his first bright and beautiful student.

Most often, late at night, Princess Rayhana would come to the observatory to watch Mohammad observing the sky. She would be mostly quiet, not wanting to disturb Mohammad's concentration. Mohammad, however, was always aware of Princess Rayhana's presence. Her perfume would give it away. She had been coming every night. During many nights when the moon was shining and Mohammad was lost in the universe, she had her own dreams. She would wait for a chance to ask Mohammad some questions about the universe. Then when he was answering her questions, she would think, "Look at his face. How honest! How attractive! The words coming out of his mouth are so in order, so insightful. He is my young handsome scholar.

I like him. I have utmost respect for him. He is my best friend. I love him! I wish he knew about my feelings for him."

Late one night, Lady Rayhana went to the observatory. Mohammad, as usual, was busy gazing at the sky. She entered softly and quietly, then waited a few minutes before saying hello. Mohammad noticed her perfume before her beautiful voice. He said, "Hello to you, my beautiful princess." She asked Mohammad, just out of curiosity, "What is that tool?" Mohammad first told her the name then explained how it is used in an observatory. She asked about another tool and then about another. Finally, she said, "Why don't you just go ahead and tell everything you know about all the tools and equipment here." He smiled, shook his head, and said, "Look at this ring. We use it to measure the sun's altitude. These four cylinders are used to measure the moon's transition. That tool in the corner on the black marble platform is used to measure the latitude of a place. This one is the ring of longitude. This concave mirror . . . that parallelepiped . . . that ruler . . . this compass . . . and, finally, this astrolabe."

Princess Rayhana stopped him by asking, "How many kinds of astrolabe do we have?" It was like he was expecting such a question. He was ready to name fifteen different types of astrolabes in less than a few seconds, from the full astrolabe to the cane of Moses.

"Who invented the astrolabe?" asked Princess Rayhana. Mohammad responded, "It was Muhammad Ibn Musa Khwarazmi. He was born right here in our city in 780 and died in 850 C.E. in Baghdad. He lived in Baghdad under the caliphates of Mamun and Mutasim in the first golden age of Islamic civilization. His algebra book, the first in the world, was a compilation of rules for arithmetical solutions of linear and quadratic equations. He is the one who gave us the word *algorithm*. In his geography book he calculated coordinates of many towns, for the first time. He actually corrected many mistakes made by Ptolemy. As our hometown scholar, we should be proud of him."

Princess Rayhana was enjoying Mohammad's lecture. She said, "I am astonished by the wealth of knowledge you have accumulated. You came from a village and learned so many things from my brother, yet I am so ignorant." This remark made Mohammad somewhat upset. It sounded like an insult to him as if people from rural areas are not capable of learning. Thus, he said, "My Lady, Princess Rayhana, my father was not a peasant. He was your uncle's court astronomer. He was exiled for no reason." The princess said, "Sorry, I did not mean to insult you. You know I respect you very much. . . . What is the meaning of the word *exile*? Why are you called Biruni? People say you are from outside!"

Mohammad smiled and said, "My Magnificent Lady, Princess Rayhana, you should know that the farmers are the oldest and the most important class in our society. Without them life would not be very easy." Princess Rayhana noticed that this young scholar had a very tender and delicate heart. She did not mean to make him sad. She reached for Mohammad's hands. She wanted to apologize. "Please do not be upset with me," said the princess.

Mohammad looked up and saw, for the first time, Lady Rayhana's pretty eyes, which were so full of elegance and beauty. And in a way, they were familiar to him. They looked like the sky: extensive, endless, and mysterious. They were filled with sparks. Her graceful and cheerful eyes were aflame with desire. In the candlelight, those eyes were like diamonds absorbing and emitting light. What a lovely sight. Such a soothing look!

Mohammad was getting a strange feeling of warmth deep inside. He had some sweat forming on his forehead. He never had experienced such a feeling before. He wanted to get on his knees and, with tears in his eyes, tell her how much he loved her. Her violet perfume was in the air. Her soft and silky hand was inside his. She was hugging him. She was in his arms. She put her beautiful lips near Mohammad's ear and said murmuring, like a very exquisite music, "I love you, I love you, I love you very much. You are my young scholar. You know everything. You are going to discover the secrets of the universe and the creation. And I am nothing. I have lost my mind and my heart. And, more importantly, I will love you forever."

Mohammad almost started to laugh. He was unsure that this light-spirited princess, this joyful girl was serious. This magnificent lady with more than four hundred years of pure royal blood was expressing interest in him. In split seconds, he felt that she was really serious. Her lovely eyes were wet. Yes, she was crying with smiling eyes.

He said in a low tone, "My dear princess, I am no match for you. I am nobody. You yourself are the secret of the universe. You are the most beautiful flower of my world. You are the mystery of the Milky Way, of course. Everybody is jealous of your beauty, elegance, and wealth. What am I? Who am I to deserve your attention? I'll always be your scholar. But love . . ."

They were standing face-to-face. For the longest time they were just staring into each other's eyes. Their lips were ready to kiss. But the princess took Mohammad's hands in hers and kissed the top of his left hand. It was like fire or electricity sent through Mohammad's body. He was burning. He took his hands out, turned around, and ran toward his room. Princess Rayhana was alone in the middle of the hall. She felt like her world was gone. She was cold. She slowly and softly walked toward the house. In her dreams, she was with her young handsome scholar.

When Mohammad reached his room in the school yard, Beejan, his room-mate was still studying. He looked at Mohammad and said, "What is wrong with you? You look like you are coming back from the grave. Are you sick?" Mohammad did not say anything. Yes, he was sick, but what kind of sickness? Beejan blew out the candle and said, "Damned Satan," and went to bed. Mohammad covered his body and head with a quilt. He said something that Beejan could hear too. "Goodnight my princess . . . I love you. More importantly, I will love you forever."

It was only three days later that Abu Nasr summoned Mohammad. While playing with his carnelian rosary, he asked:

"Did you tell anything to my sister . . ." Mohammad was surprised. He said, "What do I have to tell her, my Amir?"

"Think carefully. Three nights ago in the observatory, what went on between the two of you?"

"Nothing, my Amir."

"You know that I have trusted you all the time."

"Yes, I know. You have the highest gratitude and honor for me. I am indebted to you for the rest of my life."

"Then why don't you tell me the truth?"

"What truth?"

"I am disappointed with you. I didn't think that you would hide anything from me."

"There is nothing that I am hiding from you."

"Do you love my sister? Did she tell you anything about her love toward you?" Mohammad was perspiring.

"Princess Rayhana said that she respected me as a scholar and wanted to be like me and . . . and . . ."

"Then?"

"Nothing."

"Did she tell you she loved you?"

"Yes, she did. But I swear to my father's grave, I did not say anything."

"Don't you love her?"

"I was not expecting anything like that. She surprised me. I have been treated as a family member and it is not fair to think about your beloved sister with indulgence and look at her as the object of my desires. I swear that I said nothing."

"Therefore, you don't love her?"

"The thinking of mixing honest friendship with desire makes me tremble. I worship her. I kiss the ground that she walks on. But I do not think I deserve her!"

"Thank you, Mohammad. Although it is not easy, I want you to forget her. I myself will act as a suitor and find a wife for you. Please, just try to forget her. My sister is spoken for. It was through an arranged marriage. Upon her birth, she has been nominated as the future wife of my uncle's son. To us, she is engaged to him and we must honor our obligation and our tradition. She told me, with tears in her eyes, that she loves you. She said that you love her too. However, I trust you. Actually, it is too early for you to settle down. You and I have a lot of research to do together. We might unlock many mysteries of the world."

Mohammad wanted to say getting married to Princess Rayhana would not slow down his research. But he just choked. He knew that an arranged marriage was very important. He knew he was losing the love of his life because of some political reasons.

"I want you to remember Lady Rayhana as a younger sister. We have no choice. We have promised that she will get married to my uncle's son. I am very sorry. It is our tradition and you are the victim. You might suffer for the rest of your life. I have been thinking about this situation for two days. I do not have any other way out. You know that I love my sister. More importantly, you know that I love you as my brother. I know it will be painful for the two of you. But . . . !

"Yes, my Amir. I understand your political responsibilities."

Later in life, Biruni wrote a book titled *Kitab al-tafhim li-awa'il sina'at al-tanjim*, or *Book of Understanding Basics of the Art of Astronomy*, for Lady Rayhana. *Al-Tafhim*, as it is most often called for short, is in itself an enormous achievement for a scholar in the Middle Ages. In this book too, Biruni's method is to ask questions and provide answers in the simplest possible way. For example, some of the questions in the first part of the book ask, What is geometry? What is a point? What is an angle? On the other hand, Homaii argues that "although this book was written for a young Iranian Princess about a thousand years ago, yet it contains subjects and problems that still are not fully understood in our time" (p. 23). In *Al-Tafhim*, Biruni not only has laid an outstanding foundation for the science of astronomy but he has also produced an important piece of literary work. This book became a model for innovative scientific terminology in Arabic and their beautiful parallel translations in Persian. Many of these standardized keywords both in Arabic and Persian, including an upside-down map of the world, were used by future generations of scholars.

The historical Lady Rayhana was perhaps an accomplished astronomer, one of very few in the whole world. She was trained by Biruni. She may have written her own scientific books and carried her own research. Considering the fact that Biruni translated and dedicated a book to her, we can conclude that she was an important person. R. Ramsay Wright (1934) believed that "she is marked out among oriental women by her craving for scientific knowledge and by the rare distinction of having a book dedicated to her" (p. vii). Regrettably, history and geography worked against the records of her achievements, covering everything she did in a cloud of mystery.

CHAPTER FOURTEEN

Political Turmoil

The man who would become Princess Rayhana's father-in-law was called Mamun Ibn Mohammad. He was the governor of Gurganj, the second largest city of Khwarazm after Kath. He was the commander-in-chief of Khwarazm. He was the second most powerful person after Khwarazmshah, King Abu Abdulla. Since this arrangement was agreed upon after the Muslim invasion, the two leaders, the king in Kath and the governor in Gurganj, have had many problems, that is, political conflicts. The king always had been the forgiving partner and had always sought peaceful solutions to those problems. Actually the marriage between Princess Rayhana and the governor's son was arranged to lower tensions between the two sources of power.

After a few months, Abu Nasr's family was getting ready for Princess Rayhana's wedding. It was the most expensive in the history of Khwarazm. Mohammad was lost both on the Earth and in the sky. In a span of three days, he had found and lost the love of his life. He even did not touch any of the food and sweets prepared for the wedding. He was sick. And only two other people knew why. On the final day of the wedding celebrations, Rayhana in her wedding dress rode a horse at the head of a large procession leading into the city of Gurganj. Her face was covered. Therefore, nobody could see the tears she shed for leaving behind her brother's house and her heart. The procession was accompanied by loud music. Princess Rayhana's dowry was loaded on fifty camels. Late that afternoon, Mohammad was watching the procession from his room. He felt the biggest pain in his heart. He did not know who was to blame. He was lovesick. From the tiny window of his little room, he watched his heart being taken away. He was so hopeless he could not even cry. When he saw the end of the procession, he collapsed over the mat on the floor of his room. In seconds, his pillow was wet from his tears.

Unfortunately, even after Princess Rayhana's wedding, political conflicts did not end between the two ruling families of Khwarazm. Actually, the situation was worsening day by day. Abu Nasr was playing the role of a mediator between the two. He had forced his sister to marry somebody she did not love. Now he was feeling the pain too, because the two persons he loved the most in the whole world were suffering, and this political union had no positive effect on the situation.

Mamun, the governor of Gurganj, appeared to be a very brave person but he was a superficial one, with a shallow personality. He believed that he should be occupying the throne of Khwarazm in Kath instead of King Abu Abdulla. He believed that King Abu Abdulla was weak and that all he knew was to read books, do research, and sponsor scientific gatherings. If he stayed on the throne much longer, he felt, enemies would invade and Khwarazm will disappear. Mamun thought of himself as a more powerful person, however, who could expand Khwarazm's territory. Therefore, he sent several verbal messages to Khwarazmshah to resign and to go into retirement peacefully. Of course, Khwarazmshah did not like the idea. Instead, he tried to buy Mamun's loyalty and increased Mamun's salary.

In order to forget his worldly problems, Abu Nasr began spending more time in the observatory with Mohammad. Although they were doing research together, they hardly talked to each other. It was Abu Nasr who did not know what to say. This atmosphere of sadness slowly changed when Abu Nasr started to gradually talk about the problems in Khwarazm, albeit mostly political. He was predicting a gloomy future for Khwarazm. Abu Nasr said, "I wish I could see a better future for our beloved country. I regret one fact the most. You know what I am talking about, Mohammad? I should not let . . ." Mohammad said, "It has happened and now we cannot do anything about it. I wish too that our political leaders come to their senses and avoid further conflict."

Abu Nasr said, "Let's be realistic. I know Mamun well. I know that he will not give up his claim. Dear Mohammad, I know also how political conflicts, wars, revolts, and riots bring total calamity and misfortune to a country. The whole nation loses something or other, of course, but we scholars lose everything. I have read that during the Sassanid Empire a few scientists were able to harness the power of thunder and lightning. According to Chinese references, the Persians were able to produce lighting artificially. What happened to all that progress?"

Abu Nasr continued, "Dear Mohammad, I am sure you remember al-Muqanna, the veiled prophet of Khurasan whose moon would shine over the city of Nakhshab. And who can forget Abdulmalek, who stole the book containing the secrets of the science used by Maqanna. I am sure that Christian Andalusia will use those secrets against the Muslims in the future."

Mohammad was thinking how insignificant his personal problems were in comparison. He was feeling sorry for Abu Nasr and the country. His silent reverie was broken by Abu Nasr. He said, "During the Sassanid kings' reign, Persian astronomers had a complete map of the stars. This map with much accuracy was painted on the ceiling of a Zoroastrian temple in Azerbaijan. Persian physicians, for the first time, had dissected and studied the bodies of dead people in order to find out the causes of diseases. They even practiced out on living people. Chess and sugarcane were brought to Iran from India. When Buzorgmehr, who brought those two items to Iran and perfected the art of chess and became the Grand Vizier, was asked what he wanted as a prize for bringing the game of chess, he said nothing. But when the king insisted, he said just a single grain of wheat in the first square and double the amount in the next until the last one is reached. The king laughed. The vizier did not. Soon the king found out that it was impossible to pay his vizier that much wheat. This was due to the fact that, as even our very young pupils know, raising a number to the power of another number makes it very big. Later in life, Mohammad calculated the result.

The Persians in southwest Iran planted sugarcane and learned to refine sugar. It was then taken into North Africa and southern Europe. Today, sugar is a very important international trade item.

Mohammad was still thinking about al-Muqanna, so he asked, "Has anybody understood how the masked man of Khurasan invented his fireball? And how he was able to send it into the sky?" Abu Nasr said proudly, "Yes, I have. Al-Muqanna wrote everything in codes and used Chinese to explain his equations and chemical elements to produce the fireball. I have found a copy of the original plan written on deerskin. I am sure you remember Professor Heuchian, the Chinese professor of arms development in our own school. He translated al-Muqanna's writing for me. We wanted to build a catapult and use the fireball against our enemies."

Abu Nasr left for a few minutes. He reentered the great hall with a deerskin rolled up in his hands. He opened up the large skin on a table and asked Mohammad to join him in examining the writing. It was a big plan. It looked like a map with many strange symbols, numbers, and codes. Mohammad asked:

"Whose writing is this?"

"Al-Muqanna himself!"

"Why did he call himself al-Muqanna?"

"Because his face was damaged from an accident he had when experimenting with some chemicals one day. He wore a mask made of red gold. He deliberately wore white clothes, including a white turban, white robe, and white boots, to show his hostility with the Abbadis Caliphs of Baghdad, who wore black clothes. With a golden mask and white dress he had an appalling and imposing presence over his followers. For about twenty years from 725 C.E., his movement dominated Transoxania."

"Did his followers wear white clothes too?"

"Yes."

"Aren't these two among the same people who wanted to sacrifice me?"

"No, no, absolutely not. The white-dressed people of Tammami are different. They are a group of superstitious people who only wear white. The original white-dressed people were real warriors, brave and anti-Arab. They were fighting the armies of the caliphs of Baghdad. They saw the caliphs as tyrants and cruel oppressors that were a disgrace for the whole of humanity. I believe that al-Muqanna, whose real name was Hosham Ibn Hakim, was a genius. He used the Chinese 'fiery black medicine,' gunpowder, to send his fireball into the sky."

"Fiery black medicine!"

"Yes, we call it 'baroot.' It was invented by the Chinese for peaceful purposes. They use it for fireworks during national celebrations such as the beginning of their New Year or on birthdays of their emperors. This medicine is kept as a very important national secret. Everybody leaving China is inspected to prevent its export out of China."

"What do you want to do with this map?" Abu Nasr got closer to Mohammad and in a very low voice said, "I want to produce the fiery black medicine and build my own fireball. Then I will be able to prevent Mamun's army from capturing the city of Kath. If al-Muqanna was able to fight against Baghdad's army for more than twenty years, I could save Kath at least. But I need help. I cannot trust anybody else but you. Do you want to help me?"

One final question, said Mohammad.

"Why during Abdulmalek's hearing were you so calm and did not say much about . . . ?" Abu Nasr said, "We too as scientists sometimes should act as politicians."

One day Mohammad heard that Khwarazmshah's own army had rebelled against him. Their complaint was that they were paid late. Khwarazmshah tried to calm them down by promising that they will be paid on time in the future and advised them on helping him keep the nation united. He was unable to calm them down, however. They city of Kath was in turmoil for a whole day and a night. On the second day, a few of the colonels entered the palace and arrested the shah. Khwarazmshah and his family members were sent to a fort near the city of Gurganj. The fort acted as a big prison occupied only by the royal family.

It was obvious who was behind the rebellion and the arrest. In fact, merely a few hours after the shah was arrested, Mamun entered the palace and sat on the throne. The new shah was known as a brave soldier but had a shallow personality and was almost illiterate.

One day the new king of Khwarazm summoned Abu Nasr and told him that it was very expensive to keep the observatory and its associated library and school running. So he ordered Abu Nasr to close them down. The new Shah Mamun thought all those students and their teachers were useless parasites and that they were just getting fat from leading an irresponsible life. Abu Nasr agreed to close the school without any argument. Actually, Abu Nasr was very prompt and on the same day, he ordered the students and teachers to go home and then he closed down the observatory, library, and the whole school.

King Mamun was a jealous and shortsighted person. He did not like Abu Nasr. And if it was not for the sake of the marriage between his son and Princess Rayhana, he would have ordered the killing of Abu Nasr. He was afraid of Abu Nasr, because Khwarazmshah was Abu Nasr's uncle. Abu Nasr was loved by the people, who also remembered and liked their former shah. King Mamun was worried that Abu Nasr might lead a rebellion against him. Thus, he was trying to find a reason to arrest him. Abu Nasr knew this, and that was why, when ordered, he quickly closed the observatory without any resistance. That was also like Abu Nasr to know how to play the game.

King Mamun brought his vizier to Kath from Gurganj. It seemed that this vizier did not know anything but how to lie and deceive. He was a pessimist, full of suspicion, jealousy, conspiracy, and backbiting. He had been involved in frauds, cheating, and cruelty. His spies were everywhere. People were more afraid of him than the new shah. After the city of Kath was captured, the new shah was advised by his vizier to arrest more than one hundred former civil officials and many that were related to the old royal family. Many of them were innocent. This was to frighten the population and anybody that had any plans to cause trouble. Thirty of the one hundred arrested were immediately executed, based on shameless unfounded accusations from the vizier's office.

Ten days after the takeover, one night Mamun sent a group of his soldiers called the *mofrad*, meaning "Singular," who alone can fight against many, to the former Khwarazmshah's prison to get rid of him. The former shah was actually released first so he could be accused of escaping. The *mofrads* told him that they came from the countryside and that they were rebelling against Mamun, who indeed had escaped already. The poor king believed them. The former Khwarazmshah, who had lost everything, was so excited that he fell on his knees and started thanking Allah on his way out of the prison. At that very second, one of Mamun's *mofrads* dew his dagger and stabbed him. The former shah was still alive when the same soldier sat on his chest and cut off his head and put it in a bag. It was going to be gifted to the new shah on his tenth day on the throne.

Upon seeing the bloody head, King Mamun, who was drunk, said with a silly laugh, "This is a punishment for somebody who did not listen to me!" The new king and his vizier then celebrated the killing of a good king.

It is during the last week of autumn 991 C.E. when we meet the new king of Khwarazm, Mamun, in his palace two weeks after he took over the city of Kath, located south of Lake Aral in the country of Uzbekistan today.

The barber put both his hands into a bowl of musk perfume then rubbed them over the new king's face. The whole room was filled with this beautiful odor. The musk was dripping from the king's beard, which was mostly black with some white hair growing in the middle. The barber used some warm water and soap for shaving the king's neck. His neck was red, big, and wrinkled. The king was sitting on a big and high chair. There was a slave boy sitting on a small stool in front of him was rubbing his toes with a curative oil that was brought in from Gujarat in western India. The king's toes had been itching, which was bothering him. They were itching. This oil, recommended by a physician, was effective, and the itching was almost gone.

The new vizier, Khwaja Ghayasdin, entered the room. He bowed and said, "What do you order in regard to the guilty ones?" The new shah's order was clear. He said, "Send the former shah's family members to jail and execute the rest!" The new shah's order already was written on a piece of Chinese paper, and all he had to do was just sign it. And he did. Khwaja Ghayasdin's second question was about Abu Nasr.

"What should we do with Abu Nasr?"

"He is Lady Rayhana's brother. Although rude, daring, and irreligious, we cannot execute him."

"Should he be exiled?"

"No, no. The observatory is closed. The students and professors are gone. Thus, wait and see what he is up to. But keep him under surveillance.

"What should we do with the observatory?"

"Let's reopen it as an elementary school."

"I do not think we need another school. We have 133 schools in the city already."

"What about an army base?"

"It is too small for an army base."

"I have a better idea. Let's use it as my harem. I have so many wives, maids, and slave girls, and we do not have enough room for all of them in the palace."

"Good idea, my great Amir."

The slave boy was still rubbing that magical oil on the king's toes. Suddenly, the king kicked the boy in the chest and shouted, "Go get Zaryab!" Zaryab, Goldseeker, was the name of a black slave from Zanzibar, off the coast of east Africa. He was the new king's clown. He would wear red pants and cloak and a long cone-shaped hat, just for the fun of it.

Mamun, the new shah, told Zaryab, "Come here and clothe me." Zaryab waited until the barber finished his job of putting a wet towel on the king's neck. The barber was now cutting the hair growing inside the king's nostrils. He had already trimmed the king's beard. Therefore, this man of fifty-eight was ready for a night full of pleasure.

Actually, the king was planning to go to bed with the most beautiful slave girl. Her name was Angela. She was a princess originally from the island of Sicily. She was stolen by pirates while on her father's ship. She was sold to a Muslim-Arab merchant first, who brought her to the city of Damascus and sold her to the governor. As a gift from the governor then she was sent to the former Khwarazmshah's court. She had spent only a month in the palace when Khwarazmshah was deposed. She was the most beautiful slave girl in town. She was tall, with big, beautiful eyes and long black hair, a very lovely girl overall. Angel then was going to be the king's new concubine.

Mamun was daydreaming about the night waiting for her. This young slave girl about twenty years of age was a princess, too. His sweet imagination was suddenly cut short by his vizier, Ghayasdin, who asked, "What should we do with all of those astronomers that we have fired?" Mamun said, "They should wear hats like that of Zaryab and should be shown around town and let people laugh at them. The bastard Khwarazmshah paid them and fattened them, just to look into the sky!" At this moment, Abnous, a black slave girl entered the room. Mamun asker her, "How is she? Is she ready?" Before she said anything, the vizier asked, "What should we do with the fifteen high court (government) officials of the former government. My great Amir, can you see them from the windows? They are waiting for your order."

It seemed that Mamun did not hear what Ghayasdin asked or just ignored him. Mamun asked Abnous, "Is she beautiful?" Abnous responded, "Yes, your honor, the best in the world!" Ghayasdin asked, "What should we do with all of those students expelled form the observatory? Should we enlist them in the army? They are . . ." Mamun said, "Yes, yes, it is a good suggestion."

Ghayasdin repeated his questions that were ignored by Mamun. His question was about the fifteen's fate. They were blindfolded and their hands were tied on their backs. With their sharp, long, heavy machetes, the executioners were waiting for Mamun's order. The new shah suddenly remembered the fifteen! He said, "Yes, sorry, I forgot. . . . My mind has been occupied with the thought of this Sicilian girl. I mean . . . Angela. I cannot wait to see her." He waited a few seconds, then continued and said, "Kill them all. They are our enemies. I have no mercy for my enemies, and remember that it is also our tradition, before the groom sees his bride he is required to sacrifice some animals. Think of those fifteen people as animals. Think of those fifteen people as animals to be sacrificed. This takes away bad luck from my family."

The executioners got busy. In minutes, the heads of the fifteen had been cut off. Blood covered a large portion of the courtyard. The courtyard was becoming a killing place. Until recently, it was a place where beautiful women, political representatives from all over the world, and learned men walked.

The observatory had two windows overlooking the courtyard, which was covered by fresh blood. Behind those windows were two pairs of eyes watching what was going on in the courtyard. Those eyes belonged to Abu Nasr and Mohammad. Although a very brave man, Abu Nasr was frightened. He was very sad. He was silent. For the first time since he met Abu Nasr, Mohammad saw tears in his eyes. He was in pain, because those executed were not guilty of any crimes.

After a long, deadly period of silence, Abu Nasr said, "What a just and wise government we had. Khwarazmshah himself was a learned man. He paid so much attention to scholars. He built the largest and the best observatory in the world here. He built dams, city walls, schools and . . . what a wonderful scientific gathering we had. What a lofty goal we had. And what is this low life, the new shah, this tyrant is doing other than killing innocent people! His most important goal, since enthroning himself, has been to sleep with this Sicilian slave girl, Angela."

Abu Nasr was unsure what to do. He knew, however, that it was not safe to stay in town. He was thinking about getting out of town, probably to go toward central Iran and reside in Rayy, Isfahan, or Shiraz.

Abu Nasr called Mohammad, his only trusted friend, student, and confidant, to find out about caravans going toward central Iran. Abu Nasr needed some information about how much it would cost him to move out of Kath altogether and when was the departure time of some of the caravans.

In the history of Iran and the Middle East, caravans have always played a major role as a means of transportation. Most often, a large number of merchant pilgrims, travelers, and explorers would accompany a caravan. The larger the number, the safer it would be to travel with a caravan. Most often, of course, caravans would be accompanied by security forces. In a good-sized caravan, at least two thousand people would sign up. In addition to horses, mules, and donkeys, a larger number of camels were used as the beast of burden.

Before the observatory was closed down by the order of the new shah, Mohammad took two pupils. This means that he was now a young, new teacher. His students' names were Kazem Birjandi and Sa'eed Qaynati. Both of them were from the Khurasan region. As it was the practice at that time, their places of birth were used as their surnames. They, Mohammad, Kazem, and Sa'eed, together went to several caravansarais to gather the information needed by Abu Nasr. A caravan-salar's, owner and/or leader of a caravan, first question would be what was the name of the person joining the caravan? As soon as a caravan-salar heard Abu Nasr's name, he would come up with some excuses like they were full or winter was coming or just no reason at all. They visited fifteen caravan-salars. They heard the same reasons over and over. There was no room for Abu Nasr and his family in any one of the caravans.

Mohammad knew the actual reason from the beginning of their search, but he still was somewhat hopeful to find a place for Abu Nasr and his family in one of the fifteen caravans. Kazem and Sa'eed were getting tired. Almost at the same time, they said, "Mr. Mohammad, don't you think that the new government is behind all of this? And we are wasting our time!" Mohammad did not respond.

It was true that the deceased Khwarazmshah was Abu Nasr's uncle. But Abu Nasr was an independent scholar and did not have very strong political relationships with the former king, yet he still was regarded with suspicion by the new king. Mohammad became very upset. He reported back to Abu Nasr that no caravan is taking him and the new government is behind it. Mohammad told Abu Nasr that he should go and see the new shah if he wants to get out of town.

Abu Nasr used to see Khwarazmshah, his uncle, anytime he wished. Not anymore. The new king was avoiding him. Abu Nasr had to ask for an appointment in writing. And it was only three days later that he was given one.

On his way home from the palace, Abu Nasr noticed that he was being followed by two beggars. They had a worn out quilt-like mantle over their heads and tried to keep a certain distance from him. The next day, he noticed that his house was under surveillance too. He and his house were being watched by spies, disguised as hawkers, peddlers, and beggars. In a week, Abu

Nasr was prevented from entering the observatory and was not even allowed to take his own equipment from the observatory.

It was at this time that a cholera epidemic devastated the city. The people believed that it was due to the new king's crimes. Allah was angry because satanic actions had been committed by Mamun.

Throughout the centuries, the Persian Empire not only has had the best armies in the world but it had espionage offices of several types. The Achaemenid kings (559–330 B.C.) beginning with Cyrus the Great called their spies the "ears and eyes of the shah." They were selected from the general population from every section of the society. The Sassanids used the same title for their spies. These spies were used very effectively during Anowhiravan's reign (531–579 C.E.).

After the Islamic takeover of the Middle East, especially during the Umayyad, Caliphs (661–750 C.E.) wanted to control Ali's descendants. Abbadis Caliphs had an office of espionage for information gathering and controlling their enemies. The first governor of Khurasan, Tahir, was poisoned on the same Friday when he was ordered to drop the name of the Abbadis caliph from a public sermon in 828 C.E. His bodyguard and servant was the caliph's spy.

Mamun, the new Khwarazmshah, reestablished the tradition of espionage. The former Khwarazmshah had a very small office responsible for gathering information on the enemies of the king, because he had no enemies. Thus, this office's activities were at a standstill level. Actually, had it been more active, it would have been able to prevent Mamun's takeover. The new Khwarazmshah, with help from his vizier's office, enlarged the office of espionage. The new government hired spies among slaves, maids, servants, eunuchs, and many more.

The omnipresent spies had reported to the shah that Mohammad Ibn Ahmad, known as Biruni, was still going to the observatory although he knew that it was officially closed. A few of the spies reportedly heard him saying, "What business does this tyrant, murderer, and foolish shah have with the observatory?" This report became the new shah's major indignation. He ordered his chief of police to arrest Mohammad right in front of the observatory and the people and "Take out and cut his tongue!" They were eating lunch when the shah ordered this. The people present at the table who heard this order included the shah's son and his wife, Rayhana. She, now called Lady Rayhana, suddenly cried out! Khwarazmshah turned his face to look at her carefully and asked, "What has happened to you? Why has your face gone yellowish? Why did you lose control? And why have you become so upset? His tongue is not the first one I have ordered to be taken out!"

Lady Rayhana was so frightened she was ready to confess all the secrets hidden in her heart. But she could not. She put herself together and said, "Dear father, according to my brother Abu Nasr, this young man whose tongue you ordered to be cut . . . is the smartest scholar the world has seen in a long time!" Khwarazmshah interrupted Rayhana and asked, "How do you know this so-called scholar?" She answered, "Dear father, everybody in the city of Kath is aware of this young man's knowledge and fame! He has taught many royal family members, including myself!"

Khwarazmshah knew that Lady Rayhana, like her brother, was a learned person. Therefore, he accepted her words and said, "But he has to get out of town. He has to be punished for his remarks, anyway." Lady Rayhana was happy at heart that she was able to save the life of the love of her life. But she still wanted to ask for a bit more. She said, "Dear father, this young man is the best astrologist in the world today. You should keep him in town. It will give you credit for sponsoring science, which in turn will provide you with respect from the people and other royal families." The shah was busy eating a small roasted fish. Thus, he was cool and calm. He still commented negatively. He said, "To hell with reputation and respect. I need brave men to fight for me. I do not need astronomers, magicians, or fortune tellers. Anyway, if he was a good fortune teller, why did he not predict your uncle's sad future? I do not need a peasant astrologer from *birun*, "outside," called Biruni!"

Lady Rayhana got very sad and tears came down her face when she heard her uncle's name. But at heart, she still was very happy that she could do something for her young scholar. Khwarazmshah's insistence on using the derogatory word "Biruni" for Mohammad became common and it was formalized. This became Mohammad's last name and stayed with him for the rest of his life, although it was a contemptuous and derogatory title. Actually, late in life he was known as Ostad Biruni or Master Biruni. The Persian word *ostad* is a reference to a professor, master, or architect or the most knowledgeable, skilled person in an occupation.

Mohammad, Kazem, and Sa'eed were standing in front of a globe, marked with all known stars, in the now-abandoned observatory. They were talking about some topics in astronomy. They were not supposed to be there. They were talking in low voices. At this time, the first stone hit the latticed wooden window of the observatory hall. A mob with a disorderly and uproaring noise was already forming. The crowd was moving closer to the main door of the observatory hall. Now, some of the words and sentences could be heard:

"Break . . . break . . . this house of Satan."

"Goddamn those magicians, imposters, and geomancers."

"Cholera has destroyed our city. Allah is angry because these magicians want intervention in his plans."

"I peeped inside the big hall last week; I saw so many satanic tools. These tools are used to call up Satan. Astronomers then ask questions from Satan about the mysteries of creation!" shouted an old man. He continued, "Cholera is killing hundreds of people every day. It is because of those crystal globes, strange writings that are in the language of the infidels. The government has spent thousands of gold dinars on the astronomers and their toys. The former Khwarazmshah has hired people from every other nation in the world. They employed Chinese, Indians, Jews, Zoroastrians, and even Christians."

A woman shouted, "I saw four of them on the roof watching the sky one night!" Another one cried, "Maybe they were talking to Satan." Mohammad had a bitter smile on his lips. He said, "Simple-minded public, observing stars seems to them as talking to Satan."

"Let's go from here, professor," suggested Kazem. "Let's ask for help from the security forces," suggested Sa'eed. Professor Biruni commented, "Nobody will help us. This mob of fools is being guided by somebody who has ordered the security forces not to help us." Rocks of every size and shape were hitting the windows. Part of the dome shaped like a half circle over the big hall was broken, making a huge sound. A young man in the crowd shouted, "They wanted to make 'the Chinese black medicine.'" Mohammad listened carefully. He said, "I can recognize that voice. It belongs to that thief, that dishonest man who stole our books and gave them to the people from Andalusia. It was Abdulmalek. He was among the crowd. He knows what the scholars were up to in the laboratories of the school and observatory. But we were making *baroot* (gun powder) for the government."

Kazem said, "Dear professor, of course Abdulmalek is not our friend. He can make up so many lies." Mohammad said, "We made a mistake. We should have talked to Abu Nasr. It was safer to go with him, if he could get out of Kath. He is gone and we are at the mercy of this tyrant." Kazem suggested, "However, we have to get of out of town as soon as possible or . . ."

There was no escape route left. The mob was led by a group of rogues and mischievous, vicious people. Now they were throwing fireballs toward the roof of the buildings. Some of the police officers, who appeared fully drunk, started helping the mob.

In the royal garden, Khwarazmshah Mamun was drinking wine. Zaryab and Abnous were waiting on him. Angela was sitting next to the Shah. Their cups were filled with a type of red wine. The shah and Angela were laughing loudly and enjoying the sight of the mob playing with fire and destroying the observatory. Khwarazmshah was encircled by a group of men from Gurganj, and there were prostitutes, dancers, and clowns too. He was firm on destroying everything associated with the former shah.

Mohammad Ibn Ahmad and his two students were losing hope. He was shouting, "Help us . . . help us. The observatory and the school are burning. The royal library is next door. The observatory and the library contain a quarter of a million books. These books are the most valuable in the whole world. Let's climb the roof and shout. Somebody may help us." The three reached the top of the observatory. Now, they could see everybody in the royal garden. Mohammad continued shouting and asking for help. He hoped that the new shah might be a reasonable person who could somehow be persuaded to help save the observatory from destruction. He kept saying, "Dear Khwarazmshah, in the observatory there are thousands of astronomical instruments that are worth millions of dinars. Some of them are made in China, some in Rome, and some came from Baghdad. Please save them!" The shah was looking at Mohammad's mouth, but he could not recognize a word of what Mohammad was saying.

Mohammad still kept shouting hopelessly, "Your honor, we are not malicious individuals. I am a poor professor from the village of Vasemereed. I learned many subjects from my master Abu Nasr. Please help yourself and your government. A quarter of a million books are in danger of being burned. It took a thousand years to build these facilities. Please save them." Khwarazmshah could not hear what Mohammad was saying because of the distance, noise, and consumption of wine. The royal garden itself was crowded and the mob in front of the observatory was very noisy. More importantly, the shah was drunk.

Khwarazmshah asked his vizier, "What is that young man on the roof of the observatory saying?" Ghayasdin said he could not hear him. But he was lying. He could recognize most of what Mohammad was saying. The Shah said, "Could somebody tell me what that clown on the roof of the observatory is saying?" Somebody said, "He is Biruni." The shah said, "He is the one who claims that he knows everything. He and his little beard! Hey, Biruni, *Birun show* (meaning "get lost" in Persian). You are an unpleasant peasant. Not a learned man." The king was unable to stand straight. He was holding on to Angela.

Ghayasdin could understand Mohammad's cry for help. He thought that Mohammad was right. Those tools and books were very valuable. So he came up with a plan. The vizier's plan was to save the equipment and books, then sell them. There were many people who would pay a large sum of money for some of those books and equipment. And he could keep the money for himself. But it was too late to save anything.

When drunk, Khwarazmshah would behave like a real wild animal. He was dancing in the middle of a group of clowns. Then he took a sharp knife and stepped toward the fire, where a lamb was being roasted. He cut a big piece of the lamb, which was hardly ready, and tried to eat it. He did not like the taste of the raw meat. He spat out everything and picked up a bowl of wine instead.

The observatory was ablaze. First, the wooden doors and windows, then the silk curtains, and in no time everything else were on fire. The flames were taking over. The mob could enter the big hall now. They were breaking everything. The vizier ordered the arrest of the three on the roof of the observatory and accused them of arson. He said, "Those three carried out Abu Nasr's orders to destroy our observatory and library." Mohammad, Kazem, and Sa'eed were taken to jail.

Meanwhile, the fire was continuing to rage. It was expanding to every corner of the building, including the educational and research facilities. Then the mob heard the loudest noise in their lives. Somebody said, "That was the Chinese black medicine that exploded." The roof of the observatory blew off and broke into pieces in midair. The whole library was uprooted and destroyed. Big, frightening explosions, one after another, even scared the mob and got the drunken shah's attention. He stopped dancing and just stood there watched the facilities ablaze.

Ostad Biruni and his students were sent to jail. In the jail, they were beaten up and then put into a dark room. The three just sat there resting their heads on their hands. Even with their eyes closed, all they could see was fire.

It was sometime after midnight when the jail cell door opened. A colonel entered the room with a candle in his hand. He said in a low but decipherable tone, "Quick, get out of here." It was like the three were ready. He said, "We should get out from the back door. Behind the building are three horses waiting for you. Just get out of town as soon as possible. You are scheduled to be executed tomorrow." Biruni looked at this big colonel in arms; unable to believe they were being helped and their lives were being saved by a stranger, he asked, "Who are you? Could you tell me where Abu Nasr is?"

The big colonel answered, "My name is Aladin Tarmazi, and I am the chief of the palace guards. I believe that Abu Nasr has already left town. I do not know anything more." Mohammad asked while getting out of the jail, "What makes you commit such a generous and brave act for us?" The colonel responded, "Lady Rayhana has ordered me to save your life. Although I do not know you personally, I have heard that you are the most famous scholar in the world. She has sent you a special greeting. She has asked you not to worry about her. Because her husband, although Mamun's son, is a different person. She is happy with her life with him. And you better get out of town immediately."

The colonel was leading the three through the jail hallways. They made a left turn, when Mohammad saw flames of fire and smoke marking the observatory from a little window. He said, "It is still ablaze." Nobody said anything. Before stepping out of the jail, Colonel Tarmazi gave Mohammad, Kazem, and Sa'eed three violet cloaks. He said, "These are our night watchers' uniforms. Wear them over your clothes. They may help disguise you. Please do not wait. Just get out of town soon."

"Do you want us to go alone?"

"No, I am sending one of my officers up to the city gate with you."

CHAPTER FIFTEEN

The Wandering Years

After his escape from the city of Kath, Biruni was unable to settle down for three years. First, he stayed in a large village. But he did not like rural life. As a professor, researcher, and scholar, he needed to live in a large city that had a large library and a generous royal family to support him. Therefore, he decided to go to the city of Rayy, located south of present-day Tehran. It was a large prosperous city with a flourishing economy. The library of the Buyid Dynasty was one of the largest in the Muslim world. It is believed that this library had more than three hundred thousand books.

Kazem and Sa'eed, Biruni's students, now his friends, accompanied him. The Buyid kings were very generous and supported science, art, and poetry. One famous personality from the city of Rayy was Mohammad Ibn Zakarya Razi. He discovered alcohol and is one of the most well-known Persian-Muslim physician. Later in life, Biruni had acknowledged using Razi's books.

Fakhrodola was the Buyid king in Rayy. He was a learned man and a very generous person. Actually, he supported Biruni's research. However, Fakhrodola had his problem of overindulgence. He had been eating and drinking too much and it was taking a toll on his health. One of the main reasons Biruni wanted to stay in Rayy was that the people and the royal family followed the Shiah branch of Islam, similar to the people of Kath. The Shiah Muslims believed that Ali, Prophet Mohammad's nephew and son-in-law, was his rightful successor. In addition, the Shiah Muslims had always been more politically active and open to change. In Rayy, many scholars could get together and discuss many subjects freely.

About the same period of time, Sultan Mahmud of the Ghazavid Dynasty, who was a Sunni Muslim, wanted to expand his territory. After Fakhrodola died due to overeating and overdrinking, his wife Sayyida Banoo enthroned herself. Meanwhile, Sultan Mahmud was becoming restless about taking over Central Iran, including the city of Rayy. He even suggested marrying Sayyida Banoo. Her answer was no and she told him she was ready to fight him. Her message was that whether he loses or wins a war, he was still going to leave a bad name in history. She wrote to Sultan Mahmud, "If you defeat me, historians will say you only defeated a woman, but if I defeat you, then you will become the most famous Sultan in the world, one who was defeated by a hopeless woman." As long as she was alive, Sultan Mahmud avoided conflict with her.

It was after Sayyida Banoo's death that Mahmud and his powerful army surrounded the city of Rayy. In a short time, Mojaddola, the last king of the Buyid Dynasty, was jailed. Later he was executed. His guilt was that he had fifty concubines in his harem. Taking concubines as wives is allowed in Shiah but not in Sunni Islam. Sultan Mahmud himself took many concubines however. As a king he could, of course, do anything he wished. It is believed that Sultan Mahmud ordered the hanging of four hundred scholars in Rayy because they were Shiah Muslims.

Biruni's life in Rayy was getting tough. After Mahmud's takeover, he lost his source of income and, more importantly, his life was in danger. Ostad Biruni and his students suffered poverty in Rayy. He later wrote that he was ridiculed by his peers, and his ideas in astronomy were rejected because of his appearance.

One day, he heard that in Tabarestan (now called Mazandaran), in the southeast corner of the Caspian plains, there was an amir who might give him refuge. He was Marzban Ibn Rustam Ibn Shirvin of the Bavand family. He himself was a learned man who had written a book called *Marzban-Nameh* (*Book of Marzban*). Animals were the main characters of this book, who dispensed moral advice. Being in an inaccessible mountainous region, the Bavand family was saved by the geography of their territory. It was almost impossible for the Muslim-Arab armies and the armies of other neighboring kings to take over Tabarestan.

In Tabarestan, Biruni wrote his first book of astronomy. He presented this book to the king, Marzban, who ordered ten copies to be made and bound. Most of the copies were sent to major libraries in the large Islamic cities of the time.

Tabarestan, however, was small for Biruni. He decided to go to another place. After his book reached the city of Bukhara, he was contacted and invited there by one of his students. In the late 990s, the city of Bukhara was a very large and prosperous urban center. Bukhara was the capital city of the Samanid Dynasty's empire. On arrival, Biruni was ordered to build an observatory by Mansur II.

Unfortunately, the city was being attacked by Ilak Khan's tribe. And Bukhara's affairs were going from bad to worse. Even the king himself advised Biruni to move out of town. King Mansur II was hoping that Sultan Mahmud would provide some help before the collapse of the city and the dynasty. At least verbally, he had promised to. On the surface, Sultan Mahmud had respect for the Samanid kings, because his father, Alptakin, was a slave in the Samanid court. But in reality, Mahmud wanted to see a weak king in Bukhara at the mercy of a Turkish tribe so he could exploit the situation. At one point, Bukhara's army began deserting the city as there was not enough food in the city. And, more importantly, typhus was killing many people. Thus, a large number of people left Bukhara.

One day, Ostad Biruni, now a well-dressed, rich scholar, was wandering in Bukhara's main bazaar when he heard someone call him by name. As a famous astronomer, he would be recognized very easily. The man said he had important news from Khwarazm. "King Mamum had a heart attack and has gone to hell," he said. Biruni stopped. He could not believe it. He asked, "Who has replaced him? Maybe another tyrant!" The stranger said, "No, actually his son Ali, who is loved by everybody. He is indeed undoing what his father had done. King Ali, the new Khwarazmshah, even has apologized to the people for his father's wrongdoings. Everybody knows he is influenced by his wife Lady Rayhana." Biruni just said "Thanks" and called Kazem and Sa'eed, who never were that far from him and said, "Let's go back home!"

When the three reached Khwarazm and entered the city of Kath, they found the city in ruins. They really got very sad thinking how one man, King Mamun, could destroy the whole city and the country in such a short time.

The three settled down but were not living very comfortably. Only Biruni was excited, because he was waiting for an eclipse of the moon that year. It was very significant to him because he had already written to a fellow astronomer in Baghdad by the name of Abul Wafa Buzjani (940–998 C.E.) to record the time of the eclipse carefully, and Biruni himself wanted to do the same in the city of Kath. Biruni believed that the difference in time of the eclipse in the two cities indicated that the Earth was not flat and he could calculate the distance between the two cities.

Biruni was able to meet the new Khwarazmshah, Ali Ibn Mamun, who was Rayhana's husband. He found King Ali to be a very pleasant person, worlds apart from his father. The new Khwarazmshah was a self-possessed, sedate, logical person. He liked to support scholars and their research. He most often would listen to his wife, Lady Rayhana. He shared many political decisions with her. Biruni became very happy to see his love in a long time. He became happy because she was happy and touching many lives and helping her subjects.

These memorable, beautiful days did not last long, however. It was Ostad Biruni's fate not be able to settle down. The country of Khwarazm, especially the two cities of Gurganj and Kath, like Bukhara, came to be targeted by Ilak Kahn's invading forces. Floods and epidemic diseases killed many people too. Soon, Mohammad and his student-friends, Kazem and Sa'eed, had to take to the road again.

CHAPTER SIXTEEN

The City of Gorgan

The modern city of Gorgan is located near the southeast corner of the Caspian Sea in Iran. Sometimes spelled Gurgan, in Old Persia, it was known as Varkana. It is the ancient city of Hyrcania. The Arabs called it Jurjan. In more recent times, it was also called Astarabad.

The city of Gorgan has been the center of Astarabad, modern-day Mazandaran Province. This region forms a link between dry northeastern Iran covered by steppe grass and the province of Gilan to the west, which has a humid subtropical climate. The province of Mazandaran has two major rivers, Atrak and Gorgan. The prosperity of the province and the city has been based on the generous natural elements of fertile soils and abundance of rain and freshwater sources. This in itself has been a fortunate mixed blessing.

During the Sasanid period (226–651 C.E.), several fortresses were built here as a defensive measure against the nomads of the steppes. It is believed that toward the north of this province a long wall was built for the same purpose. But the city and the province fell to the Muslim-Arab armies in 717 C.E. The city was among the most prosperous and beautiful places in the whole world by the tenth century. It was surrounded by many gardens irrigated by the Gorgan River. The city itself was divided into two parts by the river. Parts of the town were connected by a bridge of boats. The city had nine gates.

The revival of a Persian dynasty goes back to the early 900s when Mardavij, son of Ziyar, founded a kingdom in Gorgan in 928 C.E. The House of Ziyarid survived for about a hundred years. The famous dome-shaped tomb of Qabus, pronounced Qabous (died in 1012), still exists as a major memorial of this period (see Ghirshman, Minorsky, and, Sanghvi, 1971, p. 124).

The city of Gorgan was destroyed by the Mongols in the early thirteenth century. Although Timur, Tamer Lame, built a palace on the bank of the Gorgan River in 1392 C.E., the city never attained its former economic success and well-being. At present, in the early years of the twenty-first century, nearly a quarter of a million people live in Gorgan.

The year was 998 C.E., and the Persian celebration of Norouz, marking the beginning of spring and a new year, was in full swing. The fresh spring air saturated with the odor of citrus fruits was very delightful. Orange and tangerine trees were plentiful, with abundant fruits everywhere. Hyacinths, angelicas, and jasmines were in full bloom, available to customers. People were getting ready for this once-a-year ancient celebration of the new year.

This was Qabus's fifth year on the throne. He and his government made sure to honor and have one of the best New Year celebrations. The city boulevards, which were lined with palm trees, were full of people and one could see *Hajji Firoozes* (the Iranian version of Santa Claus) in their red uniforms spreading good cheer and making everyone happy.

Three beggars just entered the city on this first day of spring. They were surprised by the site of plenty and abundance. They were equally surprised by seeing so many foreigners in town. The people of Gorgan looked taller, red faced, and well dressed. But the most visible, bigger, taller people that the three beggars were watching were from Russia. They were wearing fur coats and hats, boots, and most of them had a reddish beard. These were Russian merchants in search of fur to be imported to Europe. The city of Gorgan, being a major trade center, had many taverns. Non-Muslim merchants such as Christians, Jews, and Zoroastrians would enjoy the best wines in the city. In Islamic cities, taverns were allowed to serve alcohol to their many foreign clients.

The city and the region itself was a major producer of cotton silk in the world. Its black silk clothes were world famous. European merchants, especially the Russians, would take raw silk from Gorgan and sell it in various European countries, including Germany, Holland, and England.

The three beggars who had just entered the city were looking like very poor people from the countryside. They were walking aimlessly. They were young, but looked to be sick and dirty. When they reached the city's Grand Bazaar, they could not believe how rich a shopping center can be. The Grand Bazaar was really filled with merchandise of all types. The three were looking at some of those items for the first time in their lives. On that first day of spring, the bazaar was filled with the odor of *hallva*, a sweet, pasty pudding, pottage, and many different kinds of food. The three were very hungry and penniless.

The three beggars were stopped by the police in the middle of the bazaar. They were told, "You seem to be strangers, lost, and smell bad. So, move on. Do not bother the people here." This meant they were not allowed to stay here for long.

"Ostad Biruni, did not you tell us that you knew somebody in this town?" One of the beggars asked. It was Kazem who posed this question. Kazem then asked Sa'eed, "What about you?"

They came to Gorgan because they had heard so much about the peace and prosperity here. Unfortunately, on their way to Gorgan, their caravan was attacked by highway robbers, and they lost everything they had, including their clothes. Escaping naked, they took refuge in a cemetery. The cemetery attendant gave them some dirty used clothes of the dead people buried in his graveyard.

"Look at those beautiful dark-brown dates. I have never seen anything like them in my life," said Kazem.

"Look at those cakes, and . . ." Mohammad even had not even finished his sentence when he saw a restaurant next to a butcher store. Workers in the restaurant were getting ready for lunch. In front of the restaurant, two of them were making kabob.

"The highway robbers were really very unfair to us. They didn't leave us any pocket money either. We had 500 silver and 100 gold coins. God-damned! They took everything, including our clothes. At least we should be thankful to the graveyard attendant . . ." said Biruni.

They left the bazaar behind and reached a street. Here, they heard drums beating and saw that the procession of the New Year was on its way. The king's formal astrologer was going to see Qabus, king of the House of Ziyarid. The three, among a large crowd, were watching this procession. It was led by four drummers, followed by one hundred African slaves dressed in red uniforms. Then one hundred riders arrived on their horses, dressed in blue uniforms. They all had ostrich feathers on their hats. They were congratulating the arrival of spring to the public and singing songs. Next, a group of well-dressed merchants, scholars, and other important people walked. They were on their way to see King Qabus.

The three stinking beggars did not know what to do, when the shah's special astrologer showed up. He was a young man riding on a big mare. The three were expecting to see an old person. Biruni looked at him very carefully and suddenly shouted, "Dear friends, I know the astrologer. He was my roommate in the Sultani School in Khwarazm in the city of Kath. His name is Beejan Tabarestani. We are saved!"

When the astrologer passed in front of the three, Mohammad shouted, "My dear friend, Salam to you. Dear Mr. Tabarestani . . ." The astrologer's eyes were half open. It seemed like he was daydreaming. He spoke some words that hardly could be heard. And when he turned around, he saw a large number of people, including three beggars. He could not, however, recognize a soul. He was not even sure that somebody actually called his name. He rarely was addressed as Mr. Tabarestani. He was known as Master Astrologer. His servants shouted, "Move away please. Let us pass by."

Mohammad had absolutely no doubt that the king's special astronomer was none other than Beejan, his roommate, the tall, simple-minded, well-mannered person who would eat raw garlic with every meal in Khwarazm. Now, still young, somewhat heavier, and big-bellied, Beejan could not recognize his roommate among the beggars.

"Dear Beejan, you really do not recognize your friend and roommate."

"No, no. Who are you . . . you lousy beggar. How do I know you? Such a strange world!" Kazem said, "Damn those selfish people." Beejan's servant said, "Such a rude and importunate beggar." Sa'eed cried out, "Professor Beejan, you do not remember your roommate Mohammad Ibn Amhad!" Beejan sped up his mare. He, of course, did not hear what Sa'eed said.

The crowd could not understand what was going on between the three beggars and the shah's special astrologer, on his way to predict good fortune for King Qabus. Mohammad knew it was his last chance to get Beejan's attention, so he shouted, "Those days in Khwarazm you smelled like garlic all the time, now you stink all over!" This time, Beejan stopped his horse and said with a smile, "Those days you still looked like beggars. The pot calls the kettle black!" Without saying anything further, he left.

Now, the crowd noticed the three beggars and started giving them some change. Kazem received three silver coins, Sa'eed got more, and Mohammad received some silver and gold ones. The three were left wondering! Beejan's last statement indicated that he had recognized Mohammad, but . . . With the money they got from the crowd, the three went to a small restaurant and purchased some soup. While enjoying his first meal in many days, Mohammad kept saying, "I am sure it was him. It was Beejan. I think he recognized me. But why? Why did he leave?" It was in this minute that a big man entered the little restaurant and addressing the three, said, "Master Astrologer has sent me to invite you to his house. He is waiting for you."

In less than an hour, they were in front of Master Astrologer's magnificent house. They entered a room where four sick women were sitting. One of them was breast-feeding her baby. The big man, Beejan's foreman, told Biruni and his friends, "Please wait a few minutes. I will tell master that you are here. But hold on. Please forgive me, but I think it is a good idea if you three took a bath and washed up . . . and changed. Your clothes and stuff may arrive late, by the next caravan." The three agreed and did not say anything about the fact that there was no next caravan bringing their stuff.

The big man led the three into a courtyard, then into a big garden. At one corner of the garden, they saw Beejan's private bath. The three entered the bath house. The ceramic tile on the floor was warm. They washed up and took time to clean up very carefully. After some time, the big man came back with three bathrobes. These robes were all large for them. Apparently, they belonged to the master himself. When washing and cleaning, they looked at a mirror; they knew for sure they looked better now. It was about time, finally, to meet Beejan.

They came back to the same magnificent house. They got some more of Beejan's clothes. Then, climbing a stairway, they reached a covered porch that was lit by four torches. They then entered a hallway with big candlesticks, with twenty candles in each. The smell of burning fat of the candles mixed with the odor of cooked rice was very appetizing. A slave girl opened the door of a bigger room and the three went in. They saw the king's astrologer in that room. He was leaning against a cushion next to the wall. His plump right hand was on another smaller cushion. In front of him a golden coffee pot and small cups could be seen. Big silver plates full of apples, oranges, and tangerines were also in front of him on the very expensive carpet. Four slaves, two males and two females, were tending to Beejan. When Mohammad, Kazem, and Sa'eed stepped inside that big room, the four slave servants bowed and while walking backward, they left the room. Beejan jumped up and said, "Welcome." He hugged Mohammad for a few minutes. Beejan then shook Kazem's and Sa'eed's hands. He said, "Welcome. I really apologize for not recognizing you at first." Beejan began laughing and said, "You looked awful, but I am sorry. I should not forget my best friend. I want you to feel at home. I am the king's best friend and advisor. I am sure the Son of High Concepts (this was the official title of Qabus, because of his literary abilities and his patronage of great scholars) will help you."

After three days of rest, Beejan took Mohammad and his friends to see the Son of High Concepts, King Qabus. Actually, the king had already heard Biruni's name and was very pleased to meet him in person. On the same day that they had their first meeting with King Qabus, Ostad Biruni was hired as the royal astronomer and Kazem and Sa'eed as his assistants.

Qabus, son of Washmgir, the Quail Catcher, was a bright and very generous man. As was typical of rulers of his time, he was stern, harsh, suspicious, and at times a dictator. In other words, he was not a patient politician. This meant that he had made a few enemies among the noblemen in his own court.

King Qabus got very surprised when he saw Ostad Biruni. He said, "I was expecting to see a very old man with a long white beard. Beejan so often talked about you. I never asked him about your age. I did not know you two were roommates. I thought you were Beejan's professor.

King Qabus was a man of letters himself. He had an aptitude for writing both Arabic and Persian poems. He made sure he spent one day every week with men of science and another day with men of letters, mostly poets. Actually, those meetings were cosponsored by his daughter, Azarmidoukht. She was one of the very few knowledgeable and educated women in the whole world. She was also very beautiful.

All of those invited to attend any one of the high-caliber meetings were on the royal family's payroll. And all of them had a good life and prosperous living. Beejan Tabarestani, Mohammad Biruni, Kazem Birjandi, and Sa'eed Qaynati were only a few of those fortunate individuals associated with King Qabus.

Biruni's peaceful, quiet, and very comfortable living in Gorgan was also very fruitful. It was in this city, in this period, that he wrote one of his most important books, an encyclopedia of world history of chronology. The idea of writing such a book was Qabus's himself. Qabus was disturbed by the fact that most information about ancient Persia was lost. He said to Mohammad, "We have lost our dignity and our nationality. We do not know who we are anymore. Beejan has told me that in addition to being knowledgeable about the pure sciences, you are a historian. So what do you think about writing about Iran's history in particular and the world's history in general?"

Biruni, of course, liked the idea. King Qabus then told him, "I will instruct my daughter Azar (the Fire, short for Azarmidoukht) to utilize your knowledge and abilities in writing such a book of time measurement and lost history."

CHAPTER SEVENTEEN

Azarmidoukht

King Qabus had two sons and two daughters. His sons were named Manuchihr and Dara. His daughters were called Azarmidoukht-e Grangoushvar and Zareen Gees. Each word in the older daughter's name has two parts. *Azar* means fire and *doukht* means daughter. *Grangoushvar* also contains two words. *Gran* means grand, expensive, and heavy. *Goushvar* means earring. These names are original Persian. Many Iranian families, particularly the royal families, deliberately used these names to revive Persian culture and nationalism after the collapse of the Sasanid Dynasty in the early part of the seventh century.

Azarmidoukht-e Grangoushvar was young, very beautiful, strong, and tall. She was very brave and showed her skills while hunting in the jungles of Tabarestan. She used to be the envy of her brothers. She was one of the few learned women in the whole world at that time, about the end of the tenth century. She was a very good poet too. Many believe that her poems were better and stronger than her father's, King Qabus.

The moment she met Mohammad Ibn Ahmad, she recognized that he was all that she had heard about him and more. Unlike her brothers, she recognized that Biruni was one of the most knowledgeable scholars in the world. Her brothers were not impressed so much. Maybe because Biruni was and looked too young or they were simply jealous.

Indeed, we know that Qabus ordered his daughter to utilize Biruni's talent. Therefore, Mohammad was working with Azarmidoukht very closely. He was even allowed to call her by her shortened name Azar, a name that was used only by her family members and very few close friends.

One day Mohammad was invited to go to Azarmidoukht's mansion. On that day, she took Mohammad to the royal library, personally. They walked together toward the library that was located in the middle of a large garden filled with citrus fruit trees. She gave the key to the library to Mohammad. While inside, sitting in a very comfortable chair, she said, "I wish you would write your first major book as soon as possible. For a man like you, it may take no more than six months!" Mohammad said, "I'll try my best but, let me not promise anything now." It took Mohammad about two years to finish his first major book titled *Athar al-Baqiya an al-Qurun al-Khaliya*. He wrote his book in Arabic rather than in Persian, his mother tongue. Literally, the title of this book means *Traces of Leftovers from the Empty Centuries*. This book was translated into English by Edward C. Sachau in 1879 and was published in London. Sachau translated the title of the book as *The Chronology of Ancient Nations*. Because this book was so extensive, most often, it is referred to as Biruni's Encyclopedia. He dedicated his book to King Qabus.

A very important question is why he wrote such a major book in Arabic and not in Persian. The answer is that Arabic was the language of religion, science, technology, and research at that time in the Muslim Empire, the largest in the world, both in land area and population. Qabus and Biruni wanted to make the book understandable to the great majority of people around the world, especially Muslim scholars. As a major vehicle of Islam and as a lingua franca, Arabic was used all over the old world. The Arabic language of a thousand years ago can be compared to the English of today. Presently, to make their research and concepts readily available to the rest of the world, most scholars use English even if neither their mother tongue nor their national language is English. This practice is very useful for the whole world. It is because of the geographical extent of English, similar to Arabic ten centuries ago.

To write his first major book, he used the royal library of Gorgan that had more than three hundred thousand books. And, of course, he had a mind himself. He could remember most of the subjects he learned while in Khwarazm and Rayy. The most important element, however, was Abu Nasr's teaching. Abu Nasr was like a moving encyclopedia of all the knowledge in the world and Mohammad was his best student.

After finishing his first major book, shortly after the year 1000 C.E., Mohammad was getting closer to his thirtieth birthday. He still did not have a nickname. This was uncommon. Every respectable man in the Muslim world had a nickname. One day, Qabus inquired about this fact. He asked Beejan, "What is Mohammad Ibn Ahmad's nickname?" Beejan's response was, "He does not have one. He has not married yet, so he does not have children, and therefore he cannot have a nickname." Most often nicknames were related to one's children's name, that is, father of so and so.

Qabus then inquired about another fact by asking Beejan, "Why is he not getting married?" Beejan said, "My dear Shahanshah, I only have heard that he was in love with a girl in Khwarazm. She was, unfortunately, engaged to a prince since birth. Therefore, he stayed a bachelor. Qabus said, "I am sure we can find him a suitable wife and after the birth of his first child, he can choose a nickname."

The next day, Beejan saw Mohammad and reported his discussion with Qabus. He told him that King Qabus was thinking about finding him a wife so he can have a nickname. Mohammad said, "Don't worry, I have a nickname! Once in Khwarazm, I was a godfather to a girl named Rayhana. Thus, my nickname could be 'Abu Rayhan.'" Mohammad's main purpose was to prove to himself that his love for Lady Rayhana had changed or he had forgotten her. He was thinking of her as his own daughter. Whatever his reason, he finally got a nickname. From now on his full name was Professor Abu Rayhan Mohammad Ibn Ahmad-e Biruni. But he was known outside Iran as Al-Biruni. "Al" is an article in Arabic with the same meaning as "the" in English. This led many European and American scholars to wrongly believe that Biruni was an Arab rather than an Iranian. In this manner, many other non-Arab Muslim scholars who used to write in Arabic are recognized as Arabs in the West. It is also an irony that many Arabs think that anybody's name that starts with an "Al" or "El" must be an Arab! Late in life, Mohammad became known as Abu Rayhan-e Biruni and his title was "Ostad."

Biruni's *Athar al-Baqia an al-Qurun al-Khaliya* could not have been written without the generous help and support of King Qabus. The 1879 English translation by Professor Sachau was titled *The Chronology of Ancient Nations.* Biruni himself could not have found a better title for his book in English than Professor Sachau. The word *chronology* describes a major portion of the book's content. In other words, in this book, Biruni was mostly concerned about time. The book, however, is really an encyclopedia of the knowledge available to him. Every topic and every chapter of the book is accompanied by an explanation of time. For example, when Biruni talks about the origin of days and nights and their changing length, he refers to the global shape of the Earth and its movement around the sun carrying seasonal changes.

This book has a total of twenty-one chapters, mostly dealing with the questions of time, history, and calendars, including times of festivities of different nations. He uses mathematics, astronomy, geography, geometry, and many other sciences to answer many questions posed by the public and scholars in the tenth century. He explains differences between the lunar and solar calendars. He also provides the basic logic for having 365 days in a calendar year, which was later used by Omar Khayyam to produce the most accurate calendar in the world. Called the Jalaly calendar, this system is still being used in Iran. The year is divided into six months with thirty-one days and five months with thirty days. The last month, Esfand, has also thirty days. During the leap years, however, the last month has only twenty-nine days.

Biruni talked about the different ways of measuring time among different nations and cultural groups in the world, namely, Jews, Christians, Hindus, Egyptians, and many others. He again explains why different nations had different methods of measuring time.

During the tenth century, some scholars believed that the planet Earth was only five thousand years old. Biruni is probably the first who rejected this idea. He studied rock erosion and even looked at fossils to argue that our planet was much, much older. He also rejected the Zoroastrian belief that our planet was twelve thousand years old. He also rejected the Buddhist idea that the world was a million years old.

He believed that the title of the Roman emperors, Caesar, Qaysar in Arabic, gave us the term *caesarean operation* due to the fact that the first Emperor was delivered by a caesarean section. In his book, Biruni makes fun of those who come up with fake family trees for royal families. Then he himself came up with the most accurate family tree for King Qabus.

Azarmidoukht was the first person to read every chapter of the book on completion. She enjoyed reading those chapters so much, she would send Biruni a gift or two after reading each. When she read about her own royal family tree, she was so happy and pleased that she sent Biruni the biggest present. Biruni documented and proved that her royal blood was related to the last great Persian dynasty, the Sasanid. He found the same family origin for another Persian royal family centered in the city of Bukhara, the Samanids. Biruni believed that the Samanid and Ziyarid families were directly related to the Sasanid kings.

Biruni had been against all pseudo-scientists and fake scholars. Whenever he found out any ideas that were wrong, he would fight the proponents of those ideas with all his might. He usually would reject a wrong idea and then he would provide a better and correct alternative. He apparently did not like Alexander the Great, called Eskandar. Biruni presented a story that one night, while having supper, Eskandar got angry and killed one of his best friends. The most important guilt of Eskandar, according to Biruni, was that he burned down Persepolis with his own hands. Persepolis was the capital of the Achaemenid Dynasty and a very important city from the perspective of Persian history.

Biruni provides us with some information about what was known as Es-kandar's Dams. He argues that these dams were not built by Alexander but by the Roman and Persian kings to control flood on the river Aras, located in the northwestern corner of Iran, which marks the border with Armenia and Azerbaijan. These dams used to prevent tribes from invading into Ro-man and Persian lands. According to Biruni, these dams had iron gates that controlled the amount of water behind the dams.

We know that Biruni was a mathematician, and he would look at a prob-lem logically as a mathematical case. Therefore, he was bitterly against false information, myth, and superstition. He could not believe in stories about three-eyed animals or two-headed people and animals. He strongly believed that these were only exceptional cases that were products of nature, similar to the rare case of a small orange growing inside a big one, an egg with two yolks, and so forth. These phenomena did not indicate anything important such as the end of the world or God's anger.

Biruni was a logical, wise, and systematic person. Although he loved his country and culture, when he was writing about the Old Persian religion of Zoroastrianism, it seemed he did not accept many of its beliefs; especially he rejected its myths. After Islam became the religion of Iran and Arabic al-phabets were used to write Persian, Iranian historians did not know how to read and interpret cuneiform writing from pre-Islamic times.

It was Henry C. Rawlinson who deciphered cuneiform inscription in 1836. But when Biruni was writing his *Chronology*, he knew how to use the Old Persian inscription. Yet his writing about the three main Persian dynas-ties—including the Achaemenid, Parthian, and Sasanid dynasties—his timetables and even the names of the shahs are accurate. This indicates that he most likely was using other sources of information than Arabic. These sources were not even available to the epic poem writer Ferdosi (935–1020 C.E.), who based his book *Shahnamah* on the prehistory of ancient Iran. Un-like Biruni, Ferdosi was not able to use those sources written in Hebrew, Syr-iac, and Urdu because Ferdosi did not know those languages. It is also possi-ble that Biruni's book either was not available to Ferdosi or, if it was, he could not understand Arabic.

Abu Rayhan Mohammad Ibn Ahmad Biruni provided the reader with a complete history of many Middle Eastern kingdoms including the Umayyad (661–750 C.E.) and Abbasid Caliphs (750–1258 C.E.). Biruni was the first scholar who predicted the downfall of the Abbasid Caliphs. He believed that they did not have real authority. Abu Rayhan wrote that the Abbasid Caliphs betrayed and murdered an Iranian hero, Abu Moslim Khorasani, to take over the world of Islam. Biruni made fun of titles and nicknames given, actually sold, to individuals by the caliphs. He called those titles as ostentatious and grandiloquent, filled with meaningless, lofty language. Sarcastically, Biruni provided the readers with examples of titles sold to rich people that had funny connotations or were opposite to the characteristic of those people. Somebody who was blind in one eye could be called Ayn-Allah, meaning God's Eye. Biruni argued that using those stupid titles is nothing but a waste of time and paper.

Abu Rayhan, when concerned with nationality, race, and culture, tried not to be biased. Thus, he equally criticized the burning of the birds in Zoroastrianism and the burning of the book by the Arab-Muslim armies. He also criticized the belief that the Arabs were a superior race, people chosen by Allah. So he repeats the fact that more than once the Arabs celebrated the burning of books in many large cities, from Alexandria all the way to Khwarazm. Biruni disliked Mansur, the second Abbasid Caliph (754–775 C.E.). He believed that Mansur was a thief, because he ordered stealing jewelry from the Sasanid, the last Persian dynasty before Islam, and Umayyad Caliphs, an Arab-Muslim dynasty, and graves. Biruni was a humanist scholar arguing for the political autonomy of ethnic minorities.

In addition to all those abilities, Biruni can be seen as an important sociologist. His idea about empty and meaningless titles and nicknames make him a brave scholar. He single-handedly was fighting the most powerful man in the world in Baghdad. The Abbasid Caliphs sold titles to anybody who could afford to pay. Biruni called this a system of bribery and corruption. He even ridiculed many of those titles.

When Azarmidoukht read the first draft of the chapter about "empty titles," she liked it very much. But, she got concerned about the fact that it was a one-man crusade against the sale of titles from Baghdad. Thus, she asked Abu Rayhan, "Are you not afraid of those men whose titles you made fun of? I am worried about your safety! You may want to lower your tone, especially in regard to the caliph himself in Baghdad!"

Biruni responded by saying, "Dear Lady Azar, do not worry. I will be fine. But this is very funny. Somebody has to say something about those meaningless titles. I used to know an Amir in the city of Rayy whose title was Sanad al-Dola. As you know, my Lady, *sanad* in Arabic means "document," so his title may mean "Document of the Nation." The river Indus is called Sind in Arabic and Persian, and *sind* is a name for a kind of cake too. I have been, therefore, wondering which one is his real title. Is he really the "document" of the nation, or is he named after a "river" or a kind of "cake"? The reader must know that these three proper names, the document, the river, and the cake are inscribed the same way in Arabic. Biruni had many stories about personal titles. He told Azarmidoukht that he knew another amir who was very lazy and hardly could take care of himself. Yet his title was "Guardian of the Nations."

Biruni showed his anger by giving more examples of waste of tax money in Baghdad. A poet, by writing a few flattering poems, may receive a large sum of money. Biruni then asked, "What do these lazy, fat caliphs do?" He provided more factual examples of Baghdad's extravagant living. One caliph had five thousand musicians although in Islam music is forbidden. Another caliph would marry virgin girls three times in one night. Yet in a single night seven babies were born to another caliph.

Biruni strongly rejected the idea of reincarnation. He believed that humans are the product of their natural environment. He disagreed with ideas that a star is simple luck or not lucky. He looked at all days and months as the same and disagreed with the idea that certain days or months were auspicious or otherwise.

Biruni's book is the first major reference about the life and time of Mazdak. Mazdak claimed that he was a prophet during the sixth century in Iran. At that time, it was hard to find wives in Iran. This was due to the fact that some rich men had a few hundred wives. The shahs sometimes had several thousand. Mazdak preached for a kind of land reform and encouraged the noblemen to divorce their wives, who he said should marry single young men.

Several times Biruni wrote that he was proud to be an Iranian. He called his country Iranshahr, "the Land of Iran" or "City of Iran." But the reader immediately recognizes the fact that he was an unbiased scholar. He was truly an international scholar.

In his book, Abu Rayhan wrote that the readers of his book belong to three groups: (1) scholars of similar rank who should appreciate his work, (2) scholars of higher rank who should forgive him when and if they see any mistakes, and (3) scholars of lower rank and the general public who should find his book very useful. And he did not forget to thank Abu Nasr and King Qabus for giving him the opportunity and making him able to write this book.

As a mathematical history of time, *The Chronology of Ancient Nations* was similar to Biruni's doctoral dissertation. In this book, like in all other texts that he had written, Biruni attacks all kinds of sham, hoax, imposture, and hypocrisy with bitter scientific sarcasm. This book is a careful mathematical calculation and critical research with a modern tone very similar to the scientific research started in the sixteenth century in Europe. We are safe to say that Biruni was at least five hundred years ahead of European scientists. Many nations, particularly the Jews, are indebted to Biruni for rediscovering their chronology. A student once asked Biruni, "Why it is so hard to understand your books?" Biruni's answer was that he wanted to "make the readers think with scientific reasoning." Biruni continued by saying that he has never been afraid of strong reasoning and has never escaped from stronger scientific ones.

In the *Chronology*, definitions are exact and his calculations are impossible to challenge. For the first time in the history of mankind, he calculated the number of an object, namely, a grain of wheat, doubled in each square of the chess board. Simply put, one grain of wheat in the first square, two in the second, four in the third, eight in the fourth, sixteen in the fifth, and so on. According to Biruni's calculations the result was 18,446,744,073,709,551,610, which is equal to $(2)^{64} - 1$.

The question, however, is why Biruni wrote such an impressive book? Actually, he has answered this question himself. He writes that "a learned man once asked me regarding the eras used by different nations, and . . . their roots . . ." (Biruni, translated by Sachau, 1879, p. 2). But was that it? Just a question? And in order to answer that question, Biruni would spend two years to write a book on chronology of ancient nations.

Another possible explanation is related to the timing of writing of the book, the year 1000 C.E. This is known as the end of the first millennium. Let us call this the Y1K hype or doomsdays, the day of the last judgment. Many Christian communities around the world, mostly in Europe, believed that the end of the world was near, creating a type of madness and mayhem, and Biruni had to fight this nonsense.

Like an epidemic, a religious hysteria in which the year 1000 was expected to bring the end of the world afflicted most of Western Europe. A mass pilgrimage took place including "crowned heads and mitered bishops, fat abbots and helmeted barons joined the simpler people on the road to Jerusalem" (Tuchman, 1984, p. 34). According to some chronicles, hordes of Europeans poured into the holy land, and a large number of them never returned.

Biruni, as a scientist who only argued with strong reason and verifiable evidence, of course did not believe this nonsense, Y1K. To him time was absolute but measurable using different methods. The number 1000 was arrived only based on a reference point in time. To Christians it was 1000 C.E., but to Muslims it was only 378 solar and 390 lunar years after Hijra. To Biruni, the sun was the best mathematics teacher.

When Biruni finished his book of *Chronology*, he was only thirty years of age; thus the year was probably 1002 C.E. He was indeed a very young scholar, and his book was more than just a chronology; it was an encyclopedia of knowledge written one thousand years ago.

One day Abdulmalek Qazvini showed up in Gorgan. He asked for Biruni and very easily was able to find Biruni's mansion. He asked the servants to be taken to Biruni, saying he had to talk to him. Biruni now was a well-known personality. His large mansion was located near the river and he was living in peace and prosperity. Now he had his own library. At all times it was ready for him to work in. Even in winter at night, a large fireplace was waiting for him. He would sit behind a short desk on a very expensive Persian carpet and read, write, or do research. His books would be scattered on the floor. As long as he was working, two slave girls were waiting on him. They were young and beautiful. Most often, after dinner, they would bring him hot milk or a coffee pot filled with mocha coffee from Yemen. At other times, he would ask for different herbal liquids, including liquorice and valerian.

Although it was common to drink wine in the royal families, in noble houses and rich families, Abu Rayhan preferred fruit juice, sherbet, and potions made of herbs and spices. It is interesting to note that in the political center, the capital city of the Muslim empire, some of the Abbadis Caliphs were known as "Drunken Amirs." It is believed that Mutasim (833–842) would drink from sunset to sunrise. But Abu Rayhan did not even have the time to get drunk.

Abdulmalek entered the yard. He was led through a big garden filled with flowers and herbs, to Abu Rayhan's library. The slave girl opened the door, and Abdulmalek entered the library where Abu Rayhan was working. Upon seeing him, Abu Rayhan got surprised, shocked, and very saddened. But we know that Abu Rayhan was a gentleman. Thus, he said calmly, "I told you three years ago, just leave me alone. I am not willing to talk to you." Abdulmalek replied, "Dear Mohammad Ibn Ahmad, how could you simply ignore our friendship. We were roommates after all!" Abu Rayhan said, "I have nothing to add. In order to get out of this town, I pay you twenty-five silver coins from my research budget. I want you to go back to your family in Qazvin."

Abdulmalek tried to bargain with Biruni by saying, "Dear Mohammad, I am thirty-one years old. I have no job and do not have a family. Even if I decided to go back to my hometown, it will cost me more than twenty-five coins. So, could you please pay me fifty gold coins?" Abu Rayhan shook his head and commented, "I teach mathematics and astronomy in the Sultani's school of Gorgan, everyday, except Fridays, I only receive forty gold coins. Why do you think you deserve to receive more than what I promised you? I look at you only as a beggar! I do not want to remind you what you have done!"

"Qazvini said that he has heard that Beejan has paid you so much money to stay in Gorgan. You are a very rich man. Why do you not want to help me get back to my hometown?" Biruni responded, "But Abdulmalek, you are not a good man. If you think of your nation as your family, remember, you cheated on your larger family. You are a traitor . . . ! All I can do is to add another five silver coins to what I promised. Therefore, you will be given thirty silver coins to leave town."

Qazvini said, "Alright, since you are not giving me any gold coins and calling me a traitor, I know what to do. I know everything about you! I will destroy you!" And he rushed out of Biruni's mansion. He went to see Manuchihr, Qabus's son, on the same day. As mentioned before, the two sons of Qabus did not like Biruni or their sisters, Azarmidoukht and Zareen Gees. They were jealous of him that this nobody at that age knew so much. Manuchihr, especially, was ignorant and ambitious. He was waiting to find something bad about Abu Rayhan so he could punish him.

Abdulmalek Qazvini told Manuchihr that Biruni was (1) a Qarmati, adherent of a branch of Ismailiyya-Shiah Islam; (2) he was insulting and cursing Allah's representatives on Earth, namely the Caliphs in Baghdad; (3) he had stolen astrology tools from the Khwarazm observatory; (4) Biruni set on fire the royal library of Khwarazm before he escaped from the town; (5) Biruni is a Zoroastrian and likes Mazdak. And Biruni believes that we should "share our land and wives!" and that (6) Biruni did not do his daily required prayers.

Manuchihr did not even ask who Qazvini was and how he knew Biruni. Manuchihr accepted everything Abdulmalek said. In reality, Abdulmalek fully contradicted himself and how a man like Biruni could be all that and more. How he could be a Qarmati and a follower of Zoroaster and Mazdak at the same time. In one case, however, Abdulmalek was right. Abu Rayhan was not a religious fanatic, and he was very relaxed about carrying out his religious duties. Thus, he often missed his daily prayers, both in Khwarazm and in Gorgan.

Manuchihr decided to give Biruni a lesson. He asked his brother Dara to go with a few of his men and arrest him. When Dara and his *jandars* arrived in front of Biruni's mansion, they found him studying. Biruni invited Dara to go in, but Dara said that he had to accompany them to the governor's office, headquarters of the security forces. We know Dara too did not like Biruni.

Manuchihr ordered Abu Rayhan put in a wet, smelling, dirty jail in the basement of the governor's office. Biruni's servant, called Kooktash, informed Azarmidoukht as soon as he could. Biruni spent about twenty-four hours in that jail before he was freed by Azarmidoukht. She immediately went to her father and told him about Biruni's being arrested by Manuchihr. She said, "I do not know how foolish my brothers are to do so. They are simply jealous. They have heard that we are in the process of establishing our own observatory here in Gorgan with Biruni's help; therefore, they are creating problems for us!"

For the first time, this wise woman, Azarmidoukht asked, "Who was the man accusing Abu Rayhan anyway? Do we even know his name? Why does my brother Manuchihr trust him?" Qabus said that he would look into the case. Azarmidoukht said, "Dear father, this may take you many days. I know how busy you are! So I will free Abu Rayhan myself."

While sitting in a large room in Biruni's mansion, Azarmidoukht asked him, "Who was the man accusing you? I want to know!" Abu Rayhan said, "We should find him and you yourself, my Lady, could ask him any questions you have in mind." Azarmidoukht ordered her own servant to go to Manuchihr asking him to locate the man accusing Biruni. The security forces searched the whole city but they found no trace of Abdulmalek. He seemed to have disappeared altogether.

CHAPTER EIGHTEEN

Maria Again

Due to the fact that Gorgan was a cosmopolitan city, one could find people from all over the world. One day, as Abu Rayhan, accompanied by one of his servants named Ramazan, was coming out from a restaurant located near the slave bazaar after having his lunch, he was approached by a person who introduced himself as Constantine, a slave trader from Greece. He began describing his slaves to Biruni. From his appearance, Constantine must have recognized that Biruni was a rich man. Constantine went on, saying he had many slave girls and that the most beautiful and youngest ones were inside his shop. He insisted that the two go inside and see for themselves. He claimed he had princesses from China and even Bulgaria. My Amir, he said, "You should see my girls from Russia. They are beautiful, powerful, tall, and red-haired."

Biruni was quiet. Thus, Ramazan told Constantine, "You shut up. It seems you have daughters of all the kings in the world." Ramazan was also Biruni's bodyguard. Biruni was walking in front of all those slave girls from different nationalities and backgrounds. He was smiling. He was still quiet, because Ramazan was doing most of the talking. The Greek man shouted at Ramazan, "Leave us alone. I want to talk to my Amir."

Biruni was quiet because he was thinking about his professor, Abu Nasr, who was fluent in Greek. Biruni wished he was here so he could completely understand this Greek guy. Constantine shouted, "Do you want to buy a white European girl? I have two of them. One is little and younger. The other one is somewhat older but more beautiful. She is from Andalusia." And he pointed at this very attractive mature woman at the back of his shop. Abu Rayhan, Ramazan, and Constantine got closer to her. The Greek kept talking, "Look at her eyes. They are warm and mysterious, black and beautiful." Then he shouted at the slave woman, "Why don't you remove your veil so my Amir could see all of you!" He proceeded to slap the slave, but was stopped by Abu Rayhan. "Why do you want to hit this poor woman?"

With her pair of penetrating, big black eyes, she was staring at Abu Rayhan. Suddenly, it looked as if he had the shock of his life, struck by lightning. He remembered that strange night in Khwarazm. That woman with two men! He remembered her brown-reddish boots. More importantly, he even remembered her perfume. Maria of Andalusia! Without a doubt, this was the spy lady who paid Abdulmalek to steal some books and equipment from the royal observatory in Khwarazm. She looked older than thirty but still was very attractive.

"Maria . . . Maria . . . is this you?"

The slave woman was staring at the ground. Constantine and Ramazan were unaware of that name. Abu Rayhan took the slave woman by her shoulders and kind of shouted, "Maria . . . Maria." While he was trembling, the slave woman put her veil back and started saying something in a strange tongue. Unfortunately, nobody could understand her. But she seemed surprised, excited, and sad.

Abu Rayhan, like a crazy person, smelt the slave woman's long hair. She still was wearing the same perfume, he was sure. Almost ten years had passed. She had grown older, of course. Mohammad had so many dreams about that proud woman, that mysterious night, that strange event, and some of the most valuable books and equipment in the world. She now was only saying something in a foreign language, probably Spanish.

The Greek slave seller, fat, short, and bold, was quiet. He was thinking that the slave woman from Andalusia might have been Biruni's slave before and he had to return her to him. He had purchased her in a slave market in Egypt.

"Where did you buy her?"

"In Fastat, Egypt."

"What language was she speaking before?"

"This is the first time I have heard her talk! I was thinking she was dumb and deaf. She had never said anything before."

"I will buy her."

"I have a younger one."

"No, thank you."

Abu Rayhan still was in love with Lady Rayhana. He hardly looked closely at any other woman. Most of all because he was always busy or kept himself busy in order not to think about women. Now he was more than curious. Biruni wanted to find out by whom and how those books were used. Why the royal court in Andalusia was so much interested in the fireball invented by the masked man of Khurasan. Abu Rayhan did not even bargain on the price quoted by the Greek, whom he heard asking for 250 gold coins. That was what he paid. Ramazan was holding the slave woman's arm as they left the slave bazaar. Outside, Ramazan rented a mare for the slave for Biruni's mansion was at a considerable distance from the slave bazaar. Soon, the three were riding toward their destination.

Biruni's lack of interest in women was surprising to everybody around him. Azarmidoukht was more curious than anybody else. Although she was one of the most beautiful girls in the world, she had never seen Biruni look at her with eyes that might indicate desire. She even noticed that Biruni most often avoided looking into her eyes. Was it really a deliberate attempt or just coincidental? She wanted to discover that secret about her favorite scholar. Therefore, she gave Biruni a slave girl as a gift one day, and the slave girl was instructed to spy on him and report back to her. Report after report indicated that Biruni avoided women and wine.

Azarmidoukht then would ask her spies, "I do not care what he is not doing, I want you to report back to me on what he is doing." Again, report after report indicated he was busy making new tools. And when he was not busy he looked at the picture of a man that he himself had painted, silently and very sadly. His newest invention was called "Quarter Astrolabe," which could measure not only the height of the sun from a place but also the latitude of that place. He would keep busy as an ant, reading, writing, and watching the sky. He took only two days off in a year, the first day of spring and the first day of autumn, when the length of days were exactly the same, the equinoxes. Both of them were considered important Persian national holidays. Thus, in a year, he worked 363 days.

The slave woman from Andalusia was given a large room with riverfront windows and a yard filled with citrus fruit trees. Unfortunately, she was sick. She was coughing very badly and continuously. Ramazan was complaining that Constantine overcharged them. "She was not worth it. My master paid 250 . . . but she is sick."

Abu Rayhan was patient. He examined her as a physician does. He ordered Ramazan to make cowslip tea for her and put some poultice on her back. Then when the coughing continued, Biruni sent Ramazan to request a very famous physician to come and see her. It took a week for the cough to subside after the treatment was begun. After a long bath and makeup, she looked her original beautiful self.

Two weeks passed. And Abu Rayhan was beginning to lose his patience. The slave woman kept silent. Beginning with the sixteenth night, he slept in her room, hoping that she might say something! But she was not paying any attention to him. She was sleeping, eating, and looking at the river and trees. On the twentieth day, she picked up a feather and dipping it in ink, she wrote "Anjeel" (the Gospel) in Arabic alphabets. Ramazan got her a copy of the Bible from Biruni's library. But nothing else happened. Abu Rayhan was almost certain she was Maria.

One day Abu Rayhan got very angry at the slave woman and said, "I do not want anything from you. Only tell me what you did with the books and equipment you got from Abdulmalek. Then I promise to set you free." She would listen carefully and murmured many Spanish words. He could now make out a few of the words, mostly place names such as Europe, Andalusia, Baghdad, Constantinople, Damascus, Shiraz, Khwarazm, and Cairo. But he did not know why she was mentioning those place names. Had Biruni known Spanish, he could have understood that the slave woman was saying that Europe was going to become like the Muslim world. It was emerging out of the Dark Ages. Another time, in Arabic, Biruni told the slave woman, "I will send you back to your homeland, you just tell me . . ." And she kept saying, "Amigo, Amigo," and many other words that he did not understand.

It was during this time period that Abu Rayhan finished another one of his books called *Abstraction of Rays and Lights*. He dedicated this book to King Qabus too, in a formal ceremony.

After the ceremony, King Qabus, Biruni, Tabarestani, and another scholar by the name of Abu Sahl had a kind of private discussion. King Qabus said, "Until now, 150 copies of your *Chronology* have been made. They have been distributed among libraries in major cities in the world. We received correspondence from Cairo, Rayy, Bukhara, and several other large cities asking for you or your book. The Caliph in Egypt wants to see you. He has seen your comments about the Caliphs in Baghdad, and he has enjoyed reading them. You know about the competition between the two of course. But I want you to stay in Gorgan. Work with my vizier for three years, and then I will choose you as my Grand Vizier. You will become my first Grand Vizier."

At this moment, Azarmidoukht entered the room. Qabus stepped down from his golden throne and started walking. This throne was of pure gold and was made in Isfahan by forty jewelers. It was made for King Qabus's uncle, Mardavij, before he was assassinated by his own bodyguards. Azarmidoukht was wearing an elegant cloth. She had a very thin veil on her face. Qabus looked at her and told Biruni, "I want you to marry my daughter! So many important individuals, including Sultan Mahmud of Ghazna, have asked for her hand in marriage. But I believe that you are better than Mahmud. You are smart. You are capable of making me the Shahanshah of all of Iran."

Abu Rayhan did not know what to say. He bowed respectfully and said, "Dear King Qabus, the most generous great shah, please forgive me. I am not made as a politician. Actually, I do not like political activities. Politicians must be able to lie so easily and that I find myself unable to accept. I am only an honest researcher. Please let me continue my studies. As about your dear daughter, I do not think I deserve her. I could not even dream of marrying her."

At night, Abu Rayhan was sitting in his living room, sad and quiet. He was thinking about that day's happenings, two proposals from King Qabus, prime ministership and marriage to the most beautiful girl in the world. It was like his lucky day. His moment of silence was interrupted by the opening of the door and the movement of the silk curtain. It was the slave woman. She came in like a shadow, light and thin. She had only a pair of high heel sandals and a long black silk nightgown with exposed shoulders on. She was not wearing anything under her gown of the best black silk of Gorgan. Her hardened nipples were forming two little points in the gown, and the upper parts of her breasts were generously exposed. Her hair was long, black, and beautiful, the same color as that dark night. She was also wearing her perfume that he knew so well. She said, "I am yours. Why don't you ask for me?" in a formal Arabic with Andalusian accent.

Abu Rayhan was astonished. He stood up suddenly.

"You are Maria? Aren't you? I am glad you are talking in a language that I can understand." Maria, with a sexy smile on her lips was coming closer to Biruni. She took his hand and said, "I heard you rejected the idea of marrying Azarmidoukht. This proves that you really love me. I have been to your library. I saw a few notes about me. Once you wrote you would give your life to see that mysterious attractive Andalusian lady." Abu Rayhan got his calmness back and said sadly, "I wrote that note a long time ago!"

"You mean you do not love me now?"

"Why do you think I paid 250 gold coins to buy you? Before I tell you anything about my feelings, you should tell me what you did with the books and the tools you took out of Khwarazm."

Maria summarized her story by saying, "One of the two men you saw me with in Transoxania was my husband, Don Mikael, and the other his brother, Don Rafael. Not really in our hearts but on the surface we had converted to

Islam. We did so to get financial aids from the Moorish king to travel into the Muslim world." Abu Rayhan asked, "Then who commissioned you to go to Transoxania?" Maria replied, "The King of Castile, Don Fredrico. We sailed across the Mediterranean Sea until we reached Halifax. Then over land, with caravans, we reached Khwarazm via Damascus, Tabriz, Rayy, Toos, and Kath. After we got what we wanted, we went to Constantinople, then sailed back home. Instead of going to the Moorish king, we went directly to the King of Castile and delivered our merchandise. Only five years later the Spanish scientists were able to reinvent the fireball, which helped Don Fredrico capture a very important Muslim fort. We were thinking that Spain was finally able to throw the Muslim Moors out of the country. Unfortunately for Spain, Don Fredrico got wounded and died shortly afterward."

"Then?"

"After Don Fredrico's death, everything stopped. Nobody could read and understand a book written in codes."

"What happened to you?"

"My husband and I started farming a piece of land we got from the King of Castile. One day, when we were traveling in the state of Valencia, we were attacked by some highway robbers. My husband, Don Mikael, was killed. For a while, I became a nun. After this, I decided to make a pilgrimage to the Holy Lands, especially the city of Jerusalem. However, our ship was captured by a group of pirates and I was taken as a slave. I have been sold several times since and been abused and raped on many occasions. Every year that was added to my age, I was sold at a lower price. My brother-in-law was executed by one of the feudal lords that he was fighting against. I was losing hope until fate brought me to Gorgan and you outbid everybody else. You gave me back my spirit and dignity. I am happy to be your slave."

Abu Rayhan asked, "Maria, tell me what happened to those books and equipment?" "Honestly, I do not know," replied Maria. Abu Rayhan excused Maria and sent her to her room. It seemed he was unable to cope with three surprises in one day. Although Maria was very beautiful, willing, and available to him, Biruni had never touched her. Maria's life story moved him so much now. He could imagine how many strange men had slept with her or raped her. She was now the same proud woman he had met in Khwarazm ten years ago. One could see how she was broken down by a painful life.

Thereafter, Maria stayed in Biruni's house. She was respected as a learned woman and as a good friend. She even helped Biruni with his research. After all, she was a scholar herself and knew some of the European languages.

CHAPTER NINETEEN

Fruitful Years

Biruni was spending happy times in Gorgan, a beautiful, cheerful, pleasant, and pristine emerald green city. He was continuing his scientific research. He had just completed his latest book, called *Rise of Dome of the Earth and Situation of Stars*, and it was already making an uproar in the world. He had observed the eclipse of the moon two times by now. Based on his observations, he corrected his earlier measurement of the latitude of Gorgan, and according to his new calculation it was 38 degrees and 10 minutes north of the equator. Modern measurement of the latitude of Gorgan is a little less than 37 degrees north of the equator, or a difference of about 1 degree.

Most often, he was visited by Azarmidoukht and her younger sister Zareen Gees, Golden Haired, the younger daughter of King Qabus. Early in the evening one day, Abu Rayhan and his beautiful students were sitting in a large room in his mansion. A slave girl had just lit a few candles around this large room. It was still somewhat dark when a man entered the room without knocking and in a low tone said, "Mohammad Ibn Ahmad, do you remember me?" Abu Rayhan immediately recognized the man. He almost jumped to get up. He hit the candle on the short table and it fell. He picked it up and with the candle in his left hand, he opened his arms and said, "My Master, my dearest professor and friend, Abu Nasr. Why do you think that I may forget you?" They hugged. Abu Rayhan wanted to kiss his hand but Abu Nasr took it away and said, "Light up the candle." Abu Rayhan took a step toward a burning candle to light up the one in his hand; he stumbled on a book on the floor and almost lost his balance but Abu Nasr held him. Abu

Rayhan said, "How many times you have saved my life. I welcome you from the bottom of my heart, and I want you to completely feel at home."

Abu Rayhan introduced his professor to the two ladies before they left the room for their palaces. Mohammad asked, "Please tell me everything. Where have you been? How have you been? I am very glad to see you!" Abu Nasr replied, "I have good news from the homeland. I have been living in the city of Rayy, working on and off. As you know, my brother-in-law Ali Ibn Mamun has replaced his murderous father. According to my sister Lady Rayhana, he has nothing in common with his father. My sister has written me that in fact her husband Ali is just the opposite of his father. Apparently, he is trying to rebuild Khwarazm. And so my sister has been asking me to come back home. She has informed me that King Ali has a very good nature, trying to do all good deeds, and even asks her for counsel. In addition to my sister's letters, I recently received a letter from the king himself inviting me to come back."

Abu Nasr continued, "The king has informed me that his security forces have found and returned most of the observatory's tools stolen by the mob. Most of the equipment was stored in a house in the Falling Flowers alley. It seems like somebody was buying them from the mob members. And, equally important, another piece of good news was that most of the books were saved too. I am glad we did not use wooden shelves in the library, and the leather binding of the books helped save most of the books from burning. King Ali has written to me that they have saved, repaired, or brought back about 158,000 books. Therefore, I am inclined to give it a try and go back."

Mohammad said, "My dear honorable teacher, you may have been informed that Kazem, Sa'eed, and I went back to Khwarazm. We even met the new king, your brother-in-law, and Lady Rayhana. It was there that I recorded the eclipse of the moon in the city of Kath while my friend Abul Wafa Buzjani did the same in the city of Baghdad. As you know, the difference in the timing of the eclipse would indicate the longitudinal distance between the two cities. I also visited my family and I gave them some money. My older sister is married and my brothers attend *maktab*. I made sure that they could get financial aids and money for the tuition from the government. But . . . but, we have to be careful. I do trust King Ali and Lady Rayhana. However, one problem is the danger of invasion from a new wave of Turkish tribes headed by Ilak Khan. Other problems can be dealt with slowly."

Abu Nasr said, "I know that leaving everything behind in this beautiful and bright city is not easy. Having been in the city of Gorgan for only a short time, I have already a lot of information about King Qabus, his daughters, your library, observatory, and your wealth. You have built a life of your own, and I know it is not fair to ask you to leave everything and come with me to

Khwarazm. You stay in your own mansion and the two princesses come to you to seek knowledge. This is a rarity. You cannot find something like this anywhere else."

Abu Rayhan shook his head and said, "My honorable professor, yes, I will leave everything behind and come with you. Everything I have in my life, I owe to you. Every minute that I spend in your presence is worth years and years of research. You opened the sleepy eyes of this shepherd boy, you gave me my life back, and you gave me a new wonderful, plentiful world. You are right; I even do not know how many servants and maids I have. My mansion is one of the best in town; my pillows are made of swan feathers and covered with the best silk. I have the most beautiful slave girls and . . . But I was born to learn the mysteries of creation. Yet I have a thousand questions myself, and you are the only one I know who might be able to help me to find answers for some of those questions. Please just order me! Just say when. I am ready to follow you back to Khwarazm."

"The sooner, the better," said Abu Nasr. He continued by saying that he has also received a letter from King Ali's Grand Vizier, Ahmad Ibn Muhammad Sohayli, asking him to come home as soon as possible and bring his former colleagues with him. "He especially named you." Mohammad said, "That is interesting, because I have heard his name. He must be a wise man and a scholar himself." "That is right," said Abu Nasr.

The old friends and scholars then sat down remembering the good times in their lives. Since Abu Nasr's arrival, Abu Rayhan tried unsuccessfully to tell him about Maria, but each time something more important came up. Finally, when Mohammad got a chance, he asked Abu Nasr whether he remembered the two men and their woman companion from Andalusia who had paid Abdulmalek to steal some important books and equipment in Khwarazm. Abu Nasr said, "I remember, I do! That is not something one can forget easily!" Mohammad then gave Abu Nasr the news that was going to shock him for sure: "The woman, Maria, is now in my possession!" Abu Nasr said full of surprise, "The very same woman! It is hard to believe!" Abu Rayhan then explained everything in full and finally said, "You can question her yourself, but that is the story in short."

After a little rest, on the following day Abu Nasr and Abu Rayhan got an audience with King Qabus and his two daughters. They were all upset about Abu Rayhan's plans for departure. In a fatherly manner, King Qabus reproached Abu Rayhan for his decision to go back to Khwarazm. He said, "Why do you want to leave this comfortable life and excellent opportunity and go to a place that is filled with so many painful memories for you?" Biruni was staring at the flowers on the carpet. He was sad too. Then he raised his head and said, "My dear Amir, I miss my homeland, my family, and I have to go back and finish a lot of research we, me and Abu Nasr, started some time ago." King Qabus reminded them that Abu Nasr also was welcome to stay in Gorgan. The Grand Vizier of Qabus was repeating what Qabus was saying, in almost the same words. But the two scholars were destined to leave. They were already searching for caravans going eastward.

Professor Biruni ended his scientific research in Gorgan. His next scientific research began almost a year later in Gurganj, where he made a precise record of an eclipse of the moon.

The arrival of Abu Nasr and Abu Rayhan was warmly welcomed by the royal family. Without any delay, King Ali and his queen, Lady Rayhana, met with them. Before anything else, the king apologized for his father's behavior and said he is so fortunate to have a queen like Abu Nasr's sister. Then, King Ali and Lady Rayhana suggested building a second observatory in the city of Gurganj, in addition to the revitalized one in Kath. They accepted bearing all expenses for the new observatory, school, and library.

Unfortunately, King Ali's life was cut short unexpectedly. Seven months after the arrival of Abu Nasr and Abu Rayhan, King Ali suddenly died, and his brother Abu Abbas ascended to the throne. With King Ali's death, Lady Rayhana was widowed and became available to remarry. This time, Mohammad could not afford to wait. Thus, he brought up the idea of marriage to Lady Rayhana with Abu Nasr shortly after King Ali's state burial ceremonies. Abu Nasr said, "I am very happy to see the two of you finally together. I knew how much you two loved each other."

Finally, all traces of this unidentified sadness were removed from Mohammad's face. Since his marriage to Rayhana, he became one of the happiest men in the whole world. Their mutual love was so strong they could withstand many years of separation. Mohammad also was happy that he waited. It was worth it for sure, because Lady Rayhana was an angel on Earth. She was the queen for sometime, but still could take care of her young scholar, who loved her so much.

The eleventh century was arriving fast. Sultan Mahmud of the Ghaznavid had his eyes on all of his neighboring countries. One of his many titles was "Sultan of the East and West" and his intention was to expand his territories in both directions. The present king of Khwarazm did not want to have to worry about Mahmud's menace because he was married to Mahmud's not so beautiful sister years earlier. Therefore, King Abu Abbas was formally the son-in-law of the sultan. We further know that King Ali had a very wise man as his Grand Vizier called Ahmad Ibn Muhammad Sohayli. After King Ali's death, Sohayli was reinstated in his earlier position by King Abu Abbas. The

Grand Vizier tried to improve people's lives. He ordered the cleanup of the two cities of Gurganj and Kath. He paid special attention to building hospitals, libraries, and roads.

The capital city of Khwarazm was moved from Kath to Gurganj. In this city, after some searching, Mohammad was able to locate his family. His mother Mehrana was in good health, although approaching old age. Biruni made sure his younger brothers and sisters attended school and could use governmental financial help. He also paid for a small house for his mother. She was well aware of her son's success as an important scholar in the world.

At about this time, under King Abu Abbas and Grand Vizier Sohayli, Khwarazm was regaining its peace and prosperity. Thus, scientists, poets, and scholars were converging on Khwarazm again.

Among those famous individuals were (1) Abu Ali Ibn Sina (Avicenna), the physician-philosopher; (2) Abu Sahl Masihi, the philosopher; (3) Abu Hassan Khammar, the physician; and of course we should remember that Abu Nasr Arraq and Abu Rayhan Biruni, who were world-famous scholars, were in town.

The above five scientists were familiar with each other's work and research. The mutual respect Biruni and his teacher Abu Nasr had for each other was well known. Abu Hassan Khammar was a physician-philosopher more associated with Ibn Sina than Biruni. He was a Christian but well respected among the Muslim people. His last name, Khammar, is a reference to an occupation. It means the wine seller or tavern keeper. In the medieval times, non-Muslims were allowed to produce, sell, and consume wine and other alcoholic beverages. Abu Hassan himself was a scientist not a wine seller, but his ancestors may have been involved in this profession. We know that Abu Hassan and Abu Rayhan accepted Sultan Mahmud's offer and went to Ghazna.

On the other hand, Abu Sahl Masihi and Ibn Sina refused to go to Ghazna. They escaped from Khwarazm, and Abu Sahl probably died in the Ghuzz Desert. As a bilingual Christian scholar, Abu Sahl helped Biruni in his Greek studies. They together also studied the reasons for the extreme heat and cold in the atmosphere. Abu Sahl and Abu Rayhan had a common interest in the fields of geometry, motion, astronomy, spots of the sun, metaphysics, script, and etiquettes for the companions of kings (Said and Zahid, 1981, p. 115). Abu Nasr was not the only scholar to write books and use Biruni's name on them. Abu Sahl too wrote at least twelve books and used Biruni's name.

Abu Ali Sina was born in 980 C.E. near the city of Bukhara. When young, he moved to the city of Gurganj with his family. Ibn Sina survived the Ghuzz

Desert. He reached Gorgan and found refuge with King Qabus. He later moved to the city of Isfahan and then relocated to Hamadan in central and western Iran, respectively. He died in Hamadan by age fifty-eight, while still holding the office of prime ministry of a local king. At a very young age, he became one of the most famous philosophers in the Muslim world advocating Aristotle. He was, however, more well known as a physician. Ibn Sina was seven years younger than Biruni but more famous. The two geniuses of the Middle Ages contended for recognition of their achievements in dialog-debate form.

Biruni sent Ibn Sina a set of eighteen questions, mostly pointing to problems in Aristotle's philosophy. One of the questions was, "Why does ice float on water?" These questions indicate the fact that Biruni did not consider Ibn Sina a major scientist. These questions are a manifestation of Biruni's command of peripatetic studies as well as the exact sciences. Some of these questions were answered by Ibn Sina himself or by one of his students. Most of them, however, were left unanswered and ignored. And most of the answers were not accepted as correct by Biruni.

When Ibn Sina was unable to defend Aristotle, he attacked Abu Bakr Muhammad Zakariya Razi in return, who is considered to be one of Biruni's mentors. Razi (865–925 C.E.) was a physician and a well-known surgeon by profession who had spent most of his life in the cities of Rayy and Baghdad. He is believed to be the first person who discovered the properties of alcohol. He is credited as the first Muslim surgeon to carry out human autopsies. In his books, Razi rejected metaphysics and all prophetic institutions of revealed religions. He has been called as a "full-time freethinker" (Stroumsa, 1999, p. 87).

But Biruni criticized Razi's philosophy. Biruni collected the names of all the books written by Razi and put them in a treatise called *Al-Fihrist*, or the *Index*. In his book about Razi, Biruni also provides a list of the 132 books written by himself. Razi had many references to a historian by the name of Iranshahri and Mani. Biruni's concepts of history, mostly in relation with religions, were molded by Iranshahri. Biruni found and read Iranshahri's books very carefully. But he was unable to locate Mani's book. Biruni had searched for this book for forty years. It was one of Marzban Ibn Rustam's soldiers who found Mani's book in Kurdistan in western Iran. Mani's book called *A Trip into Secrets* was given to Ostad Biruni as a gift. He became very happy on seeing the book that he had been searching for a long time. Now he was able to review the original work rather than having to accept Razi's writings about Mani. Although Ostad Biruni did not believe in Mani's ideas, he would defend Mani against his enemies. Mani (216–274 C.E.) was more famous as a painter, because he had illustrated his book very beautifully. He is the founder of Manichaeism, which is a combination of Zoroastrianism, Christianity, Buddhism, and Taoism.

Then who won this debate? According to Said and Zahid (1981), Biruni was the clear winner. This was done "only by his superlative knowledge and alert intellect" (p. 62). Biruni took away scientific research from the static Greek approach. He gave scientific research a new life by making it more dynamic. Biruni advocated practical application of scientific research. Ibn Sina was still caught in the middle of theories in his mind. Biruni's inductive approach was involved in model building and solving real-world problems using scientific methods. We have a list of his fifty inventions, all practical applications for solving real-world problems.

At this time, Biruni was working on a hypothesis in regard to the shape of the planet Earth. About five hundred years before Galileo (1564–1642) and Copernicus (1473–1543), Biruni believed that our planet had a spherical shape. He developed this idea when he was still young. Then he worked on it while he was in Gorgan. Now, he was discussing it with his professor, Abu Nasr. Using inductive reasoning, he would argue that a longitude between an extreme northern and southern city should have one of three forms: a straight line or a concave or convex curve. He strongly rejected the idea of a straight longitude. His reason was that moving along a longitude, the number of stars always should stay the same. He also rejected the idea of a concave longitude, because the number of stars decreases if one moves northward, which is not true in reality. Therefore, according to Biruni, this longitude must be a convex curve because the number of stars increases, which corresponds to what really happens. Of course, a convex curve is similar to the exterior of a sphere.

Biruni's fame was spreading worldwide. He was well known in many large Islamic cities such as Rayy, Gorgan, Isfahan, Shiraz, Bukhara, Baghdad, Cairo, and Ghazna. But in the city of Baghdad, the capital city of the Abbasid and the intellectual center of Islam, Biruni's name created a major controversy. Biruni's writings were carefully reviewed, and now everybody liked his new and revolutionary ideas. Some of the reviewers did not agree with him and some were skeptics and pessimists. Others termed his ideas "satanic" and were asking how a man from Transoxania could not believe in what the Greek wise men, Aristotle and Ptolemy, had said about the world.

The pseudo-scientists laughed at Biruni because he said that our planet was like a ball and it was not flat. He was called crazy, foolish, and a liar. In Baghdad, Biruni was called a Magi and a follower of Zoroaster. His first major book, the *Athar*, or the *Chronology*, was reviewed by a few of the Caliph's scholars. They were ordered to read and underline in red ink and interpret Biruni's ideas.

One day the Caliph al Qadir was talking with his prime minister, the Grand Vizier, about Biruni's books. The Caliph was angry, because one of the reviewers had told him that Biruni has ridiculed titles given to rich individuals. The Caliph said, "What the hell is Sultan Mahmud doing in Ghazna? Just sitting on the throne and doing no service to us in our eastern provinces! Is he aware of this Biruni guy? Is he reading Biruni's books?" The Grand Vizier, a learned man himself, replied, "Sultan Mahmud is illiterate. He cannot read or write, your honor!" The Caliph said, "But he has gathered a large number of poets, scholars, and learned men in his court. And he does enjoy Persian poetry reading." The Grand Vizier replied, "He does that only on the surface to show he supports arts, science, and literature but at heart he does not care that much. He is a liar!"

After the takeover of Iran, the Arabs called the Iranians and non-Arab people in general "Ajam." It was an insulting title that had racial, cultural, and political connotations. The Arabs believed that they were the chosen ones, a superior race, and the rest, or *Ajams*, were of an inferior origin.

The Grand Vizier said, "My Amir, the *Ajam* people believe in such men as Sultan Mahmud. They think that somebody would revitalize the Persian Empire and Persian culture and language. They dream of an independent Iran. The *Ajam* people do not like the Arabs. They differentiate between Islam and the Arabs. That is why scholars like Biruni reflected these sentiments and made fun of the titles you give to your subjects."

With these types of comments from his prime minister, the Caliph was determined to do something about this Biruni guy. Therefore, he said, "I want you to send a spy to Khwarazm and gather more information about Biruni. I want to accuse him of heresy so we can punish him!"

The spy sent to Gurganj from Baghdad to gather more information on Biruni was originally from an Iranian family that had served the Abbasid Caliphs for a long time. His name was Yahya Hassan Naubakhti. He was sent to Gurganj as a student to study under famous professors, including Biruni. He was instructed to keep a record of everything Biruni said or did. These records and documents would be used in a trial against Biruni. He was accused of being a person with immoral life, an infidel, and blasphemous. Biruni was recognized in Baghdad as a person "whose blood may be shed with impunity."

In the new Sultani School in the city of Gurganj, Biruni had more than 250 students. After his marriage to Lady Rayhana, he was happier, calmer, and more dignified. He was the most famous professor in Khwarazm. Yahya usually would engage Biruni in questions and arguments directly related to the origin of the world, God, and creation. And Biruni's answers always were the same: that we still need to do more research to find out about the secrets of our world. And most often, Biruni would ask Yahya, "Why do you think I have the answers to your questions?" Indeed, Yahya liked Biruni very much. Yahya found out that Biruni was a very honest, hard-working scholar. Every day his respect for the man that he was going to put on trial was growing. Yahya had been in Gurganj for three years now. After this period, he had nothing but love and respect for Biruni.

Abu Rayhan Biruni lived in the city of Gurganj for fourteen years. He was respected by his students, colleagues, and the public. His lectures were so interesting that the new Khwarazmshah, Abu Abbas, came to listen to him several times. After three years, Yahya returned to Baghdad empty-handed. He had nothing bad about Biruni to report to the Caliph. He reported to Baghdad that Biruni was a good Muslim person. That unlike some of his peers, he did not even drink wine. The Caliph got angry and accused Yahya of lying to him because Yahya had Persian blood and therefore was trying to save the life of a fellow countryman. Yahya was transferred to another office and relieved of information gathering.

One afternoon, Abu Nasr, Abu Rayhan, and Professor Abdul Samad, one of the oldest teachers in the Sultani School, were discussing an important mathematical issue when Sa'eed entered the room, without knocking first. He asked, "Do you professors know what happened in the city of Gorgan?" Abu Nasr angrily replied, "Who cares, and since when do you think you can enter a room and interrupt us? It is rude, Sa'eed!" He did not even pay attention to what Abu Nasr had said. Thus, he continued by saying, "Bad news, very bad news!" The three scholars turned around and looked at him. He slowly said, "King Qabus is dead."

Despite his generosity and kindness toward the people around him, King Qabus was harsh to those in his service and was highly vengeful and vindictive. Thus, his courtiers and family members were afraid of him. Actually, King Qabus's life story is very interesting. His kingdom in the southeastern parts of the Caspian Sea was disputed by the Samanids in Khurasan and the Buyids in the southwest of the Caspian Sea. Indeed, he first reigned from 977 to 981 C.E. Then he lost control over much of his kingdom when he was defeated by the Buyid king in 982 and was exiled for about seventeen years. He was invited back to his country by his people after the Buyid king died. King Qabus's second reign covered the period between 998 and 1013.

It was during his second reign that King Qabus was associated with both Biruni and Ibn Sina. In his court both of them and many others lived in peace and prosperity. But the nearly two decades in exile had left a big scar on his heart and mind. Thus, his tyrannical rule led to a military revolt probably inspired by his son Manuchihr. The rebels murdered him by exposing him to the winter cold in 1013. His mausoleum, called Gunbade Qabus (the Dome of Qabus), is located outside the modern city of Gorgan.

Abu Nasr commented by saying, "History is repeating itself. It seems like a repetition of the tragic calamity we had here in Khwarazm. An amir is being replaced by another one. In the process, many innocent people lose their lives and property. We, the scholars, suffer the most. The direction of studies and research will change. Who knows how long we will have to wait for a man like Qabus to come along!"

One of Abu Rayhan's inventions was a map projector called "Cylindrical." This is still one of the better map projection methods used for transferring features from a globe to a flat map. Professor Biruni also calculated the total area, circumference, and radius of our planet. His calculations were very close to modern measurements.

Biruni made half a globe with a diameter of about five meters to show half of the world. He wrote the names of all known places in the world on this half-globe. In total, he put the names of six hundred places on this half-globe. King Abu Abbas had paid for the building of this hemisphere. He kept watching Biruni making and furnishing his presentation of the known world. Biruni wrote the distance between major cities on his hemisphere.

A little less than five hundred years before Christopher Columbus took to the sea in 1492, Biruni was hypothesizing that there must have been other land masses in the western hemisphere. This was based on another one of his ideas that the Earth was spherical in shape. In order for the Earth to stay on course and not collide with other planets, he assumed that opposite to the known world, there must be some antipodal land masses, that is, large continents.

Biruni's idea about unknown land masses was a major hypothesis. For the first time in the history of mankind, he "predicted the existence of land to the east and west of Eurasia, which later on was discovered to be America and Japan" (Memon, 1959, p. 216). Therefore, it was Biruni who discovered America not Columbus. Especially, we know that Columbus was not even on a mission to find a new world. He was sailing westward in order to go to the east, India. And, actually, he was lost!

Biruni's situation is similar to Le Verrier, a French astronomer who calculated the position of the "blue planet" (Neptune), the seventh from the Sun, in 1846. It was only in 1989 that the American Voyager 2 spacecraft encountered Neptune. Now we know that Neptune is located at an average distance of 2.8 billion miles from the Sun. Since its discovery, Neptune has not even finished a total revolution. It takes 164.8 years for Neptune to make a full trip around the Sun. And, of course, we know Biruni's assumptions were correct. In his mind, those unknown land masses were not too far away.

Unlike many geographers of his time, Biruni was writing about the Earth's four quarters. In one of his books titled *Limits of Places*, he has referred to a "strait" connecting the extreme parts of eastern Asia to that of the land masses of the western hemisphere. This must be the first reference in any book to what we now call the Bering Strait. Although it was explored by Russian ships under Semyon I. Dezhnyoc in 1648, it was actually discovered by Vitus Bering, a Danish captain who sailed for the Russians, in 1728. Yet Biruni was aware of such a strait.

CHAPTER TWENTY

The City of Ghazna

Ghazna is nowadays known as Ghazni and is located in Afghanistan. It is a city in the eastern part of the country. It is located abut ninety miles (145 kilometers) southwest of the capital city of Kabul. The city of Ghazna is situated at an elevation of about 7,280 feet (2,200 meters).

The original form of the name must have been a Persian word meaning "the Treasury." This may indicate that Ghazna could have been a metropolis for its large surrounding hinterland called Zabulistan in the pre-Islamic times. The oldest mention of the town, according to some historians, can be found in Ptolemy's book.

As the birthplace of Rustam, a legendary national hero in Iran, Zabulistan has played an important role in the Iranian national epic as the homeland of epic or real heroes. The armies of the Arab governor of Khurasan had penetrated into the region by the mid–seventh century. By the end of the ninth century, Saffarid Yaqub reached Ghazna. It was only by the tenth century that Ghazna became a dependency of the Samanid Dynasty.

The history of Ghazna began in 962 when a Samanid Turkish slave commander called Alptakin captured the city with an army and established himself as the Amir of the region. Fifteen years later, in 977, Alptakin's Turkish slave commander by the name of Sabuktakin rose to power and founded the Ghaznavid Dynasty, which lasted more than two hundred years. The Ghaznavid Empire was centered in Afghanistan and covered most of western Iran, parts of central Asia, and Pakistan.

By this time, Ghazna entered the two most glorious centuries of its existence by becoming the capital city of a vast empire extending, at Sultan

Mahmud's death in 1030, from central Iran to Lake Aral and to northern India. During these two centuries, it held a dominant position between the Hindu and Muslim worlds. It was an important entrepôt, a center for reexportation, for the trade between these two worlds. The merchants and the inhabitants enjoyed prosperity and ease of life here. The city dwellers were free from noxious insects and poisonous reptiles and enjoyed the benefits of its healthy climate. But it snowed extensively and it was at the mercy of floods. For example, in the summer of 1031 a torrential rain caused a flash flood that almost destroyed the city.

The countryside surrounding Ghazna was very fertile. It produced the well-known Amiri apples, rhubarb, and monster pears known as *pil-amrud*, or the "Elephant Pears." The city of Ghazna villas and mansions of the rich were located on the hill slopes to the east of the modern town, on the way to the Sultan Garden, where Mahmud's tomb lies. Sultan Mahmud himself built a palace inside a garden called the Garden of One Hundred Thousand Trees. His son Masud built a splendid new palace in its design in 1035.

The spoils of India were used in the decoration of many palaces and buildings. The precious metals and captured Hindu slaves were incorporated into the palaces as trophies of war. After his expedition into India in 1018, Mahmud built a new mosque and called it the "Bride of the Heavens." Next to this mosque, he also built a Sultani School and a large library. Mahmud's other construction works included elephant stables or *pil-khana* that could house about a thousand beasts, with quarters for their attendants and some irrigation networks, including a few dams. One of these dams in the north of the city has survived to date.

The city of Ghazna was occupied by the Saljuq armies several times, and it was taken from the Ghaznavid Dynasty in 1163 when it was occupied by a group of Ghuzz tribesmen. The Mongols sacked the city in 1221. This was the end of Ghazna's glorious time, even coins now ceased to be minted here. By the 1500s, Ghazna was no more than a small town of no importance. Its degradation continued up to the nineteenth century.

Ghazna was captured by the British in 1942. At the request of Ellenborough, governor general of the British colony, the Golden Gates of Somnath brought to Ghazna by Mahmud in 1026 were sent back to India. The majority of the population in the city of Ghazna are Sunni Muslims and Persian-speaking people. Today, Ghazna has some local importance because it is the center of the province and is located on an important highway. But one wonders, generally speaking, how and why a place like Ghazna once was the center of a mighty empire.

Abu Rayhan was contemporaneous with Sultan Mahmud (ruled 998–1030) and his son Sultan Masud (ruled 1030–1040). Mahmud's full name was Yamin al-Dawla Abul Qasim Ibn Sabuktakin. Mahmud was only two years older than Abu Rayhan. But Mahmud died in 1030. This meant that Abu Rayhan outlived Mahmud by almost twenty-three years. Without a doubt, Mahmud was the most important ruler of the Ghaznavid Dynasty. Originally he was from a Turkish slave-pagan family. His father, Sabuktakin, gained power in Ghazna and continued until 997.

Mahmud, who quarreled with his father and got rid of his brother, became the ruler at age twenty-seven. He vowed to have expeditions into India every year, the first of which large-scale campaigns started in 1001 and the seventeenth and the last one ended in 1027. Thus he was not able to carry out his campaign every year. He still created the largest Muslim empire in south Asia. Moreover, his expedition into India led to more conversion into Islam in Southeast Asia, where the world's largest Muslim nation with more than 200 million people, Indonesia, is located. Mahmud, however, laid the foundation of Pakistan, the world's first Islamic republic. Actually, India, on the surface a Hindu country, had the second largest Muslim population (more than 150 million) after Indonesia.

Sultan Mahmud was in a fortunate situation. First, because the Samanid had lost their influence and he was able to come to an agreement with other Turkish tribes by deciding that the river Oxus should be the frontier. Second, he exchanged allegiance from the Samanids to the Abbasid Caliph, al-Qadir, in Baghdad. This is why he received his honorific title, Yamin al-Dawla, from the Caliph. Mahmud then slowly annexed the Buyid territories in Central Iran and Khwarazm toward northern Afghanistan.

Mahmud decided to transform Ghazna into a great center of art and literature. He thus patronized many scholars. He encouraged Ferdosi (935–1020), the great Persian author of the epic poem the *Book of Kings*, to finish the job. Probably several hundred well-known scholars resided in Ghazna. On the other hand, the people of India, mostly the Hindus, do not have a positive view of Mahmud. In his seventeen expeditions, many innocent people were killed, Hindu temples were destroyed, and Indian treasures were carried to Ghazna. Based on historical records, Mahmud and his army arrived at the gates of Somnath in January of 1026 C.E., after a march of one month across the desert. On January 8, 1026, after killing no less than fifty thousand Hindus, he took home valuables estimated at more than 10 million British pounds in the early 1930s (Nazim, 1971, p. 118).

Iranian Shiah Muslims do not like Mahmud either. Although he had adopted Persian as the language of his court and the official language of his empire, he after all was a Sunni Muslim. Especially in the beginning of his rule, he was a devoted follower of the Sunni Caliph in Baghdad. Therefore, any non-Sunni person could have been branded a heretic and executed.

In the East of the late tenth and early eleventh centuries, Mahmud was the most powerful man. He is described by Persian historians as a tyrant and oppressor, with a very harsh temper and as a heartless person even in adversity. Wine was consumed in his court openly. He had no fewer than twelve thousand female slave concubines and wives. He had a yellowish, round face with Mongoloid features, a small amount of facial hair, and slanted eyes. He was an epileptic as well. Thus, whenever in a rage, nobody could control him.

Mahmud constantly invited famous scholars to his court. He had learned that in the court of Khwarazm there were a few scholars. It was Mahmud's sister, the Khwarazmshah, King Abu Abbas's wife and queen, who informed Ghazna about the availability of those five scholar and their full names. Mahmud was a great patron of arts and letters but, perhaps, according to Edward G. Browne, "He was in fact a great kidnapper of literary men" (1956, pp. 95–96).

One day Mahmud instructed his Grand Vizier, Ahmad Ibn Hassan Maymandi, to write a letter asking for the five famous scholars in the court of his brother-in-law in Khwarazm. Actually, King Abu Abbas was ordered by Mahmud to send the five to Ghazna as soon as possible. Mahmud never asked, he demanded. The five scholars of that time were (1) Abu Ali Ibn Sina (Avicenna), the most famous Muslim physician-philosopher; (2) Abu Sahl Masihi, the Christian, a philosopher; (3) Abu Hassan Khammar, the wine seller, a physician; (4) Abu Nasr Arraq, mathematician, astronomer, inventor, and Biruni's teacher; and, of course, (5) Abu Rayhan Mohammad Ibn Ahmad Biruni.

Ibn Sina and Masihi were not willing to go to Ghazna. Therefore, King Abu Abbas secretly helped them plot their escape from Khwarazm. Two of them, Abu Hassan and Abu Rayhan did go to Ghazna because of the accounts they had heard of Sultan Mahmud's generosity. Before moving out of Khwarazm, each one of them got a house, a slave, and one thousand gold dinars. Probably this was only one of the reasons Biruni went to Mahmud's court, not the main one, for Biruni never cared for wealth. Since his rescue from slavery and death, he was very thankful to be alive and he had never forgotten who he was. This is why he had not taken any drastic action to marry Rayhana or Azarmidoukht.

Some historians believe that later in life in the city of Ghazna, after Biruni wrote his book called *Masudi Canon*, Sultan Masud (ruled 1030–1040) offered Biruni an elephant-load of silver pieces for his work, but Biruni refused to keep the gift for himself and gave it to the Sultani School and library. Biruni, however, was a smart scholar. He had predicted the downfall of little kingdoms and the rise of Mahmud's star. He also knew he could carry out research in Ghazna and in India. He eventually became the most knowledgeable scholar about India.

It took Biruni and Rayhana a short time to pack up and go to Ghazna. On arrival, they were housed in the Turquoise palace and a few slave girls were assigned to serve them. Biruni was to meet Sultan Mahmud in a week's time. Sultan Mahmud knew Biruni as a famous astronomer. As an illiterate person and like others of his time, the Sultan was equating astronomy with fortune telling and sorcery. So when Biruni, with some other scholars, was presented to him, the Sultan said, "Professor Biruni, I have heard a lot about you! Can you read my fortune? Can you explain the unknown to me?" Biruni replied, "Dear Sultan, I only can predict according to scientific laws."

The Sultan was sitting on an elegant throne. He had shiny black boots on and the most expensive clothes and jewelry. He had a rosary in his right hand that was made of ivory and sandalwood. He was playing with the rosary. Mahmud did not like Abu Rayhan's answer. It seemed that the Sultan wanted to know everything about his fortune in an instant. So he got angry and shouted, "*Mardak* (little fellow), answer me clearly! Can you or can you not predict my future?" Abu Rayhan got upset, but said, "My dear Sultan, I think I could!"

Sultan Mahmud was sitting on this throne in his palace located in the middle of the Garden of One Hundred Thousand Trees. The throne was in a four-doored mansion in the palace complex. Mahmud asked Abu-Rayhan, "By which door would I leave the mansion? I want you to use your knowledge of stars and predict my intention and write your prediction on a piece of paper. Tell me, Ostad Biruni, by which door would I go out, Northern, Southern, Eastern, or Western?"

Abu Rayhan wrote something on a piece of paper and handed it over to the Grand Vizier, Maymandi, who put it under a quilt. Mahmud was thinking that Biruni would choose one of the four doors. Therefore, he asked for a few workers to dig a hole in the wall and build a new door and go out of that one. Then, he asked for Biruni's answer. Maymandi read Biruni's prediction. It said, "The Sultan will not go out by any one of the four doors. An opening will be made in the wall across from the throne by which the Sultan will leave the building." This surprised Sultan Mahmud. He got angry and ordered Biruni to be thrown down from the roof. Biruni, fortunately, was saved by a mosquito net. He was brought back before Sultan Mahmud safe and sound. Mahmud asked him whether he had foreseen this event. Biruni took out a notebook from his pocket and give it to the Grand Vizier and asked him to read the very last page. The Grand Vizier read that page of the notebook, which said, "Today, I shall be cast down from a high place, but reach the earth in safety and arise sound in body."

This made Mahmud angrier and he ordered Biruni to be jailed. Fortunately for Biruni, the Grand Vizier Maymandi commented on the situation by saying, "Poor Biruni made two accurate predictions, and instead of being decorated he is being imprisoned!" Maymandi, in a way, was mediating. He was a learned man himself and knew Biruni well. Therefore, he wanted to save Biruni from being sent to jail. Mahmud liked his prime minister's comment. He said, "Kings are like children. In order to receive awards from them, one must do what they want. It would have been better for Biruni to have one wrong prediction. I think I was wrong playing with a man who is serious and has no equal in the world. Therefore, I forgive him."

Now, Mahmud was in a good mood. He apologized to Abu Rayhan. Ostad Biruni was rewarded handsomely. He was given a horse decorated in gold, a royal robe, a satin turban, one thousand gold dinars, a slave, and a handmaiden. Generally speaking, Abu Rayhan did not like the way he was treated by Sultan Mahmud. He was mostly alone, and he missed his family, friends, and homeland. Therefore, he asked permission to go back to Khwarazm. Again, Prime Minister Maymandi helped Biruni by getting the sultan's permission for him to go home. He took Lady Rayhana along. This time, Abu Rayhan stayed in Ghazna only for three months.

CHAPTER TWENTY-ONE

India

The power of the Ghaznavid Dynasty reached its zenith during Mahmud's reign. He captured most of the territories west of Afghanistan including central and western Iran. He even had an eye on his own brother-in-law's territory. In 1020 he asked the Grand Vizier Maymandi to write an official letter to his son-in-law King Abu Abbas ordering him that the Friday public sermon be read in Sultan Mahmud's name. And this was not a friendly request. This meant the end of Khwarazm's independence.

Khwarazmshah, King Abu Abbas, did not know what do to, but he was afraid of Mahmud. He knew that Mahmud would get what he wanted. Mahmud was the most powerful man in the world. King Abu Abbas first consulted with three of his army commanders. All of them were against reading the Friday public sermon in Mahmud's name. Then he asked for Abu Nasr and Abu Rayhan's advice. Both of them believed that it was a good idea to do what Mahmud had asked for. The young Khwarazmshah still did not know what to do. He was desperately seeking a solution to his biggest problem.

Again, King Abu Abbas talked to Abu Nasr and Abu Rayhan. This time, Abu Rayhan suggested the formation of an alliance between Khwarazm and the two neighboring states. The king liked this idea and asked Biruni to write up the treaty and personally take it to Bukhara and Turkistan to be signed. Suddenly, this honorable man, without any experience, was being drawn into the politics of the time.

Unfortunately for King Abu Abbas, not only did Sultan Mahmud have the largest and the most powerful armies in the world but he also had the largest spy network for information gathering. Thus, it was not hard for Ghazna to learn about the formation of an alliance against Mahmud. Sultan Mahmud sent another letter to Khwarazm repeating the same demand and threatening him. King Abu Abbas showed the letter to Abu Rayhan and asked his advice. Biruni suggested reading the Friday public sermon in Mahmud's name only in the areas bordering Ghazna, but not in the capital city of Gurganj. This might have prevented a rebellion by the army against the king. Khwarazmshah liked Biruni's advice but unfortunately it did not prevent a rebellion by the army.

First, a unit of the calvary surrounded the palace in Gurganj, arrested King Abu Abbas, and beheaded him in the garden minutes later. Within a few days, another unit of the army rebelled. This time they captured the queen, Mahmud's sister, dragged her by her hair, and beheaded her in the garden next to the spot where her husband King Abu Abbas was murdered.

The news of these events reached Mahmud in no time. He swore by the Holy Book and promised to punish the murderers of his brother-in-law and sister. After all, this was a good opportunity to take over Khwarazm. It was in the year 1020 that Mahmud himself led his army that included many trained Indian elephants. The Khwarazm armies were smashed in a short time and Mahmud entered the city of Gurganj triumphantly. The leaders of the rebellious Khwarazm army units were all arrested. Some of them were hanged and some executed by having them trampled under the elephants' feet. Sultan Mahmud appointed one of his army commanders by the name of Altoontash as the governor of Khwarazm.

This, however, was not the end of Mahmud's mission in Khwarazm. He wanted a total purge of the population before going back to Ghazna. Therefore, he appointed a trusty *meanbashy*, commander of a thousand soldiers, to search and arrest all suspicious people. Abu Nasr, Abu Rayhan, and Abdul Samad, an old professor and friend of Biruni, were sitting in the main hall of the new observatory and were discussing the recent events. Abu Nasr said, "This is the beginning of a new cycle of killing, and we have to be patient to see Mahmud's departure and see what Altoontash was going to do as the new governor of Khwarazm." At this very minute a group of Mahmud's soldiers entered the observatory and arrested the three professors and took them to where Mahmud was stationed in the Rose Garden Palace.

The three professors were guided into the garden by the soldiers, where they saw a group of prisoners of war waiting to be executed. Mahmud's huge executioners dressed in red were waiting to cut off the heads of the condemned. Mahmud himself was walking in front of the prisoner with a hose, a lash-whip of some sort, in his hand. Whenever he stopped in front of a prisoner, he would ask his minister of information to identify the man and say why he had been arrested. Mahmud never talked to the prisoners directly. Based on Mahmud's decision, they were all guilty; therefore, they all must be executed.

The three professors were ordered to sit on the sand in the middle of the garden next to the only prisoner alive. He knew the three professors. He was one of the last surviving secretaries of the Khwarazmshah. Abdul Samad was sitting next to the secretary. On the right side of Abdul Samad, Abu Nasr and Abu Rayhan were waiting to be questioned. Sultan Mahmud and his spy director, or the minister of information, was facing these prisoners. Sultan Mahmud stepped in front of the secretary and asked for information about him. But the prisoner cried out loud and said, "Please forgive me, I am innocent." The minister of information interrupted him and said, "He is the secretary who wrote the alliance treaty with Bukhara and Turkistan!" The secretary said, "I just wrote it. It was my duty to do so. I was not responsible for anything else." This plea actually made the sultan angry. He kicked the prisoner and said, "From your face, I see you are guilty. Send this *mardak* to hell!"

Two of the executioners got hold of the secretary and took him a few steps away. The man's hands were tied on his back and he was ordered to sit on the sand. One of the executioners got behind him, put two fingers of his left hand in the man's nostrils and raised the man's head, and then put a sharp knife to the secretary's throat. A large amount of blood erupted out of the man's neck. The executioner pushed the body forward so it fell on the sand. That was the end of the life of an innocent individual. Fortunately, he did not say anything about Biruni.

The sultan next stepped in front of Abdul Samad. Maybe because he was an old man, about sixty-five years old, Mahmud asked him directly, "What did you do to be arrested, old man?" Abdul Samad replied, "I have no idea." The minister of information said, "He is Abdul Samad the Hakim, the philosopher." Mahmud said, "Philosophers are crazy! Send him to a mental hospital." The minister of information commented, "But he is a corrupt philosopher-geographer. He prefers Zoroastrianism and Mazdakism over Islam. He believes that our world is like a globe and rotates around itself and the Sun!"

Sultan Mahmud said, "In that case, send him to hell too!"

The two remaining professors were facing Sultan Mahmud the tyrant. They could not believe the fact that Abdul Samad was going to be murdered right before their eyes. They were now worried about their own lives. Biruni was more worried, because he was the author of the alliance treaty.

Abdul Samad was taken away by the executioners. It was Abu Nasr's turn. Although a very brave man, he was shaken by seeing so much blood. Mahmud took one step toward Abu Nasr while asking his minister of information to identify him. But Abu Nasr responded, "I am Abu Nasr Mansur Ibn Arraq. I am a nephew of the deceased king Abu Abdulla. He was overthrown by the dynasty just overthrown by you. I have nothing to do with either one of the two. Therefore, let me go." Sultan Mahmud got very angry and said, "Who gave you the permission to talk, *mardak?*" Abu Nasr asked mockingly, "Why do I need permission to talk! Who are you anyway?" Mahmud said, "You fool, you do not know who I am?"

As soon as Mahmud used the word *fool*, Abu Nasr got outrageously angry and shouted at the sultan, "You call me fool! Let's see who is a fool, you or I? You are not more than a son of a slave who is illiterate! Yet you call me a fool. It is a strange world!" This was a direct insult on the most powerful man in the world. Sultan Mahmud got very angry and said, "Silence *mardak*." At this moment, Mahmud's sickness, epilepsy, took over him. A large amount of foam was coming out of his mouth. He was shaking very badly. Mahmud suddenly took a dagger from one of his men in red and ran toward Abu Nasr. Abu Nasr's hands were tied on his back. He could not defend himself. Mahmud was a powerful man and very enraged as well. The sultan attacked Abu Nasr with the sharp dagger. Mahmud cut Abu Nasr's chest open and continued to cut toward his abdomen. The sharp dagger cut directly through Abu Nasr's heart. His dead body fell on the sand. A nice nobleman, an innocent person, and a man of honor was murdered by a lunatic king.

Abu Rayhan was half dead already. He was sweating. He was the last prisoner. He just saw three people murdered right in front of his eyes. One of them was his best friend and best teacher. Yet he was unable to do anything. Abu Nasr was fifty-eight years old. Abu Rayhan was only forty-seven years of age. Abu Rayhan began reciting a verse from the Holy Book. This was the second time he did so in his life. The first time was when he was about to be sacrificed. Now he was repeating the same verse: "We all are from Allah and return to him." And he remembered his wife, Lady Rayhana. He wished she was here to hold her hands before he died. Then he told himself, "No God, she could not take it."

Sultan Mahmud got over his rage and his epileptic fit had subsided. He took out a white handkerchief and cleaned the foam from the corner of his mouth. He took a step toward Abu Rayhan and looked at him carefully. He suddenly burst into a loud laugh and said, "I know this last prisoner. He is a very smart fortune teller. I met him in Ghazna last year. Let him loose. Let him go and continue his research. Or even better, send him back to Ghazna. We may need him. This is Biruni and I like him." Sultan Mahmud then turned toward his minister of information and said, "It is enough for today. We have given a lesson to the people of Khwarazm to be good."

Before leaving Khwarazm, Mahmud ordered sending a large number of people from this defeated country to Ghazna. According to historical documents, at least five thousand prisoners of war and hostages were taken out of Khwarazm. They were selected among the best people alive. This was one of the major reasons that Khwarazm never again reached its former glory.

Biruni's hands were untied, and he was set free by the same soldiers who arrested him and his colleagues. He did not know how he got out of the palace stained with blood. Outside the palace, he did not know what to do or where to go. All he could see was the color of blood: red. He then remembered his beloved wife. He took the shortest path home that was not too far away near the Sultani School and observatory. He was taking long, heavy steps. It was like he was stumping on the road covered with sand. He hated sand; it absorbed so much blood. He had not cried so far. He could not believe the fact that Abu Nasr was gone forever.

Abu Rayhan did not know how to explain everything to Lady Rayhana. In the front yard, she was waiting for him. She knew something was wrong. Her brother and her husband were always together. She had tears in her eyes. Abu Rayhan said, "Yes, he is gone. He was murdered by Sultan Mahmud himself. Your brother, my best friend! He is gone forever! We should go and claim the badly mutilated bloody body, the corpse." Biruni was unable to refer to his best friend by name.

This was not the first or the last time the Sultan would kill people with his own hands. Sultan Mahmud personally participated in all of his wars. According to Nazim (1971), "At the siege of Multan he killed so many of the enemy that his hand was stuck fast to the hilt of his sword with congealed blood and had to be immersed in a bath of hot water before it could be loosened" (p. 154).

Abu Rayhan and Rayhana followed Sultan Mahmud to his capital city of Ghazna. Abu Rayhan was sure he could continue his research there and Rayhana wanted to get away from Khwarazm too. Unfortunately, shortly after their arrival, Rayhana got very sick and died. For some time, it seemed that Abu Rayhan was lost. He stopped writing and doing research. After living in the suburbs of Ghazna for a while, he moved to a small village away from the city.

Later, Abu Rayhan decided to carry out research on India and so he traveled to India. He spent ten years in this country. He became the most knowledgeable scholar about India. Biruni outlived Sultan Mahmud by twenty-three years. Biruni actually saw Mahmud's grandson Mawdud on the throne. While in Ghazna, Biruni wrote at least six more major books called *Understanding Astronomy*, *The Book of India*, *Masudi Canon*, *Kitab al-Saydanah*, *Kitab al-Jamahir*, and *Kitab al-Dastur*.

Understanding Astronomy, of course, and *Masud's Canon* were in astronomy. Biruni had much better relations with Masud than with Mahmud. *Masudi Canon* is Biruni's only book that includes the name of a king in its title or is dedicated to one. This book includes an astronomical table and a table of geographical coordinates of six hundred important places in the world. Sultan Masud himself had some interest in astronomy. One day, Sultan Masud asked Biruni a question on the changes in the length of day and night during different seasons. Although Biruni explained his answer verbally, he later wrote a treatise on this very subject in the simplest way possible. The Sultan was very pleased. After Sultan Masud saw this book and his own *Canon*, he sent an elephant-load of silver to Biruni.

Biruni did not ignore medicine as a part of his scientific studies. He was very familiar with Greek and Indian medicine. *Kitab al-Saydanah* was written when Biruni was very old, and this was probably his last work, composed after his return from India and after his experience with a disease, perhaps malaria. *Sayadanah* is a comprehensive book on pharmacy. In this book, Biruni deals with medical issues such as occurrence, medicinal usage, diagnosis, natural drugs, and his approach to natural drugs. Included were etymologies, descriptions that were based on his experience, and a revision of some of the Greeks' opinions. Biruni provided the exact names of these drugs in Arabic, Greek, Hebrew, Persian, and Sanskrit.

In some circles, however, Biruni is more famous for his *Kitab al-Hind* or the *Book of India*. This book was translated by C. Edward Sachau and was published in 1887 in London. Actually, Biruni called his book *Research in India*. While in Khwarazm, Biruni studied some Sanskrit and all references about India. His main goal was to learn about Hindu astronomy. He was probably disappointed because he could hardly find anything. Most of the Muslim sources about India were one-sided. The Muslims looked down on India. This country was seen as a backward one where people worshipped idols. Sultan Mahmud's invasions in the 1020s of India thus were geared toward converting the people of the subcontinent to Islam.

In a life that continued to amaze him, the great scholar came face to face with a civilization that was totally different from his own. Biruni accompanied Sultan Mahmud on some of his expeditions. Biruni saw with his own eyes the scale of the destruction that Mahmud's armies inflicted on India.

Several times, Biruni stayed behind and continued his research in India. For the purpose of research, he also went to India alone. Living in the city of Ghazna provided Biruni with the best opportunities, historically and geographically, for pursuing his research on India. Ghazna was an important political and cultural center of Islam not far from India. Sultan Mahmud brought precious goods, prisoners of war, and scholars to this city. Thus, Ostad Biruni already had access to second-hand information, and so he visited India to secure first-hand research by himself.

Biruni was fortunate to be associated with many of the official and political representatives, that is, ambassadors, merchants, and travelers arriving at Sultan Mahmud's court. Official representatives came not only from nearby countries, but from faraway lands. Among them came delegates from the Byzantine Empire, Egypt, Khazar tribes north of the Caspian Sea, Bulgaria, and Danube region, the Gaul, Scandinavia, India, China, and from lands beyond the Amur River. The last group may have had a lot of information not only about Siberia but also about Alaska.

The Scandinavian representatives gave Biruni much information about the frozen bodies of water in extreme northern Europe. One day a merchant from Scandinavia at Mahmud's court claimed that he had seen the Sun rotate around the Earth. As usual, the Sultan got upset and accused the man of heresy and ordered him to be executed. Fortunately, Ostad Biruni was in attendance and had to explain to the illiterate Sultan that what the merchant claimed was true. Biruni said, "The Sun does not rotate around the Earth. Polar regions have only two seasons. In summer, the Sun is in the sky for about six months." The Sultan believed Biruni, and the merchant's life was saved. It was highly likely that Ostad Biruni would have learned about the Viking voyages into northern America around the year 1000. This may have influenced his idea of unknown land masses, that is, the Americas.

Biruni completed his *Book of India* in 1030 right after Sultan Mahmud's death. He was well aware of his research limitations. One of the reasons he gave why it was so hard to penetrate into the essential nature of any Indian subject was that "they differ from us in everything," he wrote later. Biruni believed that his book was "nothing but a simple historic record of facts. I shall place before the readers the theories of the Hindus exactly as they are and I shall mention in connection with them similar theories."

The world of Islam has seen very few historical studies. But Biruni's research was the first of its kind, and so far one of the best. It is a measure of Ostad Biruni's greatness and ability to make sure to understand and explain an alien culture. His research on India attempted to inform and enlighten his contemporaries about important religious, scientific, and philosophical traditions of the subcontinent, which were unknown to them.

On the last page of his *Book of India*, Biruni wrote that "His book will be sufficient for anyone who wants to converse with the Hindus, and discuss with them questions of religion, science, or literature, on the very basis of their own civilization. Therefore, we shall finish this treatise." Biruni believed that India and South Africa were somehow related. He was aware of the huge mountain ranges, the Himalayas, and was able to estimate the height of Mount Everest. More importantly, he believed that the plains of India were under water in a bygone age. As an accomplished geomorphologist, Biruni had "a fine grasp of things natural and therefore geographical" (Kazemi, 1976, p. 209). Biruni estimated the age of our planet Earth to be millions and millions of years. As regards the geological composition, he said the "Earth has undergone great changes in the course of long ages" (Memon, 1959, p. 216).

As a modern geologist, Biruni has written about shifts in the bed of the Amu Darya River since the time of Ptolemy and Alexander the Great due to earthquakes. He believed that this river did empty its water in the Caspian Sea rather than Lake Aral. He also concluded that in the very ancient times a gigantic body of water covered the plain of India that extended to the Arabian Peninsula and the Sea of Rome. This Mesozoic Sea is now called the Tethys Sea by modern geologists. As an expert hydrologist, he also explained the properties of natural springs and wells, including the artesian ones, flood, and drought. And he was well aware of the relationships between the moon and the formation of tides. He knew that the moon was not without its effects on human behavior. He also studied gravitational forces on all beings on the surface of our planet.

In the *Book of India*, Biruni suggested a new theory very similar to what Thomas Malthus advocated in regard to population and resources in the late 1790s in England (Spengler, 1971). Biruni argues that our world needs some sort of "Ecological Balance" and "Economy of Nature." Biruni too pointed out that natural resources are limited and cannot keep up with rapid population growth. He suggested a type of family planning and offered his own techniques related to contraceptives.

As an informed botanist, Biruni spent time simply counting the number of seeds inside many big and small pomegranates. He found that, regardless of their size, they always contain the same number of seeds. He also counted and kept records of the number of petals in the flowers of many plants. His conclusion was that flowers always have three, four, five, six, or eighteen petals but never seven or nine, thus not only observing geometry in nature but moving into a new area of algebra and trigonometry.

He then developed a basic theory of natural selection and evolution (Wilczynski, 1959). To him nature was similar to a gardener or a farmer, and only the best and the strongest could survive. Although his theory of evolution is somewhat crude for our time, at least he believed in the upward mobility of species. His evolution starts from dogs, to bears, to monkeys, and finally ends with human beings. However, he again goes beyond this simple evolutionary approach.

He wrote that intellectual evolution goes hand in hand with physical evolution in human societies. To him, societies will change from communal to unjust, then to an equal, just, democratic, and representative government. He explained that the world is a meeting ground between human inheritance and intelligence, and accumulation of experiences of all nations through time and over space will result in the advancement of human societies.

Precise measurements were among Ostad Biruni's achievements in the advancement of human scholarship. Like several Greek and Muslim scientists, he tried to calculate the radius of our planet. He attempted to do this measurement in Khwarazm, Gorgan, and Ghazna but did not like the results. Using a trigonometrical technique in a place called Nandana, now in the Jhelum district in Pakistan, he finally arrived at a measurement that is believed to be the closest to the value determined by modern instruments (Mercier, 1992, p. 182). Biruni's measurement was 7,890 English miles, that is, only 12 miles short of the actual value of 7,902. After this, it was of course easy to calculate the circumference, area, and volume of our planet.

Based on spherical trigonometry and personal astronomical observations, Biruni carried out research in the year 1020 to measure the longitude differences over long distances, for example, between Baghdad and Ghazna in Afghanistan. By doing this, he could calculate the actual distance between places. The results of his measurements can be found in the *Masudi Canon*. According to Sezgin (1987, p. 25), Biruni "may be characterized as the first in the history of geography" to do this type of measurement.

He came up with a conical-shaped instrument to measure the specific weight of eight elements, mostly precious metals and stones including gold, emerald, pearl, ruby, and sapphire. He filled his instrument with water and dropped those minerals in the water. Using hydrostatic principles, he weighed the amount of displaced water from the siphon of the instrument for each mineral. The specific weights that he calculated for those eighteen elements differ only in their third decimal points compared with modern values.

Biruni provides us with economic reasons for the caste system, respect for cows, and prostitution around Indian temples. He argues that kings used prostitutes as an attraction for their cities for financial reasons. The revenues earned from them as fines and taxes were then spent on the army. He generalizes the differences between educated and uneducated people in every nation. The former strive for abstract ideas, while the latter do not pass beyond the apprehension of the senses . . . without caring for details, especially in questions about reason in religion and laws.

Biruni's last two known books were titled *Kitab al-Jamahir* and *Kitab al-Dastur*. The first book is believed to be the best book on precious stones in the Muslim world and the second book deals with the best qualities, directions, and instructions. These books were dedicated to Mahmud's grandson, Mawdud, who ruled the country until 1049. Mawdud too had the highest respect for Ostad Biruni.

CHAPTER TWENTY-TWO

The End

As a much respected, prosperous scholar, Ostad Biruni stayed in Ghazna during the last years of his life. Similar to his teacher and friend, Biruni invented many astronomical–geographical and scientific tools. Unfortunately, most of those tools and books are lost. But we know that he invented a few newer, more improved astrolabes, a semiglobe, a few map projections, a conical-shaped instrument to measure the density and specific weight of elements, and an upside-down but more precise map of the world mentioned in the previous chapter.

Biruni lived to be eighty years of age. He wrote 183 books and treatises, amounting to thirteen thousand pages (Kennedy, 1970, p. 151). Many historians believe that this was equal to the full load of a camel. Only thirteen of these works have survived the last one thousand years of world events. Biruni died in 1053. His grave is located in the city of Ghazna, now called Ghazni, in western Afghanistan about ninety miles (145 kilometers) southwest of the capital city of Kabul.

In his quest for truth, Burini stands quite alone with a surprisingly modern scientific methodology and comparative research approach. He, however, was a well-versed humanist scholar. He believed in the oneness of all higher human civilizations. Even by the time Biruni was very old and fragile, he continued his enormous output of scientific works right up to the time of his death.

A story is told about when Ostad Biruni was about to die. A friend, a former student, came to visit him. Biruni asked him about the solution of some mathematical problem that they had discussed earlier. This problem was related to a mathematical analysis of inheritance. The friend was astonished that he was thinking about such matters in that condition! Biruni replied, with a great effort, that he wanted to know if it was not desirable that he should die with the knowledge of the solution of that problem rather than without it. "Why do you think I should die ignorant?" Biruni asked. As soon as the friend stepped out of Biruni's house, he had to return. He heard loud cries of his teacher's family members. After eighty years of amazing life, Biruni died in his own bed peacefully.

The first fifty years of the eleventh century rightfully and correctly are called the "Age of Biruni" by George Sarton (1927, p. 693). Biruni's death in reality did not mark the end of the Age of Biruni. Many shahs, kings, sultans, princes, princesses, and brahmans in Khwarazm, Rayy, Gorgan, Ghazna, and India learned to have the highest respect for Ostad Biruni. Many of his teachers, colleagues, and friends enjoyed conversing with him. His legacy as a man of honor and integrity and as a humanist with the highest scientific quality overshadowed the European Renaissance. Men like Newton, Torricelli, Copernicus, Galileo, Bacon, and Darwin learned something from Professor Biruni. They together made the world a better place for us.

The End

Glossary

Abbasid Caliphate (750–1258 C.E.): Claiming descent from Abbas, the Prophet Mohammad's uncle, centered in Baghdad, controlled most of the Muslim world.

Abu: Father of . . . . Usually used in many Arabic-Muslim names in combination with the name of the first-born son.

Abu Nasr Mansur Ibn Ali Arraq (970–1036 C.E.): Abu Nasr Mansur was a native of Khwarazm, where his family ruled the region. His association with Biruni started in 990. He was an astronomer-mathematician. It is believed that he wrote as many as twelve books in Biruni's name.

Abul Wafa Buzjani (940–998 C.E.): He was a Muslim astronomer-mathematician who was born in Buzjan and died in Baghdad.

Allah: The Arabic name for God.

Amir: Also spelled as Emir and Ameer. It means a prince, chief, commander, leader or army general, and governor of a province.

Amu Darya: Also called the Oxus by the Greeks and Jeyhoon by the Arabs. Amu Darya is the Persian name for one of the longest rivers in central Asia. This river originates in the eastern Pamir Mountains in Afghanistan and empties its waters in Lake Aral in Uzbekistan.

Andalusia: Muslims' reference to most of Spain.

Andijan: Also Andijon, is a city in the extreme eastern region of Uzbekistan, lies in the southeastern part of the Fergana Valley.

Andijani, Ahmad Ibn Ali: Name of Biruni's father.

Anushirvan (Ruled 531–579 C.E.): Also Anoshirvan, Khusro Anushirvan was one of the most powerful kings of the Sassanid Dynasty. His title was the "Just."

Aral Sea: Actually a lake, it is a shallow salty body of water located east of the Caspian Sea in central Asia. Syr Darya and Amu Darya are its major sources of water.

Arbab: Landlord, chief, boss, master, employer, and owner.

Avicenna: *See* Ibn Sina.

Awqaf: A plural form of *vaqf* or the religious endowment in Islam.

Azerbaijan: Name of two provinces in Iran and an independent country west of the Caspian Sea.

Bahram the Zebra Hunter: A king of the Sassanid Dynasty who was a skillful hunter of zebras or wild asses. Bahram X was Yazdgird's son and reigned from 420 to 438 C.E. It is believed that he was drowned in a swamp in central Iran chasing a wild ass.

Balkh: A town in northern Afghanistan that was formerly called Bactra, the capital city of Bactria. It is located about 14 miles (22 kilometers) west of the city of Mazar-e Sharif.

Bazaar: A shopping center or a public marketplace in a Persian town or city. It is synonymous with the Arabic word *suq*.

Beeaban: A Persian word for desert.

Beeaban-e Ghuzz: The Ghuzz Desert.

Bin: Son of . . . . *See also* Ibn.

Birun: A Persian word that means "outside."

Bukhara: A city in the country of Uzbekistan founded no later than the first century C.E. It was the capital of the Samanid Dynasty in the ninth and tenth centuries. This city is located in a natural gas region.

Buyid Dynasty (945–1055 C.E.): Also Buwayhid, was a native Persian dynasty mostly in Daylaman, northern Iran, also in western Iran and Iraq in the period between the Arab and Turkish conquests.

Caliph: The Arabic Khalifah or the successor is a reference to a ruler of a Muslim community.

Caravansarai: A lodging for travelers, merchants, pilgrims, and their goods. They were often fortified and usually located on the trade routes.

Caspian Sea: World's largest inland lake.

Dakhma: Also called the "Tower of Silence." Literally, it means the basement chamber, cave, or tomb, but it is a circular building where the Zoroastrians lay the bodies of their dead.

Darya: Persian word meaning the sea.

Dinar: Was a gold coin in ancient times. Modern version of it is now the national currency of several countries.

Dirham: Silver or copper coins in the ancient Muslim world. At present, it is the national currency of the United Arab Emirates.

Farsang: Also *farsakh*, is a unit of long-distance measurement that is about six kilometers.

Ferdosi, Abul Qasem (935–1020 C.E.): Also spelled Ferdowsi, Firdowsi, and Firdusi. He is considered to be one of the greatest poets of Iran. Author of the *Shahnamah* or *Book of Kings*, a great epic poem that presented the legends and much of the history of pre-Islamic Iran.

Geleem: Also Kelim. It is the name of a handmade rug or a coarse carpet.

Ghazna: A city located in Afghanistan. It is called Ghazni now. It is located about 90 miles (145 kilometers) southwest of Kabul.

Ghaznavid Dynasty (977–1186 C.E.): A Turkish dynasty that ruled over Khurasan in northeastern Iran, Afghanistan, most of central Asia, and northern India.

Ghuzz: One or several Turkish tribes in central Asia. It is a general name for the Turkish Oghuz people.

Gilan: Name of a province in northern Iran southwest of the Caspian Sea.

Gorgan: Also Gurgan and Jurjan. This is a city and region located southeast of the Caspian Sea in Iran.

Gurganj: Also Organj, and the Arabic name of this city was Jujaniyya. Russian spelling is Urgench or Urganch. It was situated near Lake Aral, west of Amu Darya. The city of Urganch is now located in Uzbekistan.

Hammam: A steam bath house. Bathing establishments for the public.

Herat: Also spelled Harat. It is the capital city of Herat Province in western Afghanistan.

Hijra: Also spelled Hejira, Arabic for Hijrah, or Hijra. It means emigration or flight. It is a reference to the Prophet Muhammad's emigration from Mecca to Medina in 622 C.E. Hijra is the date that marks the beginning of Muslim calendar.

Ibn: Son of . . . . *See also* Bin.

Ibn Sina, Abu Ali (980–1037 C.E.): An Iranian physician, the most famous and influential among the philosophers of Islam. He was noted for his contributions in the fields of Aristotelian philosophy and medicine.

Imam: A prayer leader. It is a title for the sovereign head of an Islamic community or the spiritual leader of the Shiah Muslim people.

Ismailiyya: A branch of Shiah Islam who believed in seven Imams.

Jalad: The executioner.

Jandar: A member of the police force guarding rural areas. It is similar to a French *gendarme*.

Kabob: Also Kabab. Skewered meat or vegetables roasted over fire.

Kadkhoda: Also Katkhoda and Kadhoda. This is the title for a headman or chief administrative official of a single village.

Kath: A city east of Amu Darya and south of Lake Aral. It is now known as Khiva in Uzbekistan.

Kerman: A city and a province in southeast Iran.

Khayyam, Omar (1038–1031 C.E.): He was an Iranian astronomer-mathematician, but Khayyam is known in the West for his book of poems called *The Rubaiyyat*, which was translated into English by Edward Fitzgerald in 1859.

Khan: Historically, the ruler or monarch of Mongol origin in the early thirteenth century. The term was later used in many Muslim societies. It also means prince, leader, and a lodging for travelers and merchants.

Khiva: *See* Kath.

Khurasan: Also spelled as Khorasan. A historical region including territories now lying in northeastern Iran, southern Turkmenistan, and northern Afghanistan. Khurasan, literally "Land of the Sun," is now only the name of a province in northeastern Iran.

Khwarazm: A general name for most of the irrigated lands south of Lake Aral between and on both sides of Amu Darya and Syr Darya located mainly in the country of Uzbekistan. Both cities of Gorganj and Kath were also called by this name.

Khwarazmi, Abu Jafar Muhammad Ibn Musa: A mathematician, astronomer, and geographer. He lived in the first half of the ninth century C.E. During the Caliphate of Mamun, he was a member of the "House of Wisdom" in Baghdad. Many of his works were translated into Latin in Spain and they exercised a powerful influence on the development of medieval thought. He coined *algebra* and *algorithm* for us.

Kish: Name of an island in the Persian Gulf.

Koran: *See* Quran.

Madrasa: Also Madrasah and Madrasseh. It is an Arabic word for school. It is also a reference to an institution for the study of law and other Islamic sciences.

Maktab: Primary school. It was and is mainly a religious grammar school. It is a mosque-affiliated Islamic school.

Mani (216–274 C.E.): Mani was a self-proclaimed prophet. He was the founder of a new religion called Manichaeism.

Marzban: Protector or warden of the frontiers, watching borders.

Mawara al-Nahr: Is the Arabic name for lands beyond the Amu Darya in central Asia.

Maydan: Also Maidan and Maydone. An open public square or plaza and central ceremonial space.

Maymandi, Ahmad Ibn Hassan: Sultan Mahmud's grand vizier.

Mazdak: Proclaimed himself a prophet in about 500 C.E. His ideas were similar to communism. He is the founder of a dualistic sect, whose followers were executed by Anushirvan the Just.

Mehr: It means love and affection, and is a reference to the Sun in Persian. It is also the name of the seventh month of the Iranian calendar. It is also the origin of the words *mithras* and *mithraism*.

Merv: Is the name of an ancient city of central Asia. It is located near the modern city of Mary in the country of Turkmenistan.

Middle Ages: Also called medieval age and the Dark Ages, is name of the period in European history from the collapse of Roman civilization in the fifth century to the period of the Renaissance.

Minaret: Arabic for beacon. It is the tower of a mosque or any Muslim religious institution from which the faithful are called to prayer.

Minbar: The stepped pulpit from which the sermon or *khutbah* and preaching is delivered.

Mongols: Members of Asiatic ethnographic groups of closely related tribal people who lived on the Mongolian plateau. Under Genghis Khan's (died 1227 C.E.) leadership, they created the second largest empire in the world.

Mulla: Also spelled Mullah, is a person versed in Islamic theology and sacred law. It is the title of a teacher in a *maktab* or religious school. It is also a reference for religious and political leaders in Iran.

Al-Muqanna, Hashim Ibn Hakim: Literally, the "Veiled One." Called also the "Masked Man of Khurasan" between 777 and 780 C.E. He was a religious leader in the city of Merv in Khurasan. He claimed to be an incarnation of God and gave rise to a new heresy whose followers dressed in white, known historically as "Sapid Jamagan."

Nishaboor: Also Nishapour and Nishapur. Name of a city in Khurasan in northeastern Iran.

Norouz: Also Nowrooz and Nawruz. Literally, it means "new day" in Persian. The Norouz period includes two weeks of national celebration beginning on the first day of spring, usually on March 21.

Ostad: Persian word for a teacher, professor, master, architecture, or the most knowledgeable, skilled person in any occupation.

Qabus Ibn Washmgir (Reigned 977–981 and 998–1013 C.E.): He was a king from the Ziyrid Dynasty who ruled southeast of the Caspian Sea.

Qanat: A type of water-supply system developed and still used in arid regions around the world. It is a man-made spring. It is a collection of wells and canals that carry water from highlands to lowlands for irrigation and domestic consumption.

Qarmati: Also Karmati, name given to a branch of the Ismailiyya sect of Islam.

Quran: Arabic for recitation. It is the holy book of Islam, regarded as the true word of God as revealed to Prophet Muhammad.

Ramazan: Also Ramadan and Ramadhan. The holy month of fasting in Islam. It is the ninth month of the Muslim calendar.

Rawlinson, Henry C.: A British archeologist who deciphered the Old Persian cuneiform inscriptions in late 1836.

Rayy: Also Ray, Rey, Rai, and Old Persian Ragha. It was formerly one of the great cities of Iran. This city was located southeast of Tehran, now almost a suburb.

Razi, Muhammad Ibn Zakarya (865–925 C.E.): Celebrated alchemist-physician-surgeon-philosopher of Islam. He was born and died in the city of Rayy. In Europe he was known as Rhazes.

Renaissance: Literally "rebirth," the period in European history immediately following the Middle Ages. The Renaissance has been characterized by a surge of interest in classical learning and values.

Rustam: A legendary national hero of Ferdosi's *Book of Kings*. He is seen as the Hercules of Iran.

Saffarid Dynasty: Name of an Iranian dynasty of lower class. *Saffar* means "coppersmith" in Arabic. They ruled in eastern parts of the country between 867 and 900 C.E.

Saljuq Dynasty: Also Saljuk, Seljuk, and Seljuq. Name of a ruling Turkish Dynasty that controlled most of the Persian Empire between 1055 and 1152 C.E.

Samanid Dynasty (819–999 C.E.): It is the name of first native Iranian dynasty after the Muslim conquest.

Samarqand: Is considered to be one of the oldest cities in central Asia, now located in the country of Uzbekistan. It served as the capital city of the Samanid Dynasty.

Sassanid Dynasty: Also spelled Sasanian and Sassanian. An Iranian dynasty who ruled the Persian Empire from 224 to 651 C.E.

Simurgh: A mythical bird of great size and wisdom that is immortal. It is believed that it dwelled in the Alburz Mountains.

Somnath: A Hindu temple in the southwestern state of Gujarat that was sacked by Sultan Mahmud of the Ghaznavid Dynasty in 1025.

Stwodone: The Tower of Silence. It is a building used by Zoroastrians where they lay their dead to decompose.

Sultan Mahmud: The most powerful king of the Ghaznavid Dynasty, ruled 998–1030 C.E.

Sultan Masud: Son of Sultan Mahmud who reigned 1031–1040 C.E.

Sultan Mowdud: Son of Sultan Masud and grandson of Mahmud, ruled 1041–1049 C.E.

Syr Darya: The ancient name of Jaxartes River in the central Asian country of Uzbekistan. It was called by the Arabs Seyhoon. It is formed in the eastern part of Fergana Valley and generally flows northeast until it empties into Lake Aral. It is longer than Amu Darya but carries less water.

Tabarestan: An old name for the province of Mazandaran located southeast of the Caspian Sea.

Transoxania: Sometimes spelled Transoxiana, it is a Greek name for a region located beyond the Amu Darya River, the Oxus, in central Asia. The Arabs called it Mawara al-Nahr. It roughly corresponds to present-day Uzbekistan, parts of Turkmenistan, and Kazakhstan.

Turan: Is a reference to most areas in central Asia occupied by the Turks.

Toos: Also Tus. A very important city located in Khurasan Province, Iran. This city was destroyed by the Mongols. It is now a suburb of Mashhad, the capital city of the province by the same name.

Umayyad Caliphate: The Islamic caliphate centered in Damascus between 661 and 750 C.E.

Vizier: Also Wazir and Vizer from the Old Persian "Judge," originally the chief minister or prime minister. The vizier stood between sovereign and subjects, representing the former in all matters regarding the latter.

Zabulistan: A region located in southeastern Iran around the city of Zabul.

Ziyarid Dynasty (927–1090 C.E.): Iranian local rulers who controlled areas southeast of the Caspian Sea.

References and Further Readings

Ahmad, N. "Al-Biruni's Geography of India." *Calcutta Geographical Review*, March & December 1943, pp. 153–158.

Ahmad, Q. *India by Al-Biruni*. New Delhi, India: National Book Trust, 1983.

Ahmad, Z. "Al-Biruni: His Life and His Work." *Islamic Culture*, Vol. 5, July 1931, pp. 343–351.

Ahmad, Z. "Al-Biruni's Research in Trigonometry." *Islamic Culture*, Vol. 6, 1932, pp. 363–369.

Alshabi, A. *Biruni's Biography*. Tehran: Ministry of Culture and Art, Center for Anthropological and Folkloric Research, n.d., Translated from Arabic into Persian by Parviz Azka'i.

Barani, S. H. "Al-Biruni's Scientific Achievements." *Indo-Iranica*, Vol. 5, No. 39, 1952–1953, pp. 37–48.

Barani, S. H. "Ibn Sina and Alberuni." In *Avicenna Commemoration Volume*. Calcutta, India: Iran Society, 1956, pp. 3–14.

Barani, S. H. "*Kitabut-Tahdid* (An Unpublished Masterpiece of al-Biruni on Astronomical Geography)." *Islamic Culture*, Vol. 3, 1957, pp. 165–177.

Barthold, W. (Edited by Bosworth, C.) *Turkestan Down to the Mongol Invasion*. London: Luzac, 1968.

Biruni International Congress. *Commemorative Volume of Biruni: Collection of Persian Presentations*. Tehran: Zar Press, High Council of Culture and Art, Center for Research and Cultural Coordination, 1975.

Boilot, D. J. "Al-Biruni." *Encyclopaedia of Islam*. Leiden: E. J. Brill, Vol. 1, 1979, pp. 1236–1238.

Browne, E. G. *A Literary History of Persia*. Cambridge: Cambridge University Press, 4 Vols., 1953–1956.

Courtois, V. *Al-Biruni: A Life Sketch*. Calcutta, India: Iran Society, 1952.

Dehkhoda, A. A. *Biography of Iran's Famous Genius Abu Raihan Muhammad Ibn Ahmad Khwarazmi-i Biruni*. Tehran: Majlis Press, 1945. (In Persian.)

Embree, A. T. (Ed.). *Alberuni's India*. New York: Norton, 1971.

Ghirshman, R., Minorsky, V., and Sanghvi, R. *Persia: The Immortal Kingdom*. New York: New York Graphic Society, Orient Commerce Establishment, 1971.

Hamarneh, S. K. (Ed.). *Al-Biruni's Book on Pharmacy and Materia Medica*. Karachi: Hamdard National Foundation, 1973.

Homaii, J. (Ed.). *Kitab al-tafhim li-awa'il sina'at al-tanjim*. (Book of Understanding the Basic Art of Astrology). Tehran: Babak Publishers, 1984. Originally written by Biruni.

Ibn Fadlan, A. *Collection of Geographical Works*, edited by Fuat Sezgin. Frankfurt am Main: Institute for the History of Arabic–Islamic Science, 1987.

Iran Society of Calcutta. *Al-Biruni Commemorative Volume*. Calcutta, India: Iran Society of Calcutta, 1951.

Kamiar, M. "Abu-Rayhan Biruni and His Geographical Works." Unpublished Research Paper, Department of Geography, Michigan State University, East Lansing, Mich., Fall 1979.

Kamiar, M. "The Qanat System in Iran." *Ekistics*, No. 303, November & December 1983, pp. 467–472.

Kamiar, M. *From the Roof of Iran to the Land of Storm*. Tehran: Expansion of Iranian Libraries Company, 2001. (In Persian.)

Kamiar, M. *A Bio-Bibliography for Biruni: Abu Raihan Mohammad Ibn Ahmad (793–1053 C.E.)*. Lanham, Md.: Scarecrow Press, 2006.

Kazemi, H. A. "Alberuni's Longitudes and Their Conversion into Modern Values." *Islamic Culture*, Vol. XLIX, No. 3, July 1975, pp. 165–176.

Kazemi, H. A. "Al-Beruni on the Shift of the Bed of Amu Darya." *Islamic Culture*, Vol. L, No. 4, October 1976, pp. 201–211.

Kennedy, E. S. "Biruni." In Gillispie, C. C. (Ed.), *Dictionary of Scientific Biography*. New York: Scribner's, 1970, pp. 147–158.

Kennedy, E. S. *A Commentary upon Biruni's Kitab Tahdid al-Amakin: An 11th Century Treatise on Mathematical Geography*. Beirut, Lebanon: American University of Beirut, 1973.

Kennedy, E. S. "The Exact Sciences." In Frye, R. N. (Ed.), *The Cambridge History of Iran: The Period from the Arab Invasion to the Saljuqs*. New York: Cambridge University Press, Vol. 4, 1975, pp. 378–395.

Kennedy, E. S., and Muruwwa, A. "Biruni on the Solar Equation." *Journal of Near Eastern Studies*, Vol. 17, 1958, pp. 112–121.

Khan, A. S. *A Bibliography of the Works of Abu'l-Raihan al-Biruni*. New Delhi, India: Indian National Academy of Science; Aligarh, India: Centre for West Asian Studies, Aligarh Muslim University, 1982.

Krenkow, F. "Abu'r-Raihan al-Biruni." *Islamic Culture*, Vol. 6, 1932, pp. 528–534.

Lesley, M. "Biruni on Rising Times and Daylight Lengths." *Centaurus*, Vol. 5, 1957–1958, pp. 121–141.

Le Strange, G. *Lands of the Eastern Caliphate.* Cambridge: Cambridge University Press, 1905.

Memon, M. M. "Al-Beruni and His Contribution to Medieval Muslim Geography." *Islamic Culture*, Vol. 33, No. 1, 1959, pp. 213–218.

Mercier, R. P. "Geodesy." In Harley, J. B., and Woodward, D. (Eds.), *The History of Cartography, Volume 2, Book 1: Cartography in the Traditional Islamic and South Asian Societies.* Chicago: University of Chicago Press, 1992, pp. 175–188.

Meyerhof, M. "The Article on Aconite from al-Biruni's *Kitab as-Saidana.*" *Islamic Culture*, Vol. 19, 1945, pp. 323–328.

Motezed, K. *Abu Raihan-e Biruni.* Tehran: Expansion of Iranian Libraries Company, 1991. (In Persian.)

Nafisi, S. "Abu Raihan's Published Materials." *Indo-Iranica*, Vol. 5, 1952, pp. 1–4. (In Persian.)

Nasr, S. H., and Mohaghegh, M. *Questions and Answers (Between Ibn Sina and Biruni).* Kuala Lumpur, Malaysia: International Institute for Islamic Thought and Civilization, 1995.

Nazim, M. *The Life and Times of Mahmud of Ghazna.* New Delhi, India: Munshiram Manoharlal, 2nd Edition, 1971.

Qurbani, A. *Biruni-Nameh.* Tehran: Society for National Monuments Publications, No. 107, 1974. (In Persian.)

Sachau, E. C. (Trans.). *The Chronology of Ancient Nations.* London: W. H. Allen, 1879. (Originally written by Biruni.)

Safa, Z. "Some of Abu Raihan's Philosophical Ideas and a Summary of His Debate with Ibn Sina." *Indo-Iranica*, Vol. 5, 1952, pp. 5–12. (In Persian.)

Said, H. M. *Al-Biruni Commemorative Volume: Proceedings of the International Congress Held in Pakistan, Nov. 26th thru Dec. 12th, 1973.* Karachi, Pakistan: Hamdard Academy, 1979.

Said, H. M., and Zahid, A. *Al-Biruni: His Time, Life and Works.* Karachi, Pakistan: Hamdard Academy, 1981.

Sarton, G. *Introduction to History of Science.* Baltimore: The Carnegie Institute, Five Volumes, 1927–1948.

Schoy, C. "Moslem Geography of the Middle Ages." *Geographical Review*, Vol. 14, 1924, pp. 257–269.

Sezgin, F. *The Contribution of the Arabic-Islamic Geographers to the Formation of the World Map.* Frankfurt, Germany: IGAIW, 1987.

Sharma, A. "Al-Biruni on the Hindu Notion of Samsara." *Islamic Culture*, July 1977, pp. 165–169.

Spengler, J. J. "Alberuni: Eleventh-Century Iranian Malthusian?" In *History of Political Economy*, Vol. 3, 1971, pp. 92–104.

Stroumsa, S. *Freethinkers of Medieval Islam.* Boston: Brill, 1999.

Sykes, P. *A History of Persia.* New York: Barnes & Noble, 1969.

Tuchman, B. W. *Bible and Sword: England and Palestine from the Bronze Age to Balfour.* New York: Ballantine, 1984.

Validi Togan, A. Z. "Biruni's Picture of the World." *Memoirs of the Archaeological Survey of India,* No. 53, 1937 or 1938.

Wilczynski, J. Z. "On the Presumed Darwinism of Alberuni Eight Hundred Years before Darwin." *Isis,* Vol. 50, Dec. 1959, pp. 459–466.

Wright, R. R. (Trans.). *Book of Instruction in the Art of Astrology.* London: Luzac & Co., 1934. (Originally written by Biruni.)

Yarshater, E. (Ed.). *Biruni Symposium.* New York: Columbia University, Iran Center, 1976.

Yusuf Ali, A. "Al-Biruni's India." *Islamic Culture,* Vol. 1, 1927, pp. 223–230, 473–487.

Index

About the Author

M. Kamiar was born in a village near the city of Bijar, Kurdistan, Iran. He completed elementary school with the highest grades in the township. By age fifteen, after finishing the ninth grade, he took a teachers training college entrance exam and obtained one of the highest scores. After graduation from this teachers training college, by age seventeen, he became the youngest teacher in Iran.

Always majoring in geography, he received a BA degree from University of Esfahan, an MA degree from University of Northern Iowa, and a PhD from Michigan State University. Dr. Kamiar is presently a professor of geography at Florida Community College at Jacksonville, Florida. He has published many books and articles both in English and Farsi.

Dr. Kamiar's first book on this classical scholar, also published by the Scarecrow Press, 2006, *A Bio-Bibliography for Biruni*, was geared toward graduate students and researchers. The present book, however, is written keeping the lay reader in mind. Dr. Kamiar is also preparing a comprehensive *Standard Pronunciation Guide for Proper Names from the Middle East*. This project will be available online soon. His next book is *Wealth of a Nation: The Case of the Empire of Iran*.